TAKING BERLIN

TAKING BERLIN

THE BLOODY RACE TO DEFEAT THE THIRD REICH

MARTIN DUGARD

CALIBER

DUTTON CALIBER
An imprint of Penguin Random House LLC
penguinrandomhouse.com

Maps by Chris Erichson

LIBRARY OF CONGRESS CATALOGING-IN-PUBLICATION DATA

Names: Dugard, Martin, author.
Title: Taking Berlin : the bloody race to defeat the Third Reich / Martin Dugard.
Other titles: Bloody race to defeat the Third Reich
Description: New York : Dutton Caliber, an imprint of
Penguin Random House LLC, [2022] | Includes index.
Identifiers: LCCN 2022017499 (print) | LCCN 2022017500 (ebook) |
ISBN 9780593187425 (hardcover) | ISBN 9780593187432 (ebook)
Subjects: LCSH: World War, 1939-1945—Campaigns—Europe. |
World War, 1939-1945—Biography—Anecdotes.
Classification: LCC D756 .D79 2022 (print) | LCC D756 (ebook) |
DDC 940.54/21—dc23/eng/20220429
LC record available at https://lccn.loc.gov/2022017499
LC ebook record available at https://lccn.loc.gov/2022017500

Printed in the United States of America
1st Printing

For Callie

PROLOGUE

MAY 15, 1944
LONDON, ENGLAND
9:50 A.M.

W inston Churchill is on time.

The lecture hall entry doors are thick, pine, Victorian. The prime minister does not stand in the long line.

Nor does the king of England.

But both men know better than to be late.

This morning's presentation at St. Paul's School is the most important audience event in Western history. Rules to be obeyed. Doors closed and locked at precisely 10:00 A.M. Late arrivals denied admission. British general Bernard Law Montgomery, St. Paul's alumnus and host for today's event, has made this very clear.

As everyone entering the room well knows, Monty always gets his way.

Military police block the entrance. Large men: unsmiling Americans, polished helmets, sidearms. Generals and admirals stand single file to present their engraved summons, an assemblage of stars and bars one hundred officers strong. No invitation, no admission. Every important Allied military figure in World War II's European Theater waits in the queue.

Except the French. They're not invited.

And the Russians. But they have war plans of their own.

Churchill makes his way to the front of the room, wrapped in a black knee-length frock coat, smoldering double corona wedged into the left corner of his mouth. Inside, it's wood-paneled walls, cigarette smoke, British and American accents—and a most intriguing visual display. "On the stage was a map of the Normandy beaches and the immediate hinterland, set at a slope so that the audience could see it clearly, and so constructed that the high officers explaining the plan could walk about on it and point out the landmarks," Churchill will write.

St. Paul's students and staff have relocated to the countryside for the duration of the war. Four months ago, Montgomery transformed the empty buildings of Gothic Victorian design—peaked roofs, stained glass, chimneys everywhere—at 153 Hammersmith Road into his personal headquarters for the purposes of planning the invasion of France. The headmaster's house is now his personal quarters. Monty has organized today's event down to the minute.

Each officer takes a seat on the hard wooden benches more often used by teenaged schoolboys. The heater is broken. No one takes off their coat. Prime Minister Churchill sits in the more comfortable front row, up next to the stage, in padded armchairs reserved for himself, Montgomery, American general Dwight Eisenhower, and no less than Great Britain's sovereign, King George VI.

Today's presentation is top secret. No cameras or press. Eisenhower will later joke that Nazi German dictator Adolf Hitler could have killed every top American and British officer with a single well-placed bomb. But the invasion of Hitler's *Festung Europa*—fortress Europe—is hardly a surprise. The whole world knows that hundreds of thousands of Allied troops have been assembling in Great Britain for months, training each day for the singular purpose of wrenching control of Europe from Hitler's grasp sometime this summer.

Coincidentally, on this very day, General Montgomery graces the cover of *Life* magazine's new issue. A vivid portrait of Monty's character runs inside—"Cromwellian," in Churchill's words, "austere, severe, accomplished, tireless"—while also playing up the general's ascetic lifestyle: "He lives in complete simplicity, eats the plainest food, and has no recreation except that of reading novels and detective stories. He is often impatient of human frailty."

But an equally large feature runs under the headline "American Invaders Mass in England." A dozen photographs show Eisenhower, Montgomery, and Churchill bundled in thick coats, scarves, and gloves against the chill English spring as they observe soldiers preparing to assault French beaches or drop from the sky. Though *Life* does not know the exact number, 156,115 Allied soldiers transported in 11,590 landing craft and 6,939 other naval vessels will wade ashore on a fifty-mile stretch of Norman beaches that have been subsectioned into smaller landing zones named Omaha, Utah, Sword, Gold, and Juno.

The paratroopers will go in first. "Invasion by Air Will Be the Biggest in History" reads a *Life* subtitle accompanying a photo of one hundred parachute canopies blossoming high over the British countryside during a practice jump.

A subsequent story is more pragmatic: "A Manual of How to Treat the Disabled of This War When They Return to Civilian Life."

Hitler is well aware that Allied forces will soon attempt to land in France, but the Führer does not know the date—"D-Day," in military lexicon. Nor does anyone shivering inside this lecture hall. The only man who knows that answer is General Eisenhower—and even he is uncertain right now.*

Ten o'clock. MPs close and lock the doors. Montgomery is famous for giving an audience "two minutes to cough, sneeze, or blow your nose. After that, there will be no interruptions."

Those words are unnecessary this morning. The room quiets as Eisenhower rises to begin the proceedings. He's every officer's boss, supreme commander of the Allied Expeditionary Force. The audience is impatient to hear each last detail of this enormous plan: naval bombardment, aerial assault, bridges paratroopers must capture in the dead of night, and the location of the landing beaches where all those soldiers will confront a well-trained and highly disciplined German force that has fortified the coastline with guns big and small. Intelligence reports confirm that Field Marshal Erwin Rommel, Germany's notorious "Desert Fox," is personally overseeing an "Atlantic Wall" designed to throw the invaders back into the sea.

"I welcome you," says Eisenhower, "on the eve of a great battle."

The general's rehearsed speech is immediately cut short as a thunderous pounding on the lecture hall doors fills the room.

General Montgomery stands and glares, furious. He gives no indication for the military police to open the doors.

The pounding resumes.

Most everyone in the room knows who might be on the other side. He's the most audacious of them all, the one man whose absence was noted.

And Monty's main rival.

Eisenhower remains silent. He could order the doors opened, or even have the insistent perpetrator sent away. But this is Monty's

---

* Home nations of the Allied soldiers that will invade France during the Normandy landings: United States, Britain, Canada, Belgium, Norway, Poland, Luxembourg, Greece, Czechoslovakia, New Zealand, Australia, and France.

show. Britain's favorite general, who is not backing down, must make the final call.

More pounding. Louder. Impatient.

Reality sets in. Montgomery's carefully scripted presentation remains a sideshow so long as the hammering continues. Whoever stands on the other side is either a fool or a force of nature, so determined to walk through those doors that he is unafraid of offending anyone inside the lecture hall—supreme commander, prime minister, and king of England among them.

Bernard Law Montgomery angrily orders the doors flung open.

To absolutely no one's surprise, a 6′2″, silver-haired American general wearing a pair of ivory-handled revolvers, knee-high riding boots, and an immaculate overcoat tailored on Savile Row strides into the lecture hall, unrepentant smile on his face.

Winston Churchill recognizes the officer immediately and will order him a whiskey over lunch to celebrate this bold maneuver.

General George S. Patton Jr. always makes an entrance.

TAKING BERLIN

NORMANDY

1

General George S. Patton is being introduced.

Blustery English weather. Forecast calls for rain. Officers and enlisted brace in formation before the reviewing stand. Patton stands at attention next to an American flag and unit standards. The general took command on January 26. He has already given this speech to other divisions of his Third Army several times. Its words will be unlike anything these men have heard before.

Patton, a general unlike any these men have *seen* before, is counting on that.

These soldiers watched him drive up in a chauffeured black Mercedes, noted the polished cavalry boots and Caesar-like entrance—motorcycle escort, brass band, honor guard. It's impossible to believe that four years ago this regal being was a washed-up colonel trying to decide whether his future lay in riding a cavalry horse into battle or embracing armored warfare.

Patton wisely chose armor. Animals have no place in modern

3

tactics. The general's genius for tank warfare has been the making of him, fueling his rise to three-star general.

These assembled soldiers don't know that. They just know he's their commander, soon to lead them in battle. Curiosity courses through the audience as they wait to pass judgment.

"We are here to listen to the words of a great man," begins General William H. Simpson, today's bald and lean three-star master of ceremonies. The audience is so large that Simpson uses a microphone and loudspeaker.

"A man who will lead you into whatever you may face, with heroism, ability, and foresight. A man who has proved himself amid shot and shell. My greatest hope is that someday soon, I will have my own great army fighting with him, side by side:

"General George S. Patton Jr."

. . .

PATTON STEPS TO the microphone. "Be seated."

No jokes. No attempt at levity.

No chairs. Wet spring grass. No hesitation. Patton waits until they drop to the ground and sit cross-legged, arms hugging knees, cold water seeping against their backsides through cotton khaki pants. Left unsaid is that the mild discomfort is like nothing they will endure in combat.

Despite the spectacle, today's speech and every other talk the general has given to Third Army in the past month is top secret. Soldiers cannot write home about it, talk in the local pub about it, or in any way admit that they have seen and heard George Patton.

The general opens with a simple declarative statement: "No bastard ever won a war by dying for his country. You win it by making the other poor dumb bastard die for his country."

The audience laughs. Patton looks just the way these men imagined, a real fighting general, the very image of fitness and polish. Yet the high-pitched voice is quite a surprise.

"Men, this stuff that some sources sling around about America wanting out of this war, not wanting to fight, is a crock of bullshit. Americans love to fight, traditionally. All real Americans love the sting and clash of battle."

Heads nodding. Jaws set. Thoughts of *That's me—hopefully.*

"You are here today for three reasons. First, because you are here to defend your homes and your loved ones. Second, you are here for your own self-respect, because you would not want to be anywhere else. Third, you are here because you are real men and all real men like to fight. When you, here, every one of you, were kids, you all admired the champion marble player, the fastest runner, the toughest boxer, the big-league ball players, and the All-American football players.

"Americans love a winner. Americans will not tolerate a loser. Americans despise cowards. Americans play to win all of the time. I wouldn't give a hoot in hell for a man who lost and laughed. That's why Americans have never lost nor will ever lose a war; for the very idea of losing is hateful to an American."

Patton talks without notes. Nobody notices the high voice anymore. What began as a speech is now a monologue spoken with conviction and comradery.

"You are not all going to die. Only two percent of you right here today would die in a major battle. Death must not be feared. Death, in time, comes to all men. Yes, every man is scared in his first battle. If he says he's not, he's a liar. Some men are cowards, but they fight the same as the brave men or they get the hell slammed out of them watching men fight who are just as scared as they are.

"The real hero is the man who fights even though he is scared. Some men get over their fright in a minute under fire. For some, it takes an hour. For some, it takes days. But a real man will never let his fear of death overpower his honor, his sense of duty to his country, and his innate manhood. Battle is the most magnificent competition in which a human being can indulge. It brings out all that is best and it removes all that is base. Americans pride themselves on being he-men, and they *are* he-men.

"Remember that the enemy is just as frightened as you are, and probably more so. They are not supermen. All through your Army careers, you men have bitched about what you call 'chicken shit drilling.' That, like everything else in this Army, has a definite purpose. That purpose is alertness. Alertness must be bred into every soldier. I don't give a fuck for a man who's not always on his toes."

Fuck.

The general just said fuck. Everyone smiles, even the officers: *I really want to be like Patton. I really want Patton to like me. Come to think of it, I don't give a fuck for a man who's not always on his toes, either.*

"You men are veterans or you wouldn't be here. You are ready for what's to come. A man must be alert at all times if he expects to stay alive. If you're not alert, sometime, a German son-of-an-asshole-bitch is going to sneak up behind you and beat you to death with a sock full of shit! There are four hundred neatly marked graves somewhere in Sicily, all because one man went to sleep on the job. But they are German graves, because we caught the bastard asleep before they did.

"An Army is a team. It lives, sleeps, eats, and fights as a team. This individual heroic stuff is pure horse shit. The bilious bastards who write that kind of stuff for the *Saturday Evening Post* don't know any more about real fighting under fire than they know about fucking!"

Patton doesn't allow a beat for laughter, pushing the pace, driving his point.

"We have the finest food, the finest equipment, the best spirit, and the best men in the world. Why, by God, I actually pity those poor sons-of-bitches we're going up against. By God, I do. My men don't surrender, and I don't want to hear of any soldier under my command being captured unless he has been hit. Even if you are hit, you can still fight back. That's not just bull shit either. The kind of man that I want in my command is just like the lieutenant in Libya, who, with a Luger against his chest, jerked off his helmet, swept the gun aside with one hand, and busted the hell out of the Kraut with his helmet. Then he jumped on the gun and went out and killed another German before they knew what the hell was coming off. And, all of that time, this man had a bullet through a lung. There was a real man!"

.   .   .

PATTON LOOKS OUT into the crowd. Sees that look, the one he sees every time he gives this speech: *I'm a real man*, those faces say. *I can do that. I can kill Germans bare-handed with a bullet in my chest.*

The general pauses, lets that soak in.

"All of the real heroes are not storybook combat fighters, either. Every single man in this Army plays a vital role. Don't ever let up. Don't ever think that your job is unimportant. Every man has a job to do and he must do it. Every man is a vital link in the great chain. What if every truck driver suddenly decided that he didn't like the whine of those shells overhead, turned yellow, and jumped headlong into a ditch? The cowardly bastard could say, 'Hell, they won't miss me, just one man in thousands.' But, what if every soldier thought that way? Where in the hell would we be now? What would our country, our loved ones, our homes, even the world, be like?

"No, goddamn it, Americans don't think like that. Every man does his job. Every man serves the whole. Every department, every unit, is important in the vast scheme of this war. The ordnance men are needed to supply the guns and machinery of war to keep us rolling. The quartermaster is needed to bring up food and clothes because where we are going there isn't a hell of a lot to steal. Every last man on KP has a job to do, even the one who heats our water to keep us from getting the GI Shits.

"Each man must not think only of himself, but also of his buddy fighting beside him. We don't want yellow cowards in this Army. They should be killed off like rats. If not, they will go home after this war and breed more cowards. The brave men will breed more brave men. Kill off the goddamned cowards and we will have a nation of brave men. One of the bravest men that I ever saw was a fellow on top of a telegraph pole in the midst of a furious firefight in Tunisia. I stopped and asked what the hell he was doing up there at a time like that. He answered, 'Fixing the wire, Sir.' I asked, 'Isn't that a little unhealthy right about now?' He answered, 'Yes sir, but the goddamned wire has to be fixed.' I asked, 'Don't those planes strafing the road bother you?' And he answered, 'No, Sir, but you sure as hell do!'"

Again with laughter. But now with tension, imagining what it will be like to be in a "furious firefight." No one wants this soliloquy to end.

Everyone wants to follow General George S. Patton into battle.

. . .

"Now, there was a real man. A real soldier. There was a man who devoted all he had to his duty, no matter how seemingly insignificant his duty might appear at the time, no matter how great the odds. And you should have seen those trucks on the road to Tunisia. Those drivers were magnificent. All day and all night they rolled over those son-of-a-bitching roads, never stopping, never faltering from their course, with shells bursting all around them all of the time. We got through on good old American guts.

"Many of those men drove for over forty consecutive hours. These men weren't combat men, but they were soldiers with a job to do. They did it, and in one hell of a way they did it. They were part of a team. Without team effort, without them, the fight would have been lost. All of the links in the chain pulled together and the chain became unbreakable.

"Don't forget, you men don't know that I'm here. No mention of that fact is to be made in any letters. The world is not supposed to know what the hell happened to me. I'm not supposed to be commanding this army. I'm not even supposed to be here in England. Let the first bastards to find out be the goddamned Germans. Someday, I want to see them raise up on their piss-soaked hind legs and howl, 'Jesus Christ, it's the goddamned Third Army again and that son-of-a-fucking-bitch Patton.' We want to get the hell over there. The quicker we clean up this goddamned mess, the quicker we can take a little jaunt against the purple pissing Japs and clean out their nest, too. Before the goddamned Marines get all of the credit.

"Sure, we want to go home. We want this war over with. The quickest way to get it over with is to go get the bastards who started it. The quicker they are whipped, the quicker we can go home. The shortest way home is through Berlin . . ."

Home.

One word. So many meanings. Everyone wants to go home: *feather beds, corner bars, civilian clothes, sleeping late. Yankees, Dodgers; Cardinals, Cubs. Bottomless cup of coffee. Girlfriends.*

If Berlin is the way home, then let's get the hell into Berlin.

Patton doesn't linger on home. No time to wallow. No time to let these soldiers think about the other things back home, things they can't control from five thousand miles away. Like wondering if their special someone is dancing and drinking and fornicating with the draft-dodging 4-Fs. That's the worst thought of all. Let a man think about that too long and he won't think about anything else.

"When a man is lying in a shell hole, if he just stays there all day, a German will get to him eventually. The hell with that idea. The hell with taking it. My men don't dig foxholes. I don't want them to. Foxholes only slow up an offensive. Keep moving. And don't give the enemy time to dig one either. We'll win this war, but we'll win it only by fighting and by showing the Germans that we've got more guts than they have; or ever will have. We're not going to just shoot the sons-of-bitches, we're going to rip out their living Goddamned guts and use them to grease the treads of our tanks. We're going to murder those lousy Hun cocksuckers by the bushel-fucking-basket."

Now the meat and potatoes of the speech. Despite his talk about the men being veterans, most are newly arrived from America. They didn't fight in Africa or Italy. Patton now reminds them who they are, what they're fighting for, and plants the seed that these regular young American men are capable of becoming legendary warriors.

And Patton adds an inside secret, as one who has been there before.

· · ·

"WAR IS A bloody, killing business. You've got to spill their blood, or they will spill yours. Rip them up the belly. Shoot them in the guts. When shells are hitting all around you and you wipe the dirt off your face and realize that instead of dirt it's the blood and guts of what once was your best friend beside you, you'll know what to do! I don't want to get any messages saying, 'I am holding my position.' We are not holding a goddamned thing. Let the Germans do that. We are advancing constantly and we are not interested in holding on to anything, except the enemy's balls. We are going to twist his balls and kick the living shit out of him all of the time. Our basic plan of operation is to advance and to keep on advancing regardless of whether we have to go over, under, or through the enemy. We are going to go through him like crap through a goose; like shit through a tin horn!"

Yes!!! The revival meeting is in full force. Cheers and applause. No one says "hallelujah" but they think something like it, just as no one has ever imagined shit flowing through a tin horn but now sees it as plain as day—and it's spectacular.

"From time to time, there will be some complaints that we are pushing our people too hard. I don't give a good goddamn about such complaints. I believe in the old and sound rule that an ounce of sweat will save a gallon of blood. The harder *we* push, the more Germans we will kill. The more Germans we kill, the fewer of our men will be killed. Pushing means fewer casualties. I want you all to remember that."

Solemn agreement. *We will remember.*

Patton brings it home:

"There is one great thing that you men will all be able to say after this war is over and you are home once again. You may be thankful that twenty years from now when you are sitting by the fireplace with your grandson on your knee and he asks you what you did in the great World War II, you *won't* have to cough, shift him to the other knee, and say, 'Well, your granddaddy shoveled shit in Louisiana.'

"No, sir, you can look him straight in the eye and say, 'Son, your granddaddy rode with the Great Third Army and a son-of-a-goddamned-bitch named Georgie Patton!'

"All right, you sons-of-bitches. You know how I feel. I'll be proud to lead you wonderful guys in battle anytime, anywhere. That is all."

· · ·

LONG AFTER THE applause fades, General Patton's days are filled with meetings and travel, including a dinner with General Montgomery in Portsmouth. The two men have made peace for the time being, their mutual respect outweighing memories of their competition in Sicily. "I had a good time, and now we understand each other," Montgomery says as the two men depart after a breakfast.

But as Monty and his British 21st Army Group prepare for their D-Day assignment of capturing the vital crossroads of Caen, Patton must wait. Third Army will not go ashore in the first wave. Or second. Or at all. The general is "a secret," in his words. Hitler and his intelligence command are supposed to believe the fiction that Patton is massing a force in Dover, preparing to invade France near the port of Calais.

The German 15th Army awaits his arrival. Patton is America's best fighting general. It seems unconscionable that they leave him out of the fighting. For the sake of neutralizing the 15th on D-Day, it is vital this charade remains complete. So it is that George S. Patton will stay in England and off the battlefield for as long as it takes.

Operation Fortitude, as the deception is known, pretends that

Patton commands the First Army Group. Through clever Allied use of signals intelligence, dummy tanks, and double-agent spies, the Germans have been spoon-fed the notion that the general is based in southeast England, just thirty-one short miles from Calais. It is here that the German 15th awaits Patton's invasion.

It is all a lie. There is no First Army Group. Patton is nowhere near southeast England. And the Allied assault will take place two hundred miles southwest of Calais in Normandy.

Yet for the myth to work, Adolf Hitler can never know that General George S. Patton commands Third Army. The general must do everything in his power to keep his true role a secret.

At the same time, Patton must prepare Third Army for war. Thus, today's speech—and the admonition that everyone here today must never write home about seeing him in person.

Fortitude seems to be working so far, but Patton is not happy about it. He fears the war will be over by the time he gets to Europe. This man who is incomplete without a fight is nearing sixty. This is almost certainly his last war. He has already packed his bags for France, ready to leave in an instant. Soon he will begin wearing a shoulder holster just like he would on the battlefield, "so as to get myself into spirit for the part," he says.

But for now, all Patton can do is wait.

"Don't get excited when the whistle blows," he writes to his wife and confidante, Beatrice, on June 4, referring to D-Day. The couple married in 1910 and have three children. The general has not been informed of the precise date of the attack but suspects it will come soon.

"I am not in the opening kickoff."

2

James Gavin is a dangerous man.

He now stands for the kickoff.

America's youngest general awaits the signal to launch, the clamor and stutter and belch of spun-up aircraft thundering all around him, an old but not entirely welcome friend. He stands in the open doorway of the aircraft numbered EUR-475. Row upon row of C-47 Skytrains are parked all around him, resting on tricycle gears, noses angled toward the runway. One more night to the full moon. Night air humid from yesterday's storm. Sounds of conversation, retching, nerves getting the better of untested soldiers, the profanity and bad jokes that always accompany the last-minute loading of men and guns into their designated planes.

The general has heard it all before. Thirty-seven. Orphan. Commissioned out of West Point. Parachuted into the Sicily invasion last year.

Then those sounds of preparation are no more, overwhelmed by the cough, sputter, then raging din of hundreds of 1,200-horsepower Pratt & Whitney R-1830 radial engines. Two massive propellers per aircraft slicing into the nighttime English sky at the very same time, the drone of Napoleon's bees multiplied by millions.

Gavin thinks the same thing he always thinks at this moment in an operation: *There's no going back.*

Pilots push throttles forward, slowly easing out of their designated parking revetment and into the long line for takeoff. Right now, at this very moment, hundreds more C-47s at eight airfields in the British countryside—Spanhoe, Cottesmore, North Witham, Saltby, Grantham (just recently renamed Spitalgate), Folkingham, Barkston Heath, Fulbeck—do the same, taxiing forward to a runway in loose formation. Temporary chalk numbers on the sides of each C-47 told paratroopers which plane to board. Tips of each wing are painted with black and white stripes, which also ring the rear of fuselages. Allied fighters and bombers will soon fill the skies over Normandy. Those bands remind one and all who the good guys are.

The first D-Day wave begins.

Every plane has an olive drab upper fuselage, neutral gray underbelly, green zinc chromate interior, and absolutely no defensive armament. Sixty-three feet nose to tail; ninety-five feet wingtip to wingtip. Doorway behind the left wing. Each aircraft is loaded with a "stick" of twenty-eight paratroopers and the extraordinary amount of gear each man straps to his body or stows in large pants pockets: ready-to-fire M1 rifle plus 156 rounds of ammunition, entrenching shovel, loaded pistol with three extra clips, knife, cartridge belt, gloves, canteen, first aid kit, maps, raincoat, rations, four grenades, flares, message book.

Each emergency ration package contains four pieces of chewing gum, bouillon cubes, Nescafé instant coffee, sugar cubes, Hershey bars, Charms candy, and a bottle of purified drinking water.*

The ground remains close after takeoff, just seven hundred feet below. Pilots circle back over the airfield until the last plane is in the air, then gather in V formations spreading across the nighttime sky—nine ships to each V, two hundred feet from one another. The leader of each flight keeps one thousand feet behind the rear of the preceding flight. Downward-facing recognition lights are turned off. Upward-facing blue formation lights remain on to prevent planes from crashing into one another, though turned down as low as possible. Airspeed to the drop zone is precisely 140 miles per hour—122 knots. Flying in formation is second nature to the troop carrier aircrews. Every pilot focuses on the shape in front of him. Ability to see other planes is paramount to preventing midair collisions.

Just as General George Patton embraced armored warfare, so Gavin earned his first star by being an early proponent of airborne fighting units—paratroopers. He has literally written the book on training and tactics required to drop men into combat by parachute. Gavin's doctrine is that airborne troops be gung ho, physically fit, and unafraid. Their job tonight is to land behind German troops guarding the beaches code-named Omaha and Utah, where tens of thousands of American soldiers will splash ashore in the morning. Key towns and bridges behind the beaches must be captured to block enemy escape and reinforcement. Farther north, British paratroopers are dropping behind beaches named Gold, Juno, and Sword. In all, 23,400 airborne Allied troops will land in Normandy within the next twenty-four

---

* British paratroopers wore much the same equipment. However, a Denison smock was worn over the torso to prevent webbing and other equipment from getting tangled in the parachute. A thin layer of body armor was often worn between the oversmock and uniform. The British also carried a special "rifle valise" to protect their .303 Lee-Enfield rifle, much like a flexible gun case. Average weight carried by both groups during a jump was 85–100 pounds.

hours. Gavin and his men will drop twenty miles west of Utah and Omaha.

No matter the nationality, Allied paratroopers will be heavily outnumbered and outgunned. Fields have been flooded and mined by the Germans, anticipating their arrival. Large, sharpened poles have been planted vertically, many topped with land mines, waiting to impale and explode.

Yet the mood in EUR-475 is not fear. Some men smoke. Some sit in the dark with their thoughts. Others nap, sitting upright, heads lolling against the curve of the fuselage. The mood is tension and nonchalance. No one doubts they will do the job. These men did not hear Patton's infamous speech. They didn't need to. Jumping into Sicily with Gavin was their baptism by fire. They already know about fighting and killing.

Gavin is tall and confident, fond of commanding from the front. The general flies in the lead aircraft, navigating the hour-long journey's progress by looking down through the open doorway: southeast to Cheltenham, hard left to Portsmouth, another at the spit known as Portland Bill, where the pilots turn off the red and green wingtip navigation lights and land is left behind, endure the dark emptiness of the English Channel, then yet another left turn just before the island of Guernsey, known to be fortified with German antiaircraft batteries. If all goes well, the pilots will fly this exact heading in reverse on the flight home. Now they steer a course just out of enemy range.

"Flak, both light and heavy, came up, burst, and fell short," Gavin will write of the passage off Guernsey. "It was exactly as we had planned when we had laid out the flight plan."

Another bank to the left. Suddenly, the C-47 is flying over French airspace. Gavin orders his jumpmaster to get the men on their feet. Should the plane get hit by enemy fire, they will be poised to egress immediately. "Stand up! Hook up! Sound off for equipment check!" bawls the jumpmaster.

Starting at the rear of the plane, paratroopers call out their number and readiness: "Twenty-eight OK! Twenty-seven OK!" And on.

"Stand in the door," the jumpmaster commands when the last soldier has called out. The paratroopers form a line, right hand on the shoulder of the man in front of him. Heavy bundles of radios, bazookas, and mines will be pushed out last.

"Are we ready?" yells the jumpmaster. "Are we fucking ready?"

Yes. But the plane isn't over the drop zone yet. The men stand and wait.

General Gavin remains by the open door, first man in line. Cold air rushes into the cabin.

Time is of the essence. Precisely eight minutes and thirty seconds from that first stretch of Norman beach to the jump zone. The Cotentin Peninsula, as the landmass below is known, is just twenty-three miles wide. One side to the other at 122 knots is twelve minutes. After that, jumping means splashing into the ocean with all that gear and no chance of rescue.

The land below is reddish brown. Moonlight shows roads and small villages. Gavin knows this route well, having studied, planned, and rehearsed tonight for months. His boots are bloused as he buckles the strap on his steel pot helmet bearing a single star. Conditions are ideal. Gavin looks out into the night, where the hundreds of C-47s in tight Vs blanket the French sky. Faint blue formation lights, orange glow of exhaust stacks and flame dampeners, black and white "invasion stripes."

Gavin is not a worrier, but the sight of all those planes is reassuring. The mission is proceeding perfectly.

Then comes the fog.

"It was so thick that I could not see the wingtips of our plane. And of course, I could not see any other planes. My plane was entirely on its own, and I could see no others," the general will remember.

"I began to check our time."

Gavin studies his watch and the sky, one then the other, again and again, waiting for the fog to lift.

In the cockpit, pilots also note the time. Tracer bullets from German ground fire light up the sky, arcing lazily toward each C-47. The aircrew is under strict instructions not to return to England with a full aircraft. Everywhere above the French countryside, panicked aircrews are breaking formation, flicking on the green jump light to dump their load before making a hasty turn back to the English Channel, unconcerned that the stick leaping from their plane is jumping at too high an altitude, too brisk an airspeed, and over a target that's miles from their actual drop zone.

But Gavin's aircrew doesn't panic, remaining on course. A switch is flipped precisely four minutes from the drop zone, causing a light over Gavin's doorway to blaze bright red.

Pilot and copilot struggle to keep a true course, maintaining low airspeed and level attitude. Evasive maneuvers are prohibited. A sudden patch of clear skies shows a river shining in the moonlight, but Gavin sees no other planes. A town, a railroad, another river. Small-arms fire from German troops pings off the C-47's reinforced underbelly "like pebbles landing on a tin roof."

The pilots reduce airspeed to 110 knots for optimal jumping. Gavin feels the plane slow. Nine minutes since the coastline. Just three more until they're over water again. "We were about thirty seconds overtime. A wide river was just ahead of us, plainly visible in the moonlight. Small arms fire was increasing," the young general will remember.

Gavin secures his M1 Garand rifle between his reserve chute and his torso. The muzzle is just below his face, and the butt is between his legs. Only when his main chute opens will he move the weapon into a horizontal position for landing.

In the cockpit, another switch is flipped.

The red light turns green.

The general takes a long look at the terrain below.

One second passes. Two. Three.

"Let's go," yells the Jumping General, stepping out the door.*

---

* Despite the thick fog, troop carrier pilots successfully dropped an estimated thirty to forty percent of their paratroopers within one mile of their drop zone. An estimated eighty percent landed within five miles. Of the 821 C-47s flying the D-Day mission, 42 were lost in action.

3

Five hours later. Eleven miles off the Norman coast. General Norman Cota braces for the long drop into his landing craft.

Next stop: a beach code-named Omaha.

Gale force winds blow spume and mist off the English Channel. Brisk fifty-nine-degree morning. USS *Charles Carroll* pitches in twenty-foot swells. Another ship, the much smaller LCVP* 71 bangs violently against one side of the transport, parallel, rising and falling in rhythm with the foul sea. General Dwight Eisenhower, supreme Allied commander, delayed the invasion one day because of this weather. When asked to push the plan once again, Eisenhower chose to make do, no matter how foul the seas might be. "We go!" Ike barked to his staff, setting in motion all that is happening this morning.

Cota stands in a line of twelve officers and fourteen soldiers on *Carroll*'s deck, waiting his turn to climb over the rail, then descend a

---

* LCVP: Landing Craft, Vehicle, Personnel.

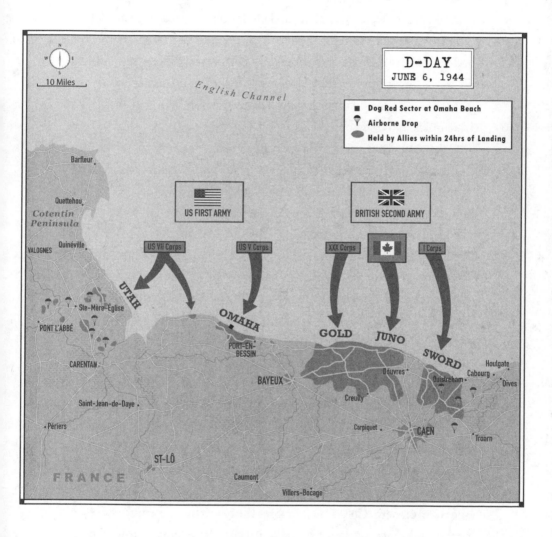

cargo net into "71." Depending upon how he judges each wave, the lower end of this rope ladder will either reach down into the landing craft or hang ten feet above the bucking steel deck.

Cota is an old soldier. He times his drop perfectly.

At 6:10 A.M., Coxswain Ricardo Feliciano pulls clear for the eighty-five-minute trip to Omaha Beach. Top speed is twelve knots but the loaded craft travels closer to nine. She is thirty-six feet long and just ten feet wide. The men stand side by side, bracing themselves in the heavy seas. Storm just passing. Sunrise a vibrant crimson. Visibility three miles. No one vomits.

Cakewalk. That's what the men have been assured. Opposition is no more, done in by relentless Allied naval and aerial shelling slamming German positions hidden in the bluffs above the beach. The bombardment has either killed all the defenders or left them completely disoriented from percussive aftershock. Craters rent from shells falling short will pock the beach, providing a divot to drop into for cover if a few of the enemy are still alive to fire back.

Cota will be the highest-ranking officer on the beach. Fifty-one. Goes by "Dutch." Born in Massachusetts. West Point class of 1917, where he played on the football team with Dwight Eisenhower.

LCVP 71 is still more than eight miles from shore when the first wave of troops lands on Omaha Beach. One hour from now, at 7:30, Cota and the second wave are due to follow. He wears a sidearm and a field jacket with a single star on each shoulder. Unlike others on board, the general does not wear a heavy pack or carry a rifle.

Six hundred yards out, a British armored motor launch directs the 71 into a landing lane swept free of mines. The landing craft gunwales are taller than General Cota. He cannot see the beach but the sounds of heavy mortar and machine-gun fire make it clear the enemy is full of fight. Loud artillery shells shriek through the air, the deathly sound of armor-piercing 88mm rounds directed toward beach targets from a mile inland.

Cota's landing craft comes under heavy fire as coxswain Feliciano motors into Dog White Beach. Timber obstacles driven into the sand poke above the surf, topped with mines and barbed wire. Clearly, demolition crews took heavy fire when they tried to detonate them just before dawn—only five of a proposed sixteen passages through the obstacles are open. Feliciano changes course to find a lane, navigating through six-foot waves to land closer to Dog Red. Small-arms fire peppers the vessel. The coxswain quickly lowers the forward ramp before German artillery can zero in on his position.

General Cota steps down the ramp into three feet of water. He wades forty yards to the beach, taking cover behind a Sherman tank. Burning armor and jeeps are everywhere. Other men from 71 lose their balance and fall onto their hands and knees, then bob their way to shore. Major John Sours is the first to die, shot in the chest and head. His body floats facedown in the water as the others move inland. He was a good man, but there is nothing to be done for him now.

Other soldiers are targeted and killed as they crawl beneath three parallel rows of mined timber obstacles at the waterline. Medics race in a crouch to the wounded, putting their own lives at risk to provide first aid.

A deafening explosion, then a giant blinding ball of orange flame and oily black smoke. The landing craft bearing the number 91—not 71—rises out of the sea like a breaching whale before collapsing onto the beach, ammunition stores ablaze. The landing craft is an inferno, every man lost.

General Cota does a quick study of the beach: There are no shell craters.

The morning smells of salt, cordite, hard decisions. Every man is drenched. Covered in sand like a sugar cookie. It is fifty yards of beautiful light brown sand the texture of kosher salt and five minutes of cautious "belly pressed to the ground" movement from the waterline to the only hiding place on Omaha Beach: a four-foot-tall seawall. Above this berm, a fifteen-foot incline leads to a beachfront road.

And that's where this invasion ends.

An impenetrable row of barbed wire is slung across the otherwise simple country lane. Two cars wide. Flatter than the beach. Coil upon coil upon coil upon coil upon coil, rusting from months in the ocean breeze, placed there quite intentionally on the orders of General Erwin Rommel, waiting to do its job. The road is deadly now, but a lovely place to walk the dog before war came to town—ocean tang, slow hiss of lazy white foam marking the tide, a stroll to let the mind wander.

But this wasn't really a town. Just a beachfront collection of very large two-story homes their fortunate owners might describe as cottages. This was where people *lived*, thinking themselves lucky to wake every morning to the sound of crashing waves and end each day reveling in the rapture of English Channel sunset. Before barbed wire and killing zones, there was long flat beach stretching from high cliffs at the left end to forever on the right as one faced the sea. Residents turned their bikes or cars from this simple road into their unpaved driveways, feeling oh so lucky to call this blissful stretch of French shoreline home.

It is nothing like that right now.

Nothing. It's perverted to think such a thought.

From now until eternity, this will be known as Omaha Beach, a place of slaughter. General Norman Cota and the men pissing themselves against the seawall see a road right above them strung in barbed wire as thick as Christmas tinsel and mines covering every inch of the sand-pitted surface. After that is the flat killing zone of grass and summerhouses now filled with German snipers all too happy to eat off the good china left behind by their owners. Each home fronting a steep row of cliffs is also manned by the best shooters in Hitler's army.

There is no way off this beach. We're fucked, the Americans agree. Completely fucked. Soldiers like to grumble. No time like now. Each man was once a private citizen, but now all are military men, trained to obey orders. And right now, no one is saying fuck all about how to go forward or backward or maybe even sideways to get out of this killing zone—any direction to let them live one more day.

Panic spreads like butter melting in a pan. German snipers kill one American after another. It is only logical that each man burrows deeper into the sand, sure the next crosshair is focused on him.

Absolutely, positively, nowhere to go. Chaos reigns.

Welcome to France. This is where we die.

Yet at the top of those bluffs, all is precision and order. The German Army has long trained for this day, placing machine guns and mortars just so, guaranteeing interlocking fields of fire. Every living thing on the sand is within shooting range. The Germans pride themselves on superior optics. Now they focus binoculars and rifle scopes on vivid details of each victim's life: rank, weight, fitness, hair color, stoicism—or terror. The trigger is pulled. The gun coughs. The shooter sees the instant each human life ends and then searches for his next target.

Or sometimes that soldier fires into the same man a second and third time, just to make certain he's dead. One German soldier will later admit that killing the Americans is so easy he can't stop thinking of all the mothers in America who will receive fateful telegrams about their son's deaths because he continues to pull the trigger.

German artillery and machine guns take particular aim at landing craft doors, firing at the precise moment the ramp is lowered. Distance is recalibrated after each shot, judging by size of the splash and line of sight. When gunners get it right, Americans are mowed down before leaving the boat. Men wearing flamethrowers are a special target, the Germans intent on robbing Americans of this key tool designed specifically to drive enemy soldiers from the massive cement bunkers in which they now hide. Radio operators are also slain—three-fourths of all radios will be destroyed this morning, robbing American forces of the vital ability to communicate.

More and more men pile atop one another at the base of the

seawall as new waves of landing craft continue to unload. The tide rolls ever closer, one foot every ten minutes. By 10:12 this morning the ocean will reach the seawall and the Atlantic will reclaim the invaders. Two and a half hours is a long time, but they will come soon enough.

All the while, the Germans take target practice, launching mortar after mortar toward the seawall, explosions coming ever closer to the pinned-down American force.

. . .

DUTCH COTA ASSESSES the situation. He predicted this. All of it. He is personally invested in this morning's landing, having been a key adviser in the D-Day planning. Cota argued against a daylight invasion, believing darkness and the element of surprise increase the odds of success. Every sight and smell here on Omaha—carnage, resistance, confusion, fire, complete and utter fubar—could have been prevented with a night landing.

But this is no time to be right.

Cota has everything to lose by doing something brash. In just five months, he will celebrate twenty-five years of marriage to the former Connie Alexander. The couple has a grown daughter who once had the honor of being the first girl born at West Point's cadet hospital. They also have a twenty-three-year-old son who flies P-47 Thunderbolts here in Europe. As a general, Cota has every right to direct this morning's action from a safe position—the tank now concealing him from German fire being an ideal location.

Yet Dutch Cota steps out from behind the Sherman.

The general begins looking for a way off the beach. He does not duck or cower. Instead, he walks calmly, standing upright, encouraging the wounded and nonwounded pressed to the sand. "Come on," he yells. "Come on. You've got to go."

Cota holds a pistol in one hand. He bites down on a cigar.

"Get off the beach," he orders the troops, one by one. He is old enough to be their father.

"If you stay here, you're gonna get killed. If you go inland, you may get killed.

"So let's go inland and get killed."

Cota walks back and forth, waving his gun around, at all times completely exposed to enemy fire. Some think he's insane. Others think he's a fool. The Germans think he's bulletproof.

Cota studies the terrain atop the seawall in search of a weakness in the enemy barbed wire. When he is done focusing on one portion of the beach, Cota strolls to another, frequently turning his back on known German gun emplacements. Five minutes pass. Ten. A half hour. Everyone except the general is crouched as low as possible, yet Dutch Cota continues to ignore the crack of bullets and mortar explosions finally forming craters in the sand.

"Several of my men called my attention to a man about one-hundred yards to my right moving along the edge of the beach," one captain will write. "He was chewing on a cigar, yelling and waving at the men in the dunes and at the seawall. He was taking no action to conceal himself from the enemy who continued to pour down small arms fire. We thought him crazy or heroic . . . I saw his insignia of rank: Brigadier General!"

Cota is everywhere, dropping to the ground only once when a shell lands too close. A nearby soldier, seeing only the general's back, complains to anyone who will listen that his matches are wet. Cota rolls over and extends a Zippo lighter.

"Sorry, sir," sputters the embarrassed soldier, glimpsing the star on the general's epaulet.

"That's OK, son," Cota replies, lighting the young man's cigarette.

The tide keeps coming in, a ticking clock determining if this invasion succeeds or fails. It is now 8:00 A.M. Cota's relentless encouragement is raising spirits, even though he has yet to find escape from the beach.

"It took courage for him to stand there in the wide open in the midst of a lot of scared kids," one soldier will write. "His leadership became infectious, because wherever you saw the general walking up and down in plain sight it inspired them to move."

Finally, Dutch Cota sees a way.

The general directs an explosive team to blast channels through the barbed wire above one section of seawall, specifically demanding that a company of elite airborne light infantry known as Rangers do the job. Cota is loud at all times, but his voice grows stronger as he shouts his order above machine-gun fire. "You Rangers have got to lead the way," he barks.*

Doing as ordered, Rangers detonate four paths through the tightly wound rolls of agricultural-grade barbed wire blocking their exit from the beach. The general arrives before the position of Ranger Company C at 8:07, demanding they press on, clear to the top of the bluffs. By 8:10, the Rangers are climbing to the German positions.

One by one, more routes are blasted through the wire. Dutch Cota joins the forward movement, climbing up to the German guns. American soldiers follow this paternal symbol of heroism, rising from the safety of the seawall, guns drawn and ready to fight. One by one, concrete German bunkers are cleared, prisoners taken, and the US Army slowly moves inland, where, as the general told these soldiers quite bluntly, many will soon die.

Dutch Cota, however, has a far different date with destiny.

---

* To this day, "Rangers lead the way" is the motto of America's Army Ranger Special Operations Forces units.

4

Winston Churchill receives the good news, but only after lunch with the king.

The D-Day landings are taking place on a Tuesday. Whether coincidence or providence, this is the day each week George VI and the prime minister have a regularly scheduled midday meal at Buckingham Palace. The tradition began in September 1940. When the king is not in London, the queen takes his place. Sometimes she sits in anyway. But mostly, it is just Churchill and George, doors closed, no servants, filling plates from a sideboard—Churchill abstaining from bread but otherwise not above disrespecting his tailor; George nibbling his light lunch with the proper manners of a man whose every movement has been studied since birth.

These meals have become a time of comfort. Buckingham Palace was bombed twice in September 1940. "Tuesdays" continued. Churchill wrote a few months later that "I have been greatly cheered by our weekly luncheons in poor old bomb-shattered Buckingham Palace."

The prime minister's personal bottle of Pol Roger rests in an ice bucket at his elbow. The king smokes. They began the war as strangers with opposing visions for their beloved nation. Now they are staunch allies. Friends.

Churchill is a scrapper, outspoken, born of a venereal father, short, growing more rotund by the day. George is dapper and reserved, an introvert who would be king only because his brother abdicated the throne in the name of love. Winston and George could not be more different.

Their similarities are found in personal handicaps and vices—and love of Mother England. Churchill is a thespian with a lisp, an unrepentant drinker. Both are athletes, the king superb on horseback and the tennis court; Churchill, despite his middle-age weight gain, is still nimbler. Once, when directed toward the lift—elevator—at Buckingham Palace, he sneered and sprinted up the stairs two at a time.

George is a sovereign ruler who stutters, a dedicated chain-smoker. The prime minister is sovereign in his own way, refusing to seek peace with Adolf Hitler when Britain appeared lost early in the war. The king could have taken his family to safety in Canada during those dark days but chose to remain in London throughout "The Blitz," as Nazi bombing of the city is known.

The British people love them both.

The two most powerful and popular men in Great Britain intended to watch Operation Overlord in person, safely out at sea aboard the light cruiser HMS *Belfast*. Both are sailors, at ease on a swaying deck as the big guns boom—although George is sometimes afflicted with seasickness. The king is a commissioned officer who saw action at sea in World War I. Churchill served twice as First Lord of the Admiralty. Prime Minister sold the *Belfast* idea to George VI as a throwback to ancient times when kings rode into battle with their armies.*

---

* HMS *Belfast* is permanently moored on the Thames in London as a museum.

The desire is not prudent, grown men playing war like schoolboys, risking national security for an adrenaline rush. Yet what other rulers could say they were at D-Day? Not America's Franklin Roosevelt or the Soviet Union's Joseph Stalin—both govern this war from the polite distance of their capital cities and country homes. And certainly not Nazi Germany's Adolf Hitler, who spends his life in a bunker, skin sallow from rarely feeling sunlight's warmth.

But Winston and George could have been there. What a triumph for the embattled British people to see their leaders' courage on display.

Yet on June 2, just four days ago, the king wrote Churchill to say they were making a mistake.

"Please consider my own position," George appealed, knowing that the headstrong Churchill would be tempted to go it alone. "I am a younger man than you, I am a sailor, & as king I am the head of all three services. There is nothing I would like better than to go to sea but I have agreed to stay at home; is it fair that you should then do exactly what I should have liked to do myself?

"You said yesterday afternoon that it would be a fine thing for the King to lead his troops into battle, as in old days; if the King cannot do this, it does not seem to me right that his Prime Minister should take his place."

The king added "Believe me" as a reminder of the best course of action, then signed off by addressing Churchill as "Your very sincere friend."

So it is that the prime minister did not spend this morning in the English Channel, wind on his pale cheeks, salty ocean mist on his tongue. Instead, Churchill addressed the House of Commons at noon, telling them in great detail that Rome fell to the Allies yesterday. This was a moment of pleasant triumph for Churchill. He had long sought to invade Europe through the "soft underbelly" of the Mediterranean and Italy rather than France. It has been six long months of fighting since British and American troops first went ashore at the Anzio beachhead. Victory is a great milestone.

But word flashed to London. Commons already knew. Members of Parliament all assumed Rome would be Prime Minister's reason for taking the floor.

Then, by way of passing, Churchill publicly announces the invasion of France. A stunned Commons roars their approval, bursting into cheers and applause. "Everything is proceeding according to plan," Prime Minister assured them. "And what a plan. This vast operation is undoubtedly the most complicated and difficult that has ever taken place."

Still basking in that success, Churchill drove to the palace for lunch to talk more about D-Day and wonder about the shipboard adventure that might have been.

. . .

BUT IT IS now, after luncheon, the taste of champagne still wet on his lips, that Winston Churchill gets down to the grown-up business of diplomacy. The time is 3:00 P.M. He returns to his office at 10 Downing Street, less than a mile from his meeting with the king. Prime Minister is sixty-nine and weathered, having shouldered the burden of war since the day he took office. His speeches are rousing and his public optimism a fine balance for his private inability to tolerate incompetence.

Great Britain's place in the postwar world weighs heavily upon Churchill's thick shoulders. His nation has grown poor in the past four years, stripped of lucrative Pacific colonies with their gas, oil, and rubber through Japanese invasion. German bombings here at home have killed thousands. A generation of Britain's young men have been killed on battlefields near and far. America will be the global power when this is all done. The Soviet Union will also be mighty, controlling Eastern Europe. Churchill must wedge Britain into the discussion.

He will do so in the spirit of collaboration.

So, Winston Churchill reaches out to Joseph Stalin. The two men strengthened their shaky friendship with a night of hard drinking in Moscow back in 1942. "The best friendships," Stalin tells the prime minister, "are built on misunderstandings." Yet Churchill does not trust the Soviet. Both have known the hot breath of Nazi Germany on the back of their necks. Germany invaded the Soviet Union in 1941. Since, Stalin has long complained that his people have shouldered the war in Europe alone, losing millions of lives while waiting for America and Britain to open a second front in France. The fighting in Italy, bloody as it may be, does not count to the Soviet.

Last November, at a summit held in the Soviet Union's Persian embassy, Roosevelt, Churchill, and Stalin gathered to plan European Front strategy. Roosevelt and Churchill agreed to invade France in 1944. The Soviet leader is not given a specific date or details of the plan for fear of German spies within the Kremlin.

Stalin understands this withholding of information. It does not matter. He has his own spies within the British military. Once the invasion occurs, he vows to launch an offensive that will prevent Hitler's armies from transferring into France to overwhelm the invasion force.

Now that D-Day has come, it is the time to hold Joseph Stalin accountable—never an easy task.

"Everything has started well," Churchill cables Moscow. "The mines, obstacles, and land batteries have been largely overcome. The air landings were very successful, and on a large scale. Infantry landings are proceeding rapidly, and many tanks and self-propelled guns are already ashore."

To Churchill's amazement, Stalin responds within a day. "It gives joy to us all and hope of further successes. The summer offensive of the Soviet forces, organized in accordance with the agreement at the Tehran Conference, will begin towards the middle of June on one of the most important sectors of the front," writes the ruthless Soviet dictator.

Just like his allies' silence about Overlord, Stalin is no more forthcoming with details. But in an astonishing and highly unlikely show of appreciation, the ebullient dictator follows up on that telegraph a few days later.

"My colleagues and I cannot but admit that the history of warfare knows no other like undertaking from the point of view of its scale, its vast conception, and its masterly execution," Stalin writes. "Only our Allies have succeeded in realizing honor [in] the grandiose plan of forcing of the Channel. History will record this deed as an achievement of the highest order."

Winston Churchill delights in the flattery. The sting of not witnessing Overlord in person is replaced by the knowledge that this was all his doing—without Churchill's refusal to surrender to Adolf Hitler during the dark days of 1940, as Britain stood alone against the Nazi bully, the world would be a much different place.

"The word 'grandiose,'" Churchill will write in his memoirs, referring to Stalin's latest message, "is the translation from the Russian text which was given me.

"I think 'majestic' was probably what Stalin meant. At any rate, harmony was complete."

Not for long.

5

The story comes first for Martha Gellhorn.

The journalist's hospital ship drops anchor off Dog Red, one day after General Norman Cota strode like the hero in a John Ford western on these sands. White exterior paint, red crosses on hull and deck so Nazis won't sink the defenseless vessel, a long green horizontal line painted below the deck rail to distinguish it as a governmental hospital ship—aid societies such as the Red Cross bear a red stripe instead. The ship's crew is British, the medical personnel American. Together, they sail into the coming hours of triage, surgery, amputation, and time of death.*

---

* Hollywood film director John Ford served as a navy captain in World War II. He was decorated with the Purple Heart and Legion of Merit for his service. During the invasion of Normandy in June 1944, he commanded US, French, Polish, and Dutch camera crews filming the landings.

Belowdecks, 422 empty white-painted bunks with fresh white sheets, a white mountain of bandages, those doctors and nurses newly arrived from Texas and Michigan and Wisconsin—also white, because integration is slow to come—and a small mountain of lifesaving containers conspicuously marked "whole blood" await the wounded.

Up on the main deck, a hungover Gellhorn gapes at her first sight of the invasion. The writer knows war but this is unlike anything she has ever seen. "It seemed incredible, there could not be so many ships in the world. Then it seemed incredible as a feat of planning—if there were so many ships, what genius it required to get them here, what amazing and unimaginable genius," she will write. "There were destroyers and battleships and transports, a floating city of huge vessels anchored before the green cliffs of Normandy."*

HMHS *Prague* draws near the deadly coast. The invasion continues even as American soldiers are already leaving the beaches behind: gun flashes from the big navy dreadnoughts miles out to sea. Staccato pip of German MG-42 machine guns hidden in the cliffs above the shoreline. A lone landing craft bobbing just offshore, in no hurry to go anywhere at all, laundry line strung across the beam as dance music plays loudly on its radio. Antennae stick up from the surf like graveyard crosses, marking the location of sunken tanks that never made it to shore, drowned crews still trapped inside.

And bodies. Everywhere bodies floating in the surf.

"People will be writing about this sight for a hundred years and whoever saw it will never forget it," she will report for *Collier's* weekly. "Barrage balloons, always looking like comic toy elephants, bounced high in the high wind above the massed ships, and invisible planes droned behind the gray ceiling of cloud . . .

---

* The total number of Allied craft supporting Operation Overlord is 11,590. Of these, 1,213 were naval combat ships, 4,126 were landing craft, 736 were ancillary vessels, and 864 were merchant ships. Eighty percent were British, 16.5 percent were American, and the rest came from France, Holland, Norway, Belgium, and Poland.

"Then we stopped noticing the invasion, the ships, the ominous beach, because the first wounded had arrived."

· · ·

ERNEST HEMINGWAY'S THIRD wife is not allowed to be on board Hospital Carrier No. 61, as the *Prague* is formally known. Martha Gellhorn is a stowaway, a thirty-five-year-old veteran war correspondent who bluffed her way onto this mercy vessel. As a woman, she has been denied a press credential that would allow her to take part in the momentous opening moments of invasion. Not so her husband, who observed Omaha Beach on D-Day from a landing craft before immediately returning to England. At the same time, a lonely Gellhorn grew weary of cold, gray London and worrying about "E." She made her own luck by striking out for Portsmouth, where ships were being launched for France.

The bright white *Prague* was parked quayside, the least military-looking vessel in a port where every ship is painted gray or camouflage. A sentry stopped Gellhorn but she quickly improvised, claiming to be on assignment, sent to interview nurses for *Collier's*. Which is a version of the truth. The MP waved her through. The blond reporter, daughter of a physician and fluent speaker of German, ascended *Prague*'s gangplank and locked herself in a lavatory. She drank whiskey from a flask to calm her nerves, only stepping from the toilet when she felt the ship weigh anchor.

Gellhorn made her way to the main deck. She stood beneath an awning. Cold rain fell, the storm growing more impatient as night turned to day. No one seemed to care she was there. Gellhorn sobered. Traveling at twenty knots, *Prague* entered a shipping lane recently cleared of mines and traveled through a long morning to France. "The only piece of news we had, so far, was that the two hospital ships which preceded us struck mines on their way over," she will tell her readers. "Everyone silently hoped that three would be a lucky number and we waited very hard. . . .

"Then we saw the coast of France and suddenly we were in midst of the armada of the invasion."

. . .

MARTHA GELLHORN IS put to work.

Landing craft pull parallel to the *Prague*. To Gellhorn's surprise, the first patient lifted on board is German. From midafternoon until dark, a steady stream of dead and dying from both sides of the war is borne to the mercy vessel. "The wounded were lifted by men standing on the LST (Landing Ship, Tank), who raised the stretchers high above their heads and handed them up to men on our deck, who caught hold of the stretcher handles. It was a fast, terrifying bucket brigade system but it worked."

The hospital ship also sends its own water ambulances to shore. The small motor launches are capable of transporting six stretchers back to the ship. Steering through the heavy ship traffic while keeping an eye out for mines and submerged tanks is a careful process. The search for wounded is relentless, each boat's skipper scanning the beach for the fallen before darting in to lift them on board. Dead men are left for later when burial details will scour the scene. The return trip is even more demanding, the boats now filled with not just six litters but also any other wounded that can fit. From 2:00 P.M. until dark, the water ambulances travel back and forth, stopping only to unload and refuel.

Gellhorn does not enjoy the journalistic luxury of emotionally detaching from the action. Alongside the medical staff, who will see patients nonstop until returning to England with every bed full tomorrow night, she is expected to work without ceasing. The writer makes herself useful in every way possible, even comforting enemy soldiers in German. She is shocked that these members of the "master race" are mere boys, scared and shell-shocked. Some are giddy that their war is over, chattering loudly despite orders to remain silent.

"*Ruhig!*" Gellhorn barks when it becomes too much.

Stunned Germans instantly shut up.

"It will be hard to tell you of the wounded," Gellhorn writes. "They had to be fed, as most of them had not eaten for two days. Shoes and clothing had to be cut off. They wanted water. The nurses and orderlies, working like demons, had to be found and called quickly to a bunk where a man suddenly and desperately needed attention. Plasma bottles must be watched. Cigarettes had to be lighted and had to be held for those who could not use their hands. It seemed to take hours to pour hot coffee, via the spout of a teapot, into a mouth that just showed through bandages."

No time to take notes. No time to think about her failing marriage or drunken, abusive husband. But Gellhorn watches and listens while she works. She will write of the young American lieutenant with a chest wound who vows to kill the German in the next bunk—if only he can summon the strength to move his arms and legs. There is the Austrian teenager who once fought on the Russian Front. The French farm boy with a shell fragment in his back, his family caught in the cross fire. American soldiers wonder when they'll get back to their unit and how the mail will find them. "What a Heinie," they groan when one haughty German requests special treatment for his pain.

Night falls, giving the *Prague*'s medical mandate more urgency. At least one hundred wounded are still spread out somewhere on Omaha Beach, in need of rescue. First, they must be found. Darkness brings a deep, damp cold that could kill the untreated. Shifting tides force the water ambulance crews to proceed to shore more methodically, using boat hooks to prod the dark water for mines and submerged vehicles. Some ambulances are already stranded on the beach, hulls stuck fast, unable to push back as the moon pulls the ocean away from the soft shoreline sand.

Gellhorn volunteers to assist in the shoreline search. Wreckage can be seen everywhere in the moonlight as they approach the beach: trucks on their side, burned jeeps, upside-down landing craft, typewriters from an administrative unit, mangled bulldozers, barbed wire, tanks at the waterline—all destroyed the very moment they emerged from the Atlantic.

"We waded ashore in water to our waists," she writes. "Everyone was violently busy on that crowded dangerous shore. The pebbles were the size of melons and we stumbled up a road . . . The dust that rose in the gray night seemed like the fog of war itself. Then we got off on the grass and it was perhaps the most surprising of the day's surprises to smell the sweet smell of summer grass, a smell of cattle and peace and sun that had warmed the earth some other time when summer was real."

Left unsaid is that the great Hemingway never set foot on Omaha Beach. Competition has been a fatal hallmark of their union. The next contest will be writing the better story.

Gellhorn returns to the sand and makes her way back to *Prague* on board an ambulance. In just a few short hours, everything belowdecks has changed. The sight is appalling: "Black-Hole-of-Calcutta . . . airless and ill lit. Piles of bloody clothing had been cut off and dumped out of the way in corners. Coffee cups and cigarette stubs littered the decks. Plasma bottles hung from cords, and all the fearful apparatus for holding broken bones made shadows on the walls. There were wounded who groaned in their sleep and there was the soft steady hum of conversation among wounded who could not sleep."

At dawn, *Prague* hoists anchor for the return to England. It's less than thirty-six hours since Martha Gellhorn locked herself in a bathroom. She jokes with the captain and chief medical officer when the safety of Portsmouth heaves into view, calling herself an "old-timer." *Prague* will be cleaned and resupplied, then sent back to France to do it all again.

As German prisoners are off-loaded for the journey to a POW camp, and Black soldiers carry the stretchers of the severely wounded into ambulances, a wave of exhaustion washes over Gellhorn. She never interviewed those nurses. Not formally. Yet she has a story to write. A great story.

First, she must deal with the military police who have come for the stowaway.

Martha Gellhorn is under arrest.

6

Adolf Hitler wants answers.

Two hundred and eleven miles south of London, sixty-two miles northeast of Paris, and four hundred and eighty-four miles west of Berlin, the Führer hunches on a stool in this great monument to what might have been, trying to conjure strategy from chaos. The Führer holds his eyeglasses in one trembling hand. In the other, a red pencil, among a clutch of colored pencils, for scoring the nearby map of France with his tactical opinions. Fifty-five. Insomniac. Puffy circles under his eyes. Untrimmed Charlie Chaplin mustache. A persistent and ongoing talent for flatulence, thanks to a high-fiber diet.

This is Hitler's first-ever—and destined to be only—visit to the lavish Wolfsschlucht II bunker complex. If the dictator is impressed by this particular hall's ornate accouterment—green tile fireplace, maple furniture, deep pile rugs—it does not show.

Field Marshal Erwin Rommel stands before a large easel on which the map rests, double Knight's Cross—it is Rommel's habit to wear the two he has been awarded at the same time—cinched around his throat. The Führer's other top commander on the Western Front, seventy-eight-year-old Field Marshal Gerd von Rundstedt, also stands by, preparing to weigh in with his own strategic advice.

Not that it matters. Despite the tactical genius of those battle-hardened leaders, Hitler will make his own decisions.

The three men are quietly at odds. Hitler defiantly insists a new wave of jet aircraft and guided bombs will turn the war in Germany's favor.

The cynical von Rundstedt, in his tailored gray uniform, favors retreat.

Rommel quietly believes the time has come to sue for peace. Once an acolyte of Adolf Hitler, basking in the Führer's praise, Rommel has lost faith in Nazi leadership.

The fifty-two-year-old Rommel and the aging von Rundstedt could not be more different, the former born in the provincial backwater of Swabia, a region known for its work ethic and a thick local accent Americans would consider hillbilly. Rommel prefers to prowl the front lines during a battle. He drives from his headquarters in the rural town of La Roche-Guyon each day to oversee the fighting. The field marshal used to be Hitler's favorite commander, lionized by German media for his creative use of armor in North Africa. But Rommel's 1942 defeat by the British at El-Alamein robbed him of his swagger. The Führer privately believes Rommel has lost the stomach to be a fighting general.

Von Rundstedt hails from aristocratic Prussia, erudite cradle of the German military for three centuries. He prefers to view the fighting from a more distant perspective, remaining in his villa just outside Paris, nursing his arthritis, heart condition, and fondness for addressing visitors in fluent French.

But both Rommel and von Rundstedt are known for tactical cunning. Which is why Hitler asked them here today.

There is a great deal to discuss. The Allies now have more than a half million men and almost eighty thousand tanks, trucks, and jeeps in France. The invasion is an unqualified success. German casualties are more than twenty-three thousand. Twenty American divisions are now on French soil, facing the fourteen divisions of Rommel's Seventh Army. One division of the Fifteenth has been transferred from Calais to join the fight, but the other twenty-one still stand vigil for General Patton's invasion force. From airpower to supplies to the stunning ability of naval gunnery in destroying German targets from dozens of miles away, the Allies are in charge.

Rommel and von Rundstedt are in agreement about the need to shift the Fifteenth Army from Pas-de-Calais to Normandy.

Once upon a time Adolf Hitler agreed.

Now he does not.

On the morning of June 8, Hitler boldly ordered the Fifteenth south to the Norman coastline. Deciding that two hundred thousand men and tanks might not be enough, he also commanded two other panzer divisions based in Poland to travel with all due haste to France.

But Wehrmacht High Command (*Oberkommando der Wehrmacht*, or OKW) convinced Hitler he was committing a colossal blunder. On June 9, the Führer changed his mind. The Fifteenth stays put. Hitler's decision all but ensures that the Allies will remain in France for a very long time.

Though this is a hard truth, Rommel and von Rundstedt are too fond of their careers to say so this morning.

The field marshals look at the map and see Allied invincibility. Rommel and von Rundstedt argue that if the Führer will not send reinforcements, the German Army should retreat. In a bold gambit, both men suggest Hitler seek a political end to the war.

Hitler hears "surrender," but the field marshals just want this all to end before the Allies bomb Germany back to the Dark Ages.

The Führer looks at the map differently. Hitler does not see a massive Allied force pressing inland. Instead, the map shows a slender crescent moon of beachhead appended to the enormity of Nazi-controlled Europe. The Führer doesn't even use the word "beachhead," correcting his staff that the landings are "the last piece of French soil held by the enemy." He knows Germany possesses the numeric advantage. Despite losing over a million men so far in the war, the Führer has 3.4 million troops at his disposal, with one million of those soldiers blocking the route between Normandy and Berlin.

In this way, Hitler has a knack for looking forward. "Only optimists can pull anything off," he tells his staff.

Thus, the Führer refuses to dwell on what could have been. And it's not just Normandy. Next week marks three years to the day since Hitler invaded the Soviet Union.

And yet . . .

If only the Führer had invaded Great Britain instead.

That's why he built this palace—"bunker" does not do justice to the enormity and luxury of this complex. Wolfsschlucht II was to have been Hitler's command post as his army squeezed the life out of England. Spread out over thirty-five square miles, the warren of buildings, train tunnels, a communications center, six hundred phone lines, hidden gun emplacements, and the opulent Führerbunker was built by twenty-two thousand slaves laboring for eighteen months.

When England took a knee, Hitler would have flown to London from this very location to tour Westminster Abbey and Buckingham Palace, as he did the Eiffel Tower and Napoleon's Tomb when Paris fell in May 1940.

But the invasion of Britain never happened because Hitler chose to attack the Soviet Union instead.

And until last night, Adolf Hitler had never set foot in this lavish bastion.

Yet if the Führer *had* conquered Great Britain . . .

Winston Churchill would be executed, gone with him the oratory that inspired a nation to stiffen their backbone against the same Adolf Hitler now sitting in this very room . . .

The Americans would be waging war only in the Pacific. There would be crushing payback against Japan for the surprise attack at Pearl Harbor but no reason for the US to attack Hitler's Fortress Europe. And even if the Americans did level their gaze against Nazi Germany after defeating the Japanese, where would they stage troops and supplies in the lead-up to the great day?

No place.

All of Europe, North Africa, and the Middle East would remain in German hands. The vital choke points at the Suez Canal and Straits of Gibraltar would be under Hitler's thumb, the Mediterranean a fascist lake. And if neutral Ireland thought for even one diplomatic minute about opening their nation to American troops, Hitler could have easily launched an invading army from Great Britain, putting a crushing end to such nonsense . . .

The Russians would not be massing at some unknown location on Germany's Eastern Front, due to race toward Berlin any day, desperate to rape, pillage, and murder with the same rabid intensity displayed by Hitler's troops as they marched on Moscow . . .

Hitler might have spent much of the last two years hunkered amid the subtle beauty of the French countryside in Wolfsschlucht II, enjoying the tea room atop his personal Führerbunker, with its view of the cathedral at nearby Soissons. Instead, the Führer has directed the war from an equally formidable but far less divine complex known as the "Wolf's Lair"—Wolfsschanze—hidden in a land of mosquito-filled forest and hard winter in eastern Poland . . .

And it would certainly not have taken the Führer so long to travel to this meeting. There was a time when Hitler simply flew into France, as when accepting the French surrender back in 1940. Fighter escorts were a formality. But now the journey begins with a flight to Metz, on the border of France and Germany, in a Focke-Wulf Condor. Four of these long-distance transports that served as Lufthansa airliners before the war were required for Hitler's retinue.

But Allied control of the skies is now overwhelming. Attempting the entire journey by plane is suicidal. Even Hitler's elite SS soldiers call American and British fighter aircraft "meat flies," for the ease with which they swarm potential human targets.

Same for the train. W-II has railroad tracks leading into and out of the compound, all painted rust red to give the appearance of disuse. A long tunnel protected by reinforced concrete provides the ideal place to hide the Führer's locomotive and railway cars. But Allied fighters harry the entire German rail network, disrupting an estimated three hundred trains a day in Germany, France, Belgium, and the Netherlands.

Sheer distance makes walking to this summit an absurd notion. Yet even if that were an option, the Allies are also ruthless in their strafing of German foot soldiers caught out in the open.

Meat flies.

That leaves a car. Traveling by road is scarcely less dangerous than flying or taking the train, but a vehicle can be hidden under a canopy of trees or quickly pulled to the shoulder. Rommel knows this well, chauffeured daily through the country roads of Normandy despite enemy aircraft. So it was that Hitler chose to complete the final 175 miles of his journey to this meeting in a convoy of armored vehicles.

Now, as if to punctuate Allied aerial superiority, today's strategy session is interrupted by the overhead drone of sixty American bombers. Maybe B-17 Flying Fortresses, maybe B-24 Liberators. No one can tell without stepping outside to look. No matter that W-II is not their target. Hitler and the field marshals hunker in a bomb shelter until the all-clear resumes their conference.

Today's summit is done by 4:00 P.M. Hitler walks Rommel to the field marshal's black Horch staff car. In two weeks' time, the Führer will relieve Field Marshal von Rundstedt of command. But he steps outside now because he still has a nostalgic faith in the Rommel that used to be.

The field marshal makes a plea for the Führer to extend his journey to France by visiting German frontline troops in Normandy. Winston Churchill recently traveled from England to encourage British soldiers in France. A similar surprise appearance by Hitler will surely elevate failing German morale.

The Führer promises to be there in the morning.

"What do you really think of our chances of continuing the war?" Rommel wonders aloud. He once served on Hitler's staff and is mostly unafraid to speak his mind. The field marshal believes the best course of action is to join with the West and halt the Soviet advance. Of course, he does not say that now.

"That is a question which is not your responsibility. You will have to leave that to me," Hitler shoots back. "Attend to your invasion front."

Which Rommel does, ordering his driver to make haste for his headquarters chateau. The journey to La Roche-Guyon is three hours and relatively safe in his luxury car. Top down. Warm summer weather. Closest Normandy battlefields more than two hundred miles away. A chance to breathe easy with the meat flies out of range.

And plenty of time to think.

Erwin Rommel is complicit in a plot to murder the Führer. Not an active participant, but he hears rumors. Date and place to come. This is how much he believes in peace.

Yet Rommel now has second thoughts. Seven hours with Hitler brings back his old optimism.

Rommel writes to his wife later in the evening, reassuring her that better days are coming. "The Führer was very cordial and in a good humor. He realizes the gravity of the situation," the field marshal assures his beloved Lucia.

Rommel looks forward to seeing the faces of his troops as the Führer pays the surprise visit. Perhaps this will turn the tide.

But Adolf Hitler does not arrive in the morning. The Führer has more immediate demands back in Berlin:

The Russians are coming.

7

Joseph Stalin keeps his promise.

The message arrives. Twenty minutes since sunrise. The Soviet dictator paces in his wood-paneled Kremlin office. He unravels the papers of a Herzegovina Flor cigarette and slides tobacco into the bowl of his pipe. His last name translates to "man of steel," but it depends upon who does the translating. Stalin's subjects call him Vozhd—the Boss. He strikes a match, puffs, takes a deep pull.*

A good night's sleep for Stalin is four hours. Waiting for the newly arrived missive made even that small rest impossible. Sixty-five. Dwarfed in height by Churchill, though Stalin is not as broad. Thick head of graying hair combed straight back. A mustache for the ages, robust and perfectly shaped. He has killed millions of his people

---

* Author George Orwell's 1945 novel, *Animal Farm*, will depict Stalin as a pig named Napoleon who "has a reputation for getting his own way."

without firing a single shot, through famine and starvation. Before his reign ends, the dictator will purge millions more.

But it is Joseph Stalin's skill as a military strategist that matters most right now—and past results are mixed. His fondness for over-ambitious offensives has proven impractical—January 1942 and the Rzhev salient, the Little Saturn operation outside Stalingrad, Kharkov and the Kursk salient. And with those setbacks, comrades dead and dying by the millions: 2,993,803 Soviet soldiers killed or missing in 1941. Almost the exact same figure—2,993,536—in 1942. Another 1,977,127 last year.*

Stalin learned. Which does not mean today's offensive is scaled back. Hardly. Operation Bagration will be bigger by far than any previous Soviet attack. Words like "overambitious" and "impractical" have no place, no matter how many lives are lost.

Three years ago, almost to this very moment, Adolf Hitler's armies swept into the Soviet Union. Operation Barbarossa sent 3.1 million German soldiers, 3,350 panzers, 5,000 aircraft, and 7,000 artillery pieces dashing into Soviet territory. Capturing Moscow—and Joseph Stalin—was the primary objective. This is not a war between two armies but between two peoples, the Germans showing the Russians none of the relative deference the French experienced while being conquered. Every man, woman, and child in the Soviet Union has become a soldier.

Moscow held. Hitler failed. And every day since, Stalin's armies slowly regained the soil of Mother Russia.

---

* Source: *When Titans Clashed*, by David Glantz and Jonathan House. As an aside, the exact number of wartime deaths throughout the entire Soviet Union remains unknown, but estimates have publicly increased since World War II. Stalin admitted to an official figure of 7 million in 1946. That number was altered to 26.5 million total deaths by Russian president Vladimir Putin in 2015, of which 12 million were soldiers and 14.5 million were civilians.

Now, three hundred miles west of Moscow, reporting from the dense woods and swollen rivers of Belorussia, Marshal Aleksandr Vasilevsky tells Stalin that the time for *maskirovka*—"deception"—is over. His great army is ready to come out of hiding and fight. White Russia, the land of impenetrable forests, mighty rivers, and thick swamps from which the operation will launch, has been ravaged by Nazi Germany. More than one million citizens are dead, among them every Jew in the region. Somewhere between 250,000 and 370,000 locals live off the land, enraged and displaced in the forest, their towns wiped off the map.

Success or failure depends on the Soviet strategy known as Deep Battle, with its four basic tenets: maintaining initiative, employing *maskirovka*, massing forces to enjoy superior numbers at all times, and immediately exploiting penetrations into enemy territory.

Bagration is staggering in its enormity and breadth, an invasion of German-held territories of such scope and scale that the battle plan mimics the enormity of the nation about to give it birth. This is a land of steppes and tundra, flaming deserts and Arctic ice, primeval forests and impenetrable swamps, ornate cities and peasant farms, revolution and ideology and religion, where the very best ancient czars and emperors preferred to be known as "The Great" if they were virtuous or "The Terrible" if they were indeed wretched; a swath of conflict and bloodshed so vast it cannot be contained within a single continent.

D-Day was "majestic."

Operation Bagration is Russian.

The name says it all. General Pyotr Bagration is not a Communist proselyte, defender of the proletariat, hero of the Soviet Union. He was Russian through and through, mortally wounded defending his homeland against Napoleon's 1812 invasion. Bagration fought so long and so brilliantly to protect Moscow that Napoleon was forced to retreat, never to invade Russia again.

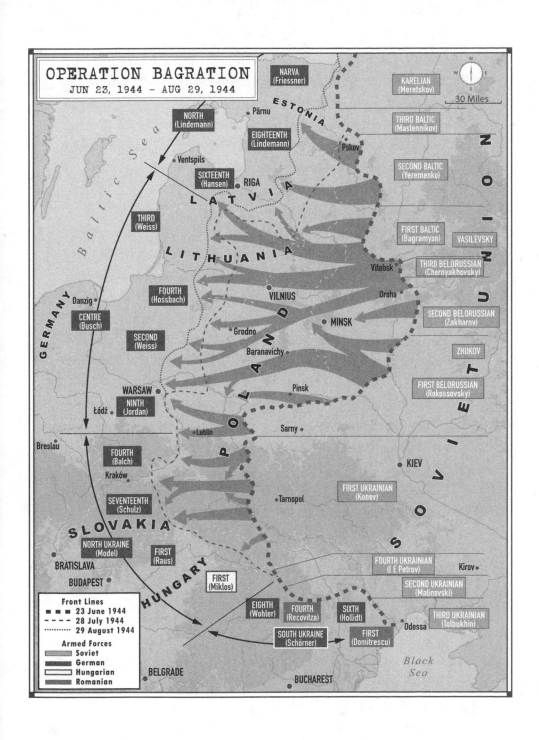

OPERATION BAGRATION
JUN 23, 1944 – AUG 29, 1944

NARVA (Friessner)

KARELIAN (Meretskov)

30 Miles

NORTH (Lindemann)

Pärnu

ESTONIA

THIRD BALTIC (Maslennikov)

EIGHTEENTH (Lindemann)

Pskov

Baltic Sea

Ventspils

SECOND BALTIC (Yeremenko)

SIXTEENTH (Hansen)

RIGA

LATVIA

FIRST BALTIC (Bagramyan)

VASILEVSKY

THIRD (Weiss)

LITHUANIA

Vitebsk

THIRD BELORUSSIAN (Chernyakhovsky)

Orsha

Danzig

GERMANY

FOURTH (Hossbach)

VILNIUS

SECOND BELORUSSIAN (Zakharov)

CENTRE (Busch)

MINSK

SECOND (Weiss)

Grodno

ZHUKOV

Baranavichy

POLAND

FIRST BELORUSSIAN (Rokossovsky)

Pinsk

WARSAW

SOVIET UNION

Łódź

NINTH (Jordan)

Sarny

Breslau

Lublin

FOURTH (Balch)

KIEV

Kraków

FIRST UKRAINIAN (Konev)

SEVENTEENTH (Schulz)

Tarnopol

SLOVAKIA

NORTH UKRAINE (Model)

FIRST (Raus)

FOURTH UKRAINIAN (I E Petrov)

Kirov

BRATISLAVA

HUNGARY

SECOND UKRAINIAN (Malinovski)

BUDAPEST

FIRST (Miklos)

Front Lines
- ▪▪▪ 23 June 1944
- --- 28 July 1944
- ⋯ 29 August 1944

EIGHTH (Wohler)

FOURTH (Recovitza)

SIXTH (Hollidt)

THIRD UKRAINIAN (Tolbukhin)

Odessa

Armed Forces
- Soviet
- German
- Hungarian
- Romanian

SOUTH UKRAINE (Schörner)

FIRST (Domitrescu)

Black Sea

BELGRADE

BUCHAREST

. . .

PALE MORNING SUN glints off the eleven Red Square domes of St. Basil's Cathedral. Joseph Stalin gives his approval to launch. Within the next three hours, six main thrusts by the Soviet Army will punch forth along a front running 450 miles north to south. More than 1.2 million valiant Soviet men and women, 2,175 tanks, 1,355 self-propelled guns, 24,000 guns and mortars, and more than 6,000 aircraft stand poised to extract revenge on Nazi Germany.

And they will not fail.

There is victory and there is death, nothing else: "*Yést chelovék, yést probléma—nyet chelovéka, nyet problémy,*" in Stalin's own words.*

At precisely 5:00 A.M., wreaths of artillery smoke puff into the clear June morning air. Flame belches from barrels and the earth shakes as big guns open fire. German troops huddle in their underground bunkers on the receiving end of those enormous projectiles, protected by pine trees laid over the top, praying a direct hit will not take their lives.

It does not matter. One way or the other, now or in a Soviet prison camp, they are all about to die.

Joseph Stalin and his army are racing to Berlin.

---

* Loosely, "Yes human, yes problem—no human, no problem."

8

General George S. Patton is also on his way to Berlin.

Sort of.

Patton's C-47 transport enters French airspace over Omaha Beach. The plane is heavy, loaded to its six-thousand-pound maximum cargo capacity. Patton, two aides, and his personal jeep fill the hold. The general's year-old white bull terrier, Willie, snores in the vehicle's driver's seat. Four P-47 Thunderbolts fly escort as the slow Skytrain descends for landing. The fighters' powerful Pratt & Whitney R-2800 Double Wasp engines are capable of 533 nautical miles per hour but are now throttled all the way back to maintain close contact with the C-47's wingtips.*

---

* Advanced Landing Grounds (ALGs) were among the first acts of engineering after the Normandy landings. The airfields were oriented east-west and initially covered in a wire known as Square Mesh Track. Later techniques to stiffen the often-muddy landing surface were steel planking and asphalt-impregnated jute. Each site was given a code number, such as A-9. In all, more than two dozen temporary airfields

Landing in France is Patton's first step in joining the war. Step two is Third Army activation, which could happen any day now. Then the general will fight.

Yet, for the time being, he's *still* a secret—and must remain so.

One month after D-Day, the German Fifteenth Army *still* stands ready, waiting for Patton at Pas-de-Calais. By order of the Führer, those troops are *still* not allowed to pivot south and destroy the Overlord invasion force.

And even though George S. Patton is a most unwilling participant, the very necessary Allied deception is working.

Still.

Everything now depends on Patton maintaining his low profile, patiently resisting the rambunctious quest for glory that seems to define his every action.

But this is no way to keep a secret. Everyone on the ground can see what's going on. Curiosity is instantly roused as the thousands of soldiers and sailors here at the airstrip witness the fighter planes just off the Skytrain's wingtips—a sure sign that a VIP is on board.

Patton sits with his back against the fuselage. Handguns, polished boots, thick wool-lined jacket. The general is grumpy, impatient, and eager—a description that applies almost every day but even more so now. An infected toe makes walking painful and he fears he will lose the nail. Sitting for the hour-long flight from England, one borrowed boot a size too large to accommodate the swollen digit, makes it worse. But most excruciating of all is the endless wait to lead men in battle. "I hope they don't win the war without us," he wrote home to Beatrice

---

were constructed on the Cotentin Peninsula in the summer of 1944. It is likely, based on descriptions of the landing site as being close to Omaha Beach, that Patton's C-47 touched down at Saint-Laurent-sur-Mer Airfield—A-21. The field closed by August 25, 1944, as Paris was liberated. The runways were returned to their previous agricultural use and, like most other ALGs, are today indistinguishable as former airstrips.

three weeks ago. She is a fiercely loyal military wife, putting up with his long absences and occasional dalliances.

Two days later, in another letter: "Still we sit and fear that the war will be over without us."

And again: "I wish I was fighting."

Patton has used the time to study French road maps, strategize when and how his Third Army will attack, and pray the war will not end before he gets another chance to draw German blood. He pays particular attention to the battle routes of William the Conqueror, reading the entire six-volume *History of the Norman Conquest of England* to learn which roads armies traveled upon in the eleventh century. Patton believes he can follow the same routes, knowing that terrain that proved passable for wooden carts and knights on horseback will be reliable in all conditions for modern trucks and tanks.

The general is also voracious in reading about the current Norman conquest. The Allied advance has bogged down since D-Day. To the northeast, British general Bernard Law Montgomery is still unable to capture the French town of Caen, an objective almost five weeks overdue. Here on the Cotentin Peninsula the beaches are secure, but American troops are moving inland too slowly, forward penetration thwarted by German troops protected in thick marshes and dense hedgerows.*

Patton's fighter escort peels away, prize cargo safely delivered. Upon landing, the two-man C-47 aircrew parks on a secure section of the airfield, separate from the wingtip-to-wingtip rows of transports and fighters—raising still more questions about the plane's occupants.

"Come on," Patton says to aide Major Alexander Stiller as the aircraft comes to a halt. Hazy outside. Light rain.

"Let's see if there is a war going on."

---

* The Cotentin Peninsula is also known as the Cherbourg Peninsula.

The door aft the wing is opened for the general. Twenty-eight paratroopers leapt from this egress in the first hours of D-Day. Now it is Patton, followed by Willie, and then the general's aides who step down a small ladder onto the airstrip.

Most telling that someone special has just arrived, a work crew scrambles to unload the jeep—an exceptional act of haste in the "hurry up and wait" world of the United States Army.

Two parallel ramps, each the width of a tire, are affixed to the open cargo door. The plane is barely wider than the vehicle. A bemused Patton kills time watching soldiers manhandle the jeep onto the narrow ramps and roll it backward out the door in halting fits and starts. One man steers in the driver's seat as four others actually stand on the ground behind the vehicle, hands pushing on the rear bumper and spare tire, putting their entire body weight into slowing the descent and preventing the jeep from hurtling out of control down each ramp—completely oblivious to their own peril.

Weighing in at more than three-fourths of a ton, this is no ordinary jeep. Patton has ordered the motor pool at his British headquarters to modify this Dodge WC57 to the unique requirements of a general who plans to roam the front lines. Armor plates protect the floor and radiator. A Browning M1919A44 .30-cal machine gun is mounted to the passenger running board, should Patton feel the need to take aim at German aircraft. A grab rail behind the front seats gives the general a handhold when he stands to address his troops. Finally, air horns on the front bumper and fender will announce his arrival above the din of combat.

So it is that the uncommon sights of the fighter escort, secure parking spot, rapid unloading, and a jeep unlike any other draw attention this morning. But it is George S. Patton himself, standing in the open with nowhere to hide, who now betrays his own secret. Patton's face has graced the cover of *Time* magazine—soon to appear on the cover of *Life* for a second time as well. Soldiers everywhere know him. His polished boots and unique pistols are iconic. Even Willie gets his picture in the paper.*

Patton is mobbed. Soldiers and sailors gather on all sides, eager for his legendary charisma to rub off on them. "A great many soldiers seemed to know me and wanted to take photographs, mostly soldiers with $5.00 Leicas," he will write in his journal tonight.

More troubling, writers and photographers for some of America's major newspapers and magazines crowd in to get the story, truly putting the general's ruse at risk. "There were some professionals present whom I warned off by assuring them I was still a secret," Patton will add. He keeps the diary for himself and posterity, anticipating that future biographers will want to learn his thoughts.

The general towers over most of the young crowd, not quite posing for pictures but not hiding, either. "When you see General Patton," one navy lieutenant will write of his own encounter, "you get the same feeling as when you saw Babe Ruth striding up to the plate: here's a big guy who's going to kick hell out of something."†

Jeep finally off-loaded, Patton steps into the vehicle and remains standing. He surveys the eager mob, knowing they want some sort of impromptu speech.

Patton's months of delivering long messages on English parade grounds is past. No more witty descriptions of what battle will be like. It will be this way from now on: Short, improvised words to inspire men in the thick of the fight. Frontline words. Words about fighting

---

* Patton first graced the cover of *Life* in July 1941. His second cover will be in January 1945.

† One month later, Patton will learn of a B-17 bomber crew forced to parachute when their aircraft is hit by ground fire. All nine land near Patton's lines in France. Upon learning their location, the general orders his driver to take him there. Patton awards each man the Bronze Star and orders them flown back to England in his personal C-47. On the way, one flier told a Patton aide, "What a guy!" Another added, "I never thought I'd get to meet him. It was worth getting shot for."

and dying. The right message delivered at the right time will make the difference between an army advancing without fear and an army too cowed to move forward.

"I'm proud to be here to fight beside you," he begins. Applause and cheers. If these men haven't already heard his famous speech, they have heard about it. They know what's coming. Officers stiffen, anticipating the profanity. Young enlisted soldiers eagerly wait to hear a three-star general talk in crude barracks language.

Patton doesn't have time for a twenty-minute address. Yet the general does not disappoint.

"Now let's cut the guts out of those Krauts and get the *hell* on to Berlin.

"And when we get to Berlin, I am going to personally shoot that paper-hanging *goddamned son of a bitch* like I would a *snake*," he finishes, voice rising and slowing for dramatic emphasis, coming down hard on the profanities and last word. It's a line he's delivered several times in the past, and Patton lands it for maximum impact.

The troops roar at the awesome thought of the great General George S. Patton using one of his legendary revolvers to shoot Adolf Hitler dead. They're going to remember this moment for the rest of their lives—however long or short that may be.

That is all.

Patton is driven away, cheers trailing in his wake.

. . .

THE FIRST HOURS in France are an education.

Patton views Omaha Beach, where ruined German pillboxes and remains of a prefabricated Allied "Mulberry" harbor recently destroyed by storm are his first glimpses of post-invasion destruction. Behind the beach, the terrain is marsh and hedgerows, cultivated fields, green everywhere he looks. Patton is surprised to see prosperous farms with cattle, chicken, horses, and ducks—war clearly came late to Normandy.

He spends the night at the headquarters of fellow general Omar Bradley near the town of Isigny. The front lines are less than five miles away. American artillery situated near Bradley's position fires through the hours of darkness, a loud reintroduction to war for Patton, who has not seen action for a year. "It was extremely noisy, possibly I had forgotten about war. In any case, the tent shook practically all night long from the discharge," he will write.

Patton rises from his cot several times to watch, Willie at his side. No leash. Patton adopted the dog from the widow of an RAF pilot lost in combat. The previous owner took Willie along on bombing raids, never completely inuring the dog he called Punch from the sound of antiaircraft fire. There are rumors Patton renamed the dog for William the Conqueror. "Willie did not like it at all," the general will tell Beatrice of their hours of tooth-rattling barrage.

July 7 is a Friday. Lunch is at General Montgomery's headquarters in Blay, just west of Bayeux. Monty is testy, refusing to take responsibility for his inability to capture Caen, the general's sole objective since D-Day. He argues that the British are fighting a much tougher force than the Americans. The general goes one step further, demanding that Patton's Third Army remain inactive for as long as it takes for Montgomery to capture not just Caen but also the city of Avranches, sixty long miles southwest.

Patton is appalled. This could take months.

Also, Third Army, once activated, has the most direct line from the Norman coast to Avranches. The slow transfer of men and matériel from England to France is almost complete. For Monty to sideline Patton for the sake of personal glory is incomprehensible.

Technically, as commander of Allied ground forces, Montgomery can make this decision unilaterally. Bradley's American troops are under the command of Monty's 21st Army Group. When Patton's Third Army is finally activated, he will also be under Monty's command. This will change when Dwight Eisenhower relocates his headquarters to France from London. No one knows precisely when that day will come. In the meantime, Monty is in charge.

Yet Montgomery's failure to capture Caen is receiving a great deal of negative publicity. Eisenhower is growing impatient. Even Churchill is having doubts about his top general. Monty now seeks a consensus rather than issuing an order, desiring the glory that will come from a swift dash to Avranches but not willing to shoulder the entire burden of blame should he fail.

Bradley sides with Patton, firmly stating that activation of Third Army will not wait on Montgomery and Caen.

"Bradley refused to bite," Patton will write in his diary. "He is using me as a means of getting out from under the 21st Army Group. I hope he succeeds."

. . .

AND STILL PATTON waits, doing his best to keep out of sight. War is all around him as the two hundred thousand officers and soldiers of Third Army swarm into France. "Lucky Forward," as his headquarters will become known, grows larger every day. But the general's life is reduced to the routine and mundane. He passes the time reading and fretting in his new combat trailer, a mobile command post complete with bed, desk, and maps. The pain in his toe is unbearable.*

"It was infected, so I had the nail pulled off after breakfast," he writes in his journal.

To Beatrice, the general adds:

"There is nothing to do at the moment but be a secret weapon."

_____

* A unit such as the Third comprises two or more Corps, each numbering between fifty thousand and one hundred thousand men. A Corps comprises two or more Divisions, each having a strength of ten thousand to eighteen thousand. Since Napoleon, the Division has been the primary fighting unit, containing all the elements necessary to sustain itself in combat. By World War II, that meant infantry, artillery, supply units, and armor instead of Napoleonic cavalry. In descending order of size, fighting units at the Division level are then subdivided into Brigades, Regiments, Battalions, Companies, Platoons, Sections, and then Squads comprising less than a dozen men.

9

The secret weapon is unleashed.

General George Patton splashes brandy into a glass, then pours another for his loyal aide, Colonel Paul "Ramrod" Harkins. The two men have traveled the same road through this war: Louisiana war games, North Africa, Sicily, and now France. All that is left is Germany.

A toast forgotten by history. Clink of raised glasses. Bent elbow. A powerful swallow. Then the sudden urge to spit it out. "Horrible brandy," Patton will describe the taste.

Yet the two men choke it down. Someone has to do it. Everyone else in Lucky Forward has gone to the mess tent for lunch. It is left to Patton and Harkins to celebrate Third Army's activation alone.

For almost two months, the Germans have waited on Patton. They know precisely how he is about to wage war and find the thought terrifying. But for all that fear, the reality of the *reisensaurei*—"one hell of a mess"—will be stupefying in its execution and slaughter.

One hell of a mess, indeed.

So Patton repeats an earlier message to his troops for emphasis, this time making sure his staff hears the words loud and clear.

"I don't want to get any messages saying that 'We are holding our position,'" Patton reminded them last night, giving a taste of what is to come. "We are not holding anything. Let the Hun do that. We are advancing constantly, and we're not interested in holding on to anything except the enemy. We're going to hold him by the nose and we're going to kick him in the ass. We're going to kick the hell out of him all the time, and we're going to go through him like crap through a goose."

Patton pauses, then shares his personal maxim, just in case any single man in the room has doubts about expectations:

"We have one motto: *L'audace, l'audace, toujours, l'audace.*

"Remember that, gentlemen."

Audacity, audacity, always audacity.

It is 683 miles from this apple orchard to Berlin—a battlefield stretching roughly the same distance as New York to Chicago. Patton believes some of the toughest fighting will come at the vital French transportation hub at Metz (348 miles, London to Edinburgh) and instructs his intelligence chief, Colonel Oscar Koch, to prepare accordingly. Koch is on record as noting that the German armies are far from defeated, "and will continue to fight until destroyed or captured."

The romantic in Patton is fascinated by the thought of liberating Paris (180 miles, New York to Washington, DC); the general's juggernaut style of tank warfare—featuring rapid forward movement even at the risk of overextending his forces and putting his flanks in jeopardy—does not allow for the house-to-house street fighting that is sure to take place in that city of four million.

Patton slept poorly in anticipation of today's activation. He visited the front lines to view the action and returned to Lucky Forward late, not switching off the light in his command trailer until 1:00 A.M. Since Patton arrived in France three weeks ago, that mobile command post has been neither mobile nor a place of command, parked between apple trees, night after night, like the small domicile of a tenant farmer with an amazing security detail.

Dawn was just as bad, all pacing and waiting. American forces are finally pressing inland from the Norman hedgerows. Avranches has fallen, and Montgomery had nothing to do with it. Patton is impatient to lead the "breakout," as the sudden American penetration into France is known.

"I was very nervous all morning," he will confide in his diary of the long wait for noon. Dreadful fears of Germany suing for peace before lunch. Third Army's activation delayed.

"It seemed impossible to get any definite news and the clock seemed to have stopped."

But noon now comes and goes without any signs of peace.

"Compared to war, all human activities are futile," Patton believes. "If you like war as much as I do."

Let the breakout begin.

10

Field Marshal Erwin Rommel believes in drastic measures.

Germany's answer to General George S. Patton sits in his home study, restless. Nothing to do but sit and heal. Outside, a Nazi command car pulls up the driveway. Slam of the passenger door. Boots walking quickly to the front door. Large white mansion. Long green front lawn. Thick pine forest right out back. This former home of a Jewish industrialist was granted to Rommel by Adolf Hitler as reward for distinguished service. Dark wood, coffered ceilings, art nouveau, bay windows. Somewhere sleeps the dachshund puppy Rommel brought back from France.

Fifteen-year-old Manfred Rommel has not seen his father since the crash. A maid lets him in. The young soldier steps past her, wearing the Luftwaffe uniform of his antiaircraft battery. He would have preferred to join Hitler's fearsome Waffen SS but his father talked him out of it. In a hurry, Manfred drops his rucksack to the floor. Mess tins clatter. The teenager washes his hands and face, then goes straight into the study.*

Erwin Rommel is waiting. Germany's fifty-two-year-old Desert Fox is not preparing for battle, nor is he in uniform. He reclines in a comfortable armchair next to a low coffee table, dressed in casual civilian coat and tie. His ruddy North African tan is no more—though Manfred pays little attention to the pale skin.

Instead, the fifteen-year-old's gaze is drawn instantly to the black patch covering his father's blind left eye, face covered in scratches and scabs, and the fractured cheekbones forming a crater from temple to jaw.

"I still get headaches," the field marshal assures his only legitimate child. "But it will all get better."

It is five weeks since Canadian Royal Air Force Spitfire aircraft strafed Rommel's staff car with 20mm cannon while he was driving back to La Roche-Guyon. The eight-inch shells tore through the vehicle. Rommel's skull broke in three places as his mortally wounded driver lost control. The field marshal was launched when his Horch careened into a ditch, sliding on his face after landing unconscious in the middle of a country road.

This is not how a lifetime in uniform is supposed to end for Germany's most famous general. He is respected by friend and foe alike, with even Churchill calling the wily tank commander "a daring and skillful opponent" and "across the havoc of war, a great general." Yet here Rommel rests, tended by wife, Lucia,† two doctors, and now Manfred.

The arc of Rommel's war mirrors that of his Fatherland: stunning

---

* German antiaircraft units were under the command of the air force, known as the Luftwaffe.

† She also went by the nickname Lucie.

early triumphs, omnipotence on the field of battle, stalemate and struggle, shocking defeats, and now near death. The field marshal is thus disillusioned about Germany's fate and his own, insights held long before his skull shattered.

But Manfred is a patriot, called up for military service just months ago and now assigned to a battery in nearby Ulm. Manfred believes in the "glory around the personage of Hitler," in his own words. Like all young Germans, he is too young to remember Germany having any other leader. Belief in Hitler's divinity is common among his peers.

Manfred does not know his father believes differently—nor that Erwin Rommel is complicit in a July 20 plot to murder the Führer. Hitler not only survived the bomb explosion but is in the process of rounding up the nearly seven thousand suspects associated with the attempt on his life. So many generals have been arrested that Field Marshal Gerd von Rundstedt is soon to be recalled to service, once again to command German forces in France. Executions have already begun—a simple hanging for those at the outer fringe of the conspiracy and the more brutal strangulation by piano wire for key plotters.

Rommel's former chief of staff, General Hans Speidel, is a prime suspect. He will most likely be arrested soon. If so, then it is only a matter of time before Hitler's torturers extract the confession that will lead them back to Rommel. Indeed, the field marshal knows that agents of the German Secret State Police—the Gestapo—are spying on the residence.

Amazingly, should Rommel's participation in the plot remain hidden, he will undoubtedly return to command. Adolf Hitler is far from defeated—and not of a mind to surrender. As the Allied forces creep closer to Berlin, there is enormous positive propaganda to be gained by sending Germany's most famous general back into the field.

"My nerves are pretty good, but sometimes I was near collapse," Rommel tells Manfred, describing the fighting in Normandy. "It was casualty reports, casualty reports, casualty reports, wherever you went.

I have never fought with such losses. And the worst of it is that it was all without sense or purpose. . . . The sooner it finishes, the better for all of us."

Manfred is unsure how to respond. Such talk is treason. Hearing it from a national hero like his father is a shock.

"Tell me, Manfred," Erwin Rommel asks. "What do the young chaps think when Hitler suddenly hangs a whole lot of people who have persuaded themselves—not wholly without reason—that the war is lost and that we should make an end of it at last?"

"They're all pretty sick of the war," Manfred responds. "Most of them still believe we can win it somehow or other."

"But it's already lost," the field marshal responds, before adding a quiet admission: "What if I, too, had declared myself ready to end it—even against Hitler's will?"

"Why do you ask that?" responds his alarmed son.

"Oh, let's leave it for now."

11

Sergeant Bud Hawk keeps his finger on the trigger.

The Allied breakout races toward Germany full gas. "Third Army has advanced further and faster than any army in the history of the war," General George S. Patton writes in his journal. He is already anticipating a quick end to the war, lamenting the inevitable return to a peacetime world. "Civil life will be mighty dull—no cheering crowds, no flowers, no private airplanes. I am convinced that the best end for an officer is the last bullet of the war."

But the war is not over yet.

The German Seventh Army is also on the run, retreating en masse from the Allied beachheads in their own desperate dash to the Fatherland. Patton's fighters—among them Sergeant Hawk—now form a roadblock to prevent that escape.

Hawk's hands, filthy from shoveling a foxhole out of the rich black soil, cradle his M1941 Johnson light machine gun. Soft summer rain

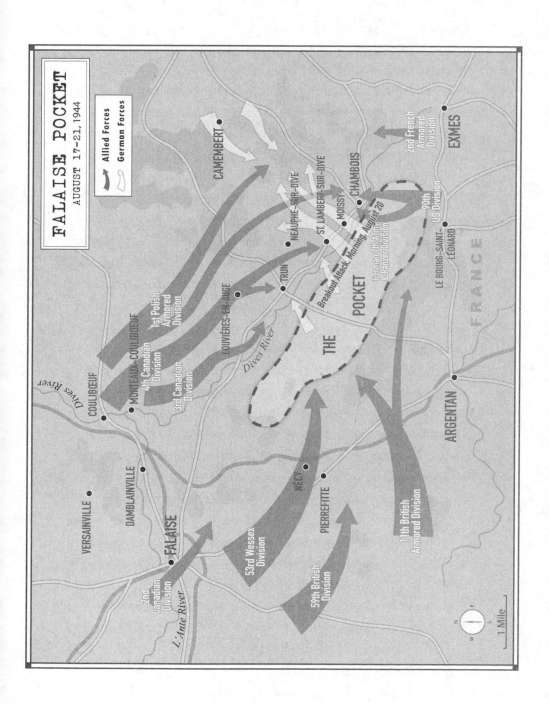

FALAISE POCKET
AUGUST 17–21, 1944

Allied Forces
German Forces

CAMEMBERT

EXMES

2nd French
Armored
Division

NEAUPHE-SUR-DIVE

ST. LAMBERT-SUR-DIVE

CHAMBOIS

MOISSY

1st Polish
Armored
Division

LOUVIÈRES-EN-AUGE

TRUN

90th
US Division

Breakout Attack Morning, August 20

German 7th Army
& Panzer Division

LE BOURG-SAINT-
LEONARD

MORTEAUX–COULIBOEUF

4th Canadian
Division

3rd Canadian
Division

Dives River

THE

POCKET

FRANCE

Dives River

COULIBOEUF

DAMBLAINVILLE

ARGENTAN

NÉCY

VERSAINVILLE

PIERREFITTE

FALAISE

11th British
Armored Division

53rd Wessex
Division

2nd
Canadian
Division

59th British
Division

L'Ante River

N
W   E
S

1 Mile

pelts the twenty-year-old squad leader. Sharp smells fill the morning air: cider apples, gunpowder, and the pungent rot of slaughtered speckled cows and young soldiers.

The rest of Easy Company, 359th Infantry Regiment, spreads out next to this orchard, awaiting the German attack. They are all Third Army—Patton's boys. The battle will take place right here. No one has a doubt. The Americans are badly outnumbered. They know the Germans have no capacity to take prisoners—captured US soldiers will simply be machine-gunned and left. There can be no retreat. No surrender.

"Who dares wins," as the British like to say.

For now, Easy sits and waits. Hawk is wiry, on the small side. Just one year removed from high school graduation but capable enough to make sergeant. His father taught him to shoot in the forests of Washington. Bud considers himself a marksman, versed in range and wind. But what shoots can also be shot. So, Sergeant Hawk keeps low—standing up to pluck a breakfast apple invites a sniper's bullet.

Somewhere out there in the morning storm hides a desperate German Army Group B. Fifty thousand Nazi soldiers are trapped within a ten-mile-wide noose known as the "Falaise Pocket." Their attempts to break free and make a run for the German border have not only failed but resulted in "absolute carnage," in Bud Hawk's description. "Animals, people, equipment, an incomprehensible slaughterhouse."

The 90th Division, to which Easy Company belongs, will record 12,335 prisoners taken this week, with another 8,000 enemy killed. This hilltop vantage point has already been christened "the balcony of death."

No less than General Dwight Eisenhower, supreme commander of Allied Forces in Europe, will describe the Falaise Pocket as "one of the greatest 'killing fields' of any of the war areas . . . scenes that could be described only by Dante. It was literally possible to walk for hundreds of yards at a time, stepping on nothing but dead and decaying flesh."

The 90th has suffered over five thousand dead, wounded, and captured since coming ashore on Utah Beach ten weeks ago—one of the highest casualty rates in the war. "We have no pictures of D-Day," the unit history will bitterly record. "Men are not in the mood to take pictures while all hell is breaking loose around them."

Yet in the two months since, the German Army has been thrown back in disorganized retreat, a chaos of men and weaponry lacking leadership and hope.

The Falaise Pocket's weaknesses are the pastures and farms east of Chambois through which German tanks and men can escape. That stretch of Norman countryside is precisely where Sergeant Hawk sits at attention right now. The Falaise Gap was closed last night when American and Polish soldiers fighting side by side captured Chambois, with its stone houses and ancient castle. Now the Germans are coming to reopen it.

The enemy has no choice but to attack straight through this apple orchard. Roads below Sergeant Hawk's position are impassable, filled with the burned-out metal ribs of vehicles pulverized by American P-47s and Royal Air Force Hawker Typhoons. Hawk listens for the reassuring whine of that protective air cover. When the weather is clear, even the night sky lights up like the Fourth of July as Allied planes find their targets. But those lethal fighters are noticeably absent this morning due to weather.

A crumple of artillery fire booms in the distance.

Just like that, the battle is on.

"My God, the sky was falling down, the earth was blowing up, and if ever there was a hell on earth, this was it," Hawk will describe the battle's first moments.

Tiger tanks grind up the hill toward Hawk and his squad. German infantry stays close, using the armor for cover. Each tank carries a five-man crew and can travel almost twenty-five miles an hour. They proceed much slower now, seeking targets. The Tiger's 88mm gun is among the most lethal on either side of the fighting, capable of launching ten shells per minute, with a range of six miles.

Hawk and his men return fire. Ears ring. Nerves at the limit. Overhead scream of mortar fire and artillery. Hawk's "Johnny gun" is forty-two inches long, weighs thirteen pounds, and fires nine hundred rounds a minute. But the thickly armored German tanks have little to fear from an American machine gun. Hawk's bullets ricochet into the downpour.

One by one, Tiger gunners find American targets. Sergeant Hawk is not spared. An artillery shell knocks his Johnny gun out of commission. The orchard is surrounded. Hawk is wounded in the leg but making up strategy as he races to find cover. Tigers advance through low shrubs just across a field, coming ever closer. A lone American soldier armed with a bazooka anti-tank gun watches the enemy but does nothing.

"What are you doing?" Hawk demands.

"I'm trying to get these tanks in the brush over there, but I've got no backup and I have to put it down to load it," the soldier responds, nodding to his weapon.

"I'll back you," yells Hawk, his words barely audible over the gunfire.

The two men go to work. Fighting lasts thirty minutes, then an hour, then several hours. The bazooka's 60mm rocket is no match for the heavily armored Tigers but drives them back nonetheless, forcing the tanks to take cover in groves of trees and behind stone farm buildings. When the supply of rockets is spent, Hawk carries on alone once again, assembling a functioning machine gun using parts from several disabled guns—anything to stop the German escape.

The panzers come out of hiding to launch a new attack. Hawk is once more outgunned and forced to take cover.

Then the tank destroyers arrive.

The American M10 is a tank itself, a modified Sherman with a fully rotating turret and 76mm gun. It does not have a name, such as the Tiger or Sherman. Its five-man crew calls it either M10 or just TD. And as the initials imply, the absolute destruction of enemy tanks is its singular mission.

Two M10s take up position on the edge of the orchard, next to a field. The Tigers line up on the opposite edge. Both sides immediately open fire.

Both sides miss.

Sergeant Bud Hawk's fate depends upon the outcome of this tank duel. As TDs and Tigers both fire again and miss, he realizes poor visibility brought on by the rain makes it impossible for the Germans and Americans to see each other. *Can't see them, can't shoot them,* Hawk thinks.

Sergeant Bud Hawk dares.

Hawk impulsively sprints into the center of the field, ignoring machine-gun bullets and the whine of Tiger fire. A small dry creek bed divides the pasture in two, its banks cutting fifteen feet down into the open pasture. He clearly sees the exact location of every hidden Tiger on the other side.

Hawk sprints back to the two tank destroyers. He gets their attention. The commanders open their turret hatches. "If I line you up, will you shoot?" he asks.

Hawk races back to the center of the battlefield, completely exposed, a human fence post. The tank destroyers use his body as a direction finder, firing directly over his head. The first shots miss, so Hawk sprints back to the M10s. "Twenty feet to the left, raise it up three feet," he yells.

The next volley blows up a wall concealing a German tank. A second volley into the same position destroys the Tiger itself.

"These guys are good," Hawk marvels. He can barely hear from all the cannon fire.

Hawk sees another hidden Tiger and once again stands tall in the great wide open to direct fire. When the shots miss, he sprints back to the TDs with another correction, then runs back out into the field to show the way. Another Tiger is destroyed.

The Germans retreat.

An exhausted Bud Hawk finds a rifle left on the battlefield. He picks it up for protection, then makes his way into the orchard and collapses under a tree. Hawk is armed and safe, at least for now.

Or so he thinks. Hawk's theatrics have not gone unnoticed. A distant Tiger commander has tracked him back to the orchard. Without warning, a German shell scores a direct hit, blasting a hole in the tree trunk, sending shards of metal and splinters of applewood through the air. A piece of this shrapnel slices into Hawk's already wounded leg, the sudden blow feeling "like a sledgehammer."

Hawk stands and hobbles away before the Tiger can fire another round. He races as best he can toward a low building. Fueled by adrenaline, waiting for the sound of the follow-up round that will surely kill him, Hawk reaches the stone wall and throws himself around the corner. Hearing is shot. Awash in panic. There is no way the sergeant can hear the rumble or smell the diesel of an idling Tiger hidden right around the corner.

Bud Hawk slams headlong into the thick steel. The collision barely makes a thud, but the Germans inside know that something just hit them. Hawk bounces off the fifty-ton tank and its four inches of frontal armor, falling hard to the ground. Stars. Hard to breathe. Hawk reaches for his rifle, feels the smooth wooden stock, curls a finger around the trigger. Still flat on the wet ground, he looks up, not sure what to do next.

The hatch opens. A curious tank commander pokes his head up through the opening.

The American and the German lock eyes.

Hawk shoots him dead.

For the second time in just minutes, Bud Hawk runs for his life.

The Tiger rumbles forward, its turret barrel gliding right and left and MG-34 machine gunner straining to get Hawk in his sights. A second Tiger, alerted by a radio call, thunders after the young sergeant.

So it is that Sergeant Bud Hawk sprints back toward the American lines, running across the same wide-open pasture where he just directed fire. He sees the orchard, the men of Easy Company, the pair of tank destroyers.

What he does not see is the wide chasm of empty creek bed. Hawk runs off the edge and drops fifteen feet into mud, where he remains hidden until the battle is over.

And when that end comes, thousands of Germans raise their hands in surrender to Third Army, throwing down their rifles and abandoning their tanks.

The Falaise Gap remains closed. For good.

But thousands of the German Seventh Army have already slipped the noose, continuing their dash to the German border.

12

Field Marshal Erwin Rommel continues the discussion.

The tank commander sits opposite his son in the large study. Face puffy, single-breasted brown suit, a million things on his mind. Comfortable armchair. It's been a month since the crash and he still can't see well. So Manfred spends this evening reading aloud from a book on current distribution of German raw materials. The teenager has a thick head of dark hair and his father's broad smile. Though a soldier, he is still very much a young boy, standing a head shorter than the field marshal. Manfred is glad for the chance to be home with his father during this crucial time. He has seen the old spark of imagination come back to life in the weeks since Erwin Rommel returned home, thinking his father "very active and impulsive again."

If only Manfred could have seen the field marshal on the battlefield, commanding vast armies with the intuition of a wizard. "Active and impulsive" would have barely scratched the surface of Erwin

Rommel's genius. Yet Manfred knows that side of his father, if only just a little. He has read the news stories, quietly enjoyed the acclaim that comes with being the son of a beloved public figure, enjoying the way the German public lionizes the ruddy man who speaks so thoughtfully to his son.

Tonight, the older Rommel listens with fascination, reveling in the detailed statistics, analyzing from a military perspective. Nazi Germany won't be able to keep fighting for long without steel and oil. Hitler would have been wise to delay the war five years, allowing enough time to build more and better tanks and ships. But the German economy, shaky in even the best of times under Hitler, would not allow it. Seizing gas from conquered Romania and machine guns from Czechoslovakia was the only answer. So many other nations provided other vital raw materials. In this way, each German conquest was like Britain's colonial empire: an island nation relying on their vassals.

As the night grows late, Manfred can see that his father is losing interest. He closes the book and places it on a table. His mother enters the room and sits down.

"Russia and the West are like fire and water," the field marshal says, thinking out loud. "There will be friction and possibly war."

"Russia's land forces are on an altogether different scale from those of the West," Manfred responds. The Soviet Army is destroying the German Army, running roughshod over Hitler's troops, drawing closer to Berlin with every passing day. The vast nation has no lack of cannon fodder. Their animosity toward Germany is equally endless.

"The Americans have control of the air and they'll keep it," says the field marshal, pointing out that the German panzers are superior to American Sherman tanks, a fact that matters not at all. "There is a sentence of death for any land army, however large, that has to fight without adequate air cover."

Rommel is thinking of Egypt and British Spitfires chasing him across the desert as he ran for his life, defying a direct order from

Adolf Hitler in order to escape. Relations with the Führer have not been the same since. The field marshal's ongoing desire to broker peace with the British and Americans is straining that fragile relationship even further—as is the ongoing Gestapo investigation into the attempted murder of Hitler last month. Rommel's neighbors here in Herrlingen are quietly being questioned by the secret police about his potential involvement. Rommel requested transfer home from France after the crash, not wishing to become a prisoner of war during the Allied advance. It now looks as if he might have made the wrong decision.

Lucia Rommel weighs in. "Maybe the Russians will wait until after the war."

"Even then the Americans and British will win," says her husband, before launching into a commander's discourse about naval power and logistics and transporting war materials to any place on the globe in order to continue the fight. He talks of railways and the precise amount of gasoline a large truck needs per mile. "Their bomber fleets would cut off the Russian Army from its supply bases, pin it to the ground and destroy it."

Manfred will remember this evening as a talk "of the future, which at the time looked very dark."

But in his own way, Erwin Rommel is warning Manfred. This is not the war to end all wars. There will be another—and likely quite soon.

If, perchance, the field marshal is not here to see that day, his son needs to see the world clearly.

Because when that day comes, making the right choices will keep Manfred alive.

13

Four hundred miles west of the Rommel compound, Private Harold Alva Garman is trained to keep his friends alive.

Fifty miles below Paris, south bank of the Seine. Not a bridge in sight. Germans everywhere on the far side, desperately contesting all attempts to cross. American troops paddle the 150-yard span of slow-moving green water in square-sterned M2 assault craft. Ten soldiers, eight oars, all crammed into a plywood rowboat thirteen feet long and five wide—as defenseless and exposed to enemy hunters as ducks on a pond. The boats go over full of men ready to fight and come back just as loaded with wounded.

Garman is twenty-six, a small man born in Illinois. His helmet with a red cross painted on both sides cocks at an angle, slightly too large for his head. The private's best girl back home is named Mary, he has four brothers and two sisters, and before he was drafted he made his living as a farmer. Garman is a Baptist but not a conscientious objector, consigned to the medical corps by fate instead of choice.

Private Garman is trained to respond to medical emergencies on the battlefield. Today that means manual labor: lifting stretchers from M2s as they return with the dying. Garman and his fellow medics then carry the litters to waiting ambulances for transportation to a field hospital. The ballet along the waterline is delicate, a medic grasping the handles of the seven-foot-long stretcher while another grabs the other end. Then the struggle to lift the limp weight of a bleeding, moaning gunshot victim from a bobbing craft and carry him up the inclined bank without dropping the wounded soldier into the mud. Sweaty work on a muggy summer afternoon. Calluses. Water-filled boots. Drenched socks. No rest until the battle ends—all the while knowing enemy soldiers might view that red cross as a bull's-eye.

Just another day in the war for Private Harold Garman from Albion, Illinois.

Then it is not.

. . .

New York to Washington, DC. That's how far Patton's army has traveled in just three weeks. "A most important part of the entire Allied operation, now busily engaged in pursuing the broken remnants of the Nazi armies in France, is entrusted to Lt. Gen. George S. Patton," writes the *Los Angeles Times*, "whose Third Army is already credited with the greatest single success of turning the enemy flank and disposing of the Nazi tanks, in a manner that out-blitzed the Germans many times over."

At this very moment, Paris celebrates liberation from the Nazis. "Never do I expect to see such scenes as I saw on the streets of Paris," one American journalist will write. "Men and women cried with joy. They grabbed the arms and hands of soldiers and cheered until their voices were hoarse."

"Two and a half months of bitter fighting, culminating for the Germans in a blood bath big enough even for their own extravagant tastes, have brought the end of the war in Europe within reach," Supreme

Allied Headquarters in London writes in an intelligence brief. "The strength of the German armies in the West has been shattered. Paris belongs to France again, and the Allied armies are streaming toward the frontiers of the Reich."

There is absolutely nothing resembling celebration here outside Montereau. Just the steady chatter of machine-gun fire on the north shore as American soldiers dig paddles into the current with extreme urgency while German soldiers take careful aim to shoot them dead. There is a rhythm to the fighting, a methodical back-and-forth marching toward an inevitable United States victory. It has been this way since Patton took charge.

Suddenly, as Private Garman awaits a new boatload, a German machine gun opens fire from the far bank. Buzz saw. Twelve hundred rounds per minute. Effective range two thousand yards.

The M2 is hit. Middle of the river. Every man for himself. Soldiers ignore wounds to jump into the water and swim for it. Two patients cling to the side of the boat, unable to swim or tread water. A third casualty, so badly hurt he can't even rise from his stretcher, has no place to hide as the M2 bobs north on the current, slowly traveling toward the hidden machine-gun nest.

Garman throws off his helmet. No time to remove his boots. He dives into the Seine and swims hard for the drifting boat. It's an incredibly stupid decision. All the odds are against his success: the minute-plus in the water just to reach the boat, those heavy boots, fully clothed, all the while raked by *maschinengewehr* bullets fired by trained sadists deliberately taking aim at the dead and dying. This is no way to make it back to Mary and the farm.

If someone told him before the war that he'd dive into a French river and risk his life in the heat of battle, Garman probably would have laughed that they were crazy. But the private is trained to respond to medical emergencies on the battlefield. And right now, that means swimming like Johnny Weismuller.

Private Garman, pushed along by the current, reaches the M2. Out of breath, jacked on adrenaline, he hangs on to the two-foot-high gunwale to survey the situation. The buzz saw never stops. Bullets whistle past his head, slap the water. Garman assesses the situation. Two wounded still cling to the boat. Nothing can be done for the man lying on deck other than get him to shore. The only way that's going to happen is for Garman to swim the M2 back.

An assault boat weighs 410 pounds. Add in the heft of the three grown men incapable of assisting and that number goes up several hundred more. There is no tow rope affixed to the bow. Yet kicking and pulling and swimming and straining, all the while tormented by a current that now works against him, Garman wrests that boat to shore.

Everyone lives.

Nine months from now, when the private is awarded the Congressional Medal of Honor for today's actions, it will be General George S. Patton placing America's highest honor around his neck. The two men will make small talk on a parade ground, that helmet with the red cross on both sides still tilted at an angle.

Just another day in the war for Private Harold Alva Garman.

With many more to come.

14

*L*es Parisiens party like the war is over.

Because for them, it is.

Four delirious days since liberation. Bleak gray skies threatening more rain. Hundreds of thousands line the Champs-Élysées, reveling in the spectacle of America's mighty 28th Infantry Division leading the city's third victory parade since the end of the Nazi reign. Martial music from the division's fifty-six-piece "Keystone" band drowns out combat boots on cobblestones. Sleep-deprived soldiers in olive drab mouth "Khaki Bill":

"Banners flying, sweethearts sighing, boys go marching along . . ."

The 28th did not liberate Paris. The French 2nd Armored Division entered first, followed by the 4th US Infantry Division. General George Patton was pivotal in taking the city but has not entered since its capitulation. Paris was not militarily vital and could easily have been bypassed in favor of a rapid advance into Germany to end the war, then retaken another day. But Patton couldn't bear the thought of Hitler burning it down.

Yet saving the City of Lights may cost him.

Allied gasoline will soon fuel Paris. Once the French capital was taken, the Allies owned a moral and ethical responsibility for turning on electricity, heating homes, and feeding the starving population. Three thousand tons per day of Allied gas and food are being sent here for just those purposes.

Supplies that could be fueling Patton's race to Berlin.

He now drives Third Army east to the German border in a flat-out sprint to destroy Hitler's shattered legions before they can regroup. The pummeling at the Falaise Pocket bruised the German fighting machine. Nazi forces remain on their feet, a staggered punch-drunk boxer wobbling around the ring in search of a neutral corner. Patton wants to deliver the knockout blow.

Yet as the war continues beyond the city limits, the people of Paris revel with abandon. "No person in the world is happier than a happy Parisian," writes the *Chicago Tribune*.

As of now, there is no electricity to power the Métro nor gasoline to fuel commuter buses. These raucous Parisians have walked, bicycled, and pushed small carts laden with cognac, champagne, green apples, and flowers to be here. Wooden shoes clop on sidewalks, leather scarce for years. Revelers in autumn coats line the boulevard six deep, hands sore from clapping too hard. Fathers hoist children onto their shoulders. Pretty girls flash the Agincourt archers' two-fingered victory V. Apartments and restaurants line the route, lotharios in pressed suits and damsels in tight dresses raising a glass from perilously overcrowded balconies.

Ernest Hemingway is in town, sharing his bed in Room 31 at the Ritz Hotel with Mary Welsh, an American journalist and author currently married to an Australian journalist. Martha Gellhorn is also in

Paris but not inclined to interrupt. Hemingway knows she's here. Gellhorn stays at the Lincoln Hotel a mile from her husband.

All are here for the party.

"After four years of German occupation," Gellhorn writes with satisfaction, "no one has read any German books, no one has adopted any German habits of thinking or living; the conquerors have left absolutely no trace of themselves in the minds of the people of Paris.

"Paris is intact and beautiful."

The City of Lights—worldwide symbol of freethinking, art, gastronomy, and above all, passion—is free. The Nazi swastika flying over the Eiffel Tower for 1,537 days and nights has been struck. "There is no public transport in this city, which is short of food and all the things that make life good," reports the *New York Times*. "Yet the people swarmed into the regions around the streets through which the procession moved to shout and laugh and cry a little."

On June 14, 1940, the victorious German Army began the occupation by marching along this same route, soldiers three abreast in a long snaking line meant to awe and intimidate.

That show of force now pales.

These columns of American soldier boys measure twenty-four across—literally curb to curb—stretching back to the Arc de Triomphe and well beyond. "The procession was a foretaste of the victory celebrations," the *New York Times* writes, "that will be held in New York and London when Berlin is in the Allies' hands."

Many feel that date may come as soon as Christmas. US war planners are already just days away from announcing plans to either bring troops home or send them to fight Japan in the Pacific. "Biggest story for millions of American fighting men and their families centers around what the army has in store for them when Germany is beaten," writes the United Press.*

---

* The syndicate would not be renamed "United Press International" until 1958.

As the column approaches the reviewing stand, Captain James Kitchen, marching in the front row, snaps his head sharply right in acknowledgment. His eyes scan the dignitaries in search of a salute. Ostensibly, the 28th has been chosen to lead the parade because of their vaunted history. Division lineage dates to a Pennsylvania militia formed by Benjamin Franklin in 1747.* Unit battle streamers show participation in every major American conflict: War of 1812; Mexican, Civil, and Spanish-American Wars; Philippine Insurrection; and World War I. Their 1918 rescue of the so-called Lost Battalion in the Argonne Forest was the division's finest hour—until now.

But there are much larger tactical reasons for sending the 28th through Paris—reasons that will not become clear until the parade is over.

The 28th is under the command of the US Army Fifth Corps, which is part of the bigger First Army, which is under the much larger Twelfth Army Group.

The generals commanding those armies now return Kitchen's gaze: hero of D-Day Norman "Dutch" Cota, from the 28th; Courtney Hodges of the First; and Omar Bradley from the Twelfth.

The Americans are joined on the review platform by towering General Charles de Gaulle of France, the 6'5" nicotine-stained believer in destiny, a man who foresaw this moment every day since France fell and all appeared lost. The general has been a burr under the Allied saddle, arrogant in his demands and spare in his thanks as he strived to see this city liberated. But that struggle is past. De Gaulle, standing ramrod straight, now snaps his right hand to the black bill of his kepi in salute.

---

* Coincidentally, Franklin lived in Paris from 1776 to 1785. He formally presented his credentials to the French court in 1779, at which time he became the first American minister—equivalent to ambassador—to France.

Captain Kitchen will remember this moment as "solemn but triumphant," marveling that "correspondents from all over the world were on hand to record details of the event, and cameramen scrambled for advantageous positions from which to take pictures."

One of those photographers is Peter Carroll of the Associated Press. His photo of Kitchen and the 28th's iconic moment in front of the reviewing stand will be issued as a set of three-cent US postage stamps.

James Kitchen will post that stamp. Four men alongside him in the front row will never know they have been immortalized—less than twenty miles from where they now march, those young soldiers will leave this mortal world.

. . .

KITCHEN AND THE 28th veer right at the Place de la Concorde roundabout to follow the Seine. They have fought their way through France since coming ashore on July 22. Casualties have been heavy, including the loss of General James Wharton, shot dead by a German sniper just hours after taking command. The infantry marched as many as eighteen miles a day the past week: swollen eyes, dusty unpaved roads, sweat, mud, sore feet.

The division reached Paris in a driving rain last night. Not just soldiers on foot—everyone. Crews of tank destroyers, antiaircraft guns, field artillery, and medics driving jeeps bearing the red cross symbol. Sleep and hot food were hard to come by. Sweat-soaked, rain-drenched uniforms made for poor pajamas, but there was no other choice.

So these men cannot be faulted for harboring fantasies about lingering in a friendly café, a soul-fortifying cathedral with its familiar aromas and rituals of Mass, or even a Parisian brothel—daydreams accentuated not by *garcons de café* or priests but by daring young women spontaneously running into the parade ranks to deliver flowers and plant kisses on lucky soldiers. As the unit historian will fondly record: "Language proved no barrier to the exuberant Parisians."

Yet the true spoils of Paris will be denied the 28th. They are not conquerors.

Just visitors.

"None suspected that the triumphal march also had been a tactical move," the division history will admit. "The parade had been a shift from one assembly area to another. While the bands played and the crowds cheered, Fifth Corps was formulating more attacks for the Keystone Division."

The party in Paris grows even larger and more boisterous as the parade continues, a thick column of humanity dividing the Right Bank in two, just as surely as the Seine divides the Left from the Right. All decorum is lost by the time the last tanks and trucks pass through, American soldiers hoisting Parisians on board to ride along. Fedoras, berets, bare legs peeking from skirts just below the knee, all clinging to turrets and 75mm Sherman barrels with broad smiles on their faces.

The American spearhead is in two parts. As part of First Army, the 28th will travel north toward Belgium and Luxembourg before entering Germany at a natural fortress known as the Hürtgen Forest. General Patton's Third Army will advance to the south on their way to the Saar region and the inevitable race across rural country into Berlin.

That is all to come. For now, the young soldiers march relentlessly toward the city limits, where more war awaits, still singing along to the prophetic words of "Khaki Bill":

"Goodbye you boys of liberty. We sing farewell, farewell to thee."

In the unit historian's words: "The race to the Reich begins."

15

General George S. Patton is winning the race to Berlin.

The contest isn't even close.

Patton stops his paperwork to pace. The heavy thud of his polished boots echoes through this commandeered chateau. Silver wire-framed reading glasses, silver hair parted just so, silver stars precisely pinned three to a side on each collar point. This idyll is the perfect place for George Patton to regroup after an August of nonstop war.

Yet that is the last thing on his mind. The general is oblivious to the stunning beauty of the Champagne countryside outside the tall windows: vineyards thick with grapes, one month to harvest, stretching mile after mile across rolling hillsides. For all that wine, Patton is not nursing a victory hangover.

This morning he is by turns angry, suspicious, and bruised. A gross miscarriage of logic is taking place, of which he is the victim— and there seems to be nothing a furious Patton can do about it.

Third Army's forward progress across France continues to be relentless, the tremble of Sherman tanks on old Roman roads as common as warbling songbirds.

Today the fight is Verdun. Patton uncharacteristically remains one hour away, with absolutely no intention of witnessing the battle in person. Unbeknownst to the general, Verdun will be the scene of his finest hour. But that is still four months away.

The Germans struggled unsuccessfully for 302 days during the First World War to capture the fortress town on the mighty Meuse River. Third Army needs just half the morning. Euphoric locals flood Rue du Maréchal-Pétain before conquest is complete, cheering Patton's soldiers while ducking at every sharp crack of rifle fire. Dive-bombing P-47 Thunderbolts own the gray skies, bulbous fuselages buzzing mansard roofs, issuing their own particular sound of freedom, defined by the snarl and chatter of .50-caliber guns pouring thirteen pounds of lead per second on enemy holdouts. Shermans meanwhile squeeze into narrow boulevards, bristling with machine gun and cannon, itchy trigger fingers searching for anything Nazi.

Conquest is over long before lunch.

Aftermath is just beginning.

"Missing" becomes the new reality: missing doll, missing dog, missing mother. Mountains of roof tile and wooden beams and white-washed plaster and shattered glass bury the answers: missing front windows, missing roof.

But that is for the people of Verdun to manage. By lunch, Third Army is leaving town, marching forward, ever forward.

"The Americans captured immortal Verdun today and plunged on beyond the River Meuse in pursuit of the retreating Germans who put up only a feeble defense," celebrates the Associated Press. "Fall of the city . . . placed the American spearheads less than 50 miles from the German frontier."

Adds AP correspondent DeWitt Mackenzie: "The Allied forces

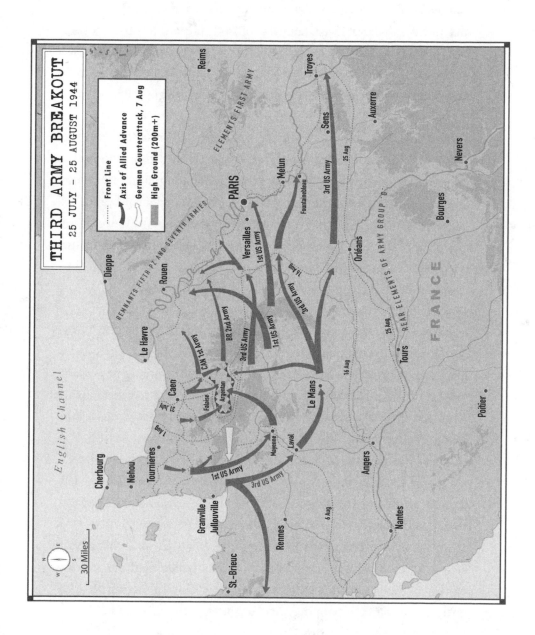

THIRD ARMY BREAKOUT
25 JULY – 25 AUGUST 1944

Front Line
Axis of Allied Advance
German Counterattack, 7 Aug
High Ground (200m+)

30 Miles

N
W E
S

English Channel

Cherbourg
Nehou
Tournieres
Granville
Jullouville
St.-Brieuc
Rennes

Caen
Falaise
Argentan
31 July
1 Aug
CAN 1st Army
3rd US Army
BR 2nd Army
1st US Army

REMNANTS FIFTH PZ AND SEVENTH ARMIES

Le Havre
Dieppe
Rouen
Reims

Versailles
1st US Army
PARIS

ELEMENTS FIRST ARMY

Melun
Fontainebleau
3rd US Army

Sens
25 Aug
Troyes

Auxerre

Nevers

16 Aug
3rd US Army

Mayenne
Laval
Le Mans

1st US Army
3rd US Army

Angers
Nantes
6 Aug

Orléans
Tours
16 Aug
25 Aug

REAR ELEMENTS OF ARMY GROUP B

Bourges

FRANCE

Potier

have at long last returned as victors to the battlegrounds where four and a quarter years ago civilization faced one of the greatest crises of all time. We shall not forget late-May of 1940. Hitler's troops, arrogant from conquest and sure in their own minds of mastering the world, swept into the Somme valley and closed the great steel trap which they had flung about hundreds of thousands of Belgian, British, and French soldiers."

Yesterday and sixty-five miles ago, the conquest was Reims—"the cathedral city," in Patton's words—taken without a shot, the lonely weathered bronze statue of Joan of Arc now flying a jauntily hung Stars and Stripes from the verdigris of her extended sword. It was a day of nice surprise: thirty downed American pilots discovered in barred jail cells, pealing church bells, and a celebration Mass in the ancient cathedral Notre-Dame de Reims, a thirteenth-century Gothic landmark now protected by a fifty-foot-high wall of sandbags.

Reims lies in the heart of Champagne, lending an even more cele-bratory tone to liberation. The vineyards are untouched by war. Local men languish in German prison camps or have been taken away as forced labor, leading to a shortage of pickers, but the grapes never stop growing. Even as Europe burned four years ago, the timelessness of wine remained a constant. Growers have been blessed by a lack of grape moths, harvest worms, or frost. Production never ceased. Lo-cals consider the 1943 a wine to be long remembered, with high hopes for the grapes to be picked in 1945. And just as the German Army left Paris intact fleeing the Allied arrival, Champagne was also spared de-struction during the hasty Wehrmacht exodus.

At the start of the conflict, citizens concealed favorite vintages in cellars, caves, and even at the bottom of wells, believing the Nazis un-worthy of drinking France's best wine. Now those bottles are out of hiding. The sound of popping corks echoes late into the night.

General George S. Patton is delaying his celebration for Berlin.

. . .

"AT THE MOMENT it is four hundred and ten miles from one flank of this army to the other," Patton writes home to Beatrice. "That is the longest swath I have yet cut but it is so big that it is mostly impersonal."

Even as Third Army presses forward, Patton remains outside Reims, in this commandeered chateau of the Count of Dampierre, local wine-maker and scion of France's oldest families.* Patton takes luxury when he can, whether in a castle, tent, or mobile command post. The chateau's fine china, oversize beds, and priceless wine cellar are not entirely lost on the wealthy general. But those niceties are an elaborate set piece in the larger drama acting out between Patton and General Bernard Law Montgomery.

Monty is sparrow bones, black beret, fussy, brilliant in his own mind. The fifty-six-year-old speaks down to everyone, including his prime minister. Churchill, sometimes a friend, describes him as "indomitable in defeat, invincible in advance, insufferable in victory."

No one describes Patton in a word. To suggest the obvious—volcanic, sentimental, eccentric—is not enough. General James Gavin calls him "an impulsive, daring commander, impatient with his subordinates, aggressive and determined to win tactical victories regardless of risks." Which is a complicated way of stating that George S. Patton is out of place in a world without a war.

And that Generals Patton and Montgomery are more alike than either wants to admit.

Which is why, in this chateau outside Reims, Patton fumes: Third

---

* In 2014, the Comtes de Dampierre will celebrate the seventieth anniversary of liberation and Patton's brief stay at the family chateau by issuing a wine in the general's honor: "Champagne Comtes de Dampierre Cuvée du Général Patton Blanc de Blancs Brut Grand Cru."

Army is ordered to halt. Do not advance. Stop beating the shit out of Hitler's army.

And let Monty win the race to Berlin.

.   .   .

PATTON'S HALT IS made necessary by the only practical aspect of war, a science known as logistics. More specifically for Patton's purposes, feeding his army gas and bullets.

Of which there are too many to count in Allied depots—but little flowing his way.

"I'll shoot the next man who brings me food," Patton grouses to General Omar Bradley, Twelfth Army Group commander, of which Third Army is now part. "Give us gasoline. We can eat our belts."

But the logistical issue is more complex than supply and demand. Patton is part of that problem. For three reasons:

First: Paris.

Second: winning.

Allied planners didn't expect Third Army to reach the German border for another six months. Patton is tearing through Hitler's army so fast, supplies can't keep up. A single Sherman burns a gallon of gasoline every mile and a half. Patton requires 380,000 gallons per day to keep his army on the move. All this gas comes from supply depots on the English Channel, clear back on the other side of a nation the size of Texas.

But Patton doesn't get all that fuel. Not by a long shot. Half that gasoline is diverted north to America's First Army.

There is plenty in Allied supply depots. The issue is getting that gas across France. Railways operate sporadically. Airlifts are successful, though flights are often grounded on rainy days like yesterday.

The solution is trucks. A convoy of six thousand vehicles known as the Red Ball Express makes the round-the-clock drive from Channel ports every day. But those heavily loaded GMCs are breaking down from wear and tear. Drivers, most of them Black in a segregated army that won't let them fight on the front lines, are exhausted. The farther the journey, the more gas the convoy needs to complete their job, meaning Red Ballers arrive at their destination with less fuel for Third Army. It takes five gallons to supply one to the front. By the time the Red Ball Express shuts down on November 16, it will be an army unto itself, nearly six thousand vehicles burning three hundred thousand gallons of fuel per day.*

Two days ago, a planned shipment of 140,000 gallons failed to arrive at Patton's supply depots. He currently has just enough gasoline for a couple hours of frisky fighting—that is, if he doesn't plan to shoot anything. Third's allotment of artillery is two and a half rounds per day per gun. Desperate to keep moving forward, Patton brazenly flirts with yet another career suicide, encouraging his men to pass themselves off as First Army to liberate gas and rounds from supply depots. There are unsubstantiated rumors that Patton himself plays traffic cop, directing Red Ball tankers into Third Army fuel dumps.

Patton's quartermaster, Colonel Walter J. Muller, even sends light aircraft on aerial searches for fuel, leading Patton to publicly state about rumors of redirected gas, "I'm sorry to learn that First Army has lost some of its gas, very sorry indeed. But I know none of my officers would masquerade as First Army officers. They wouldn't stoop to that, not even to get gas SHAEF stole from us."

Yet the closer to Germany Patton attacks, the longer that Red Ball journey gets—and with it his wait for precious fuel.

. . .

THESE VICTORIES AND their ensuing logistical headaches might be considered a good problem to have, were it not for the third reason Patton is stuck: General Bernard Law Montgomery.

---

* The most widely used trucks in the Second World War were GMC CCKW-353 2.5-ton cargo trucks. Nicknamed "Jimmies" and "Deuce and a Halfs," more than 560,000 were manufactured during the war by the General Motors Corporation.

Monty is determined to halt Patton's advance in favor of his own glorious thrust into Germany. He dreams of sprinting directly into Berlin—provided he is given every last drop of gas, bullet, and morsel of food in the Allied depots.

Despite every attempt to form a professional alliance, Patton considers the British hero a vain, inferior commander with little tactical imagination and entirely too much influence. The two came to know and dislike one another during the 1943 Sicily campaign, when Patton narrowly beat Montgomery into the capital of Palermo to claim the role of conqueror.

Now, Patton is within spitting distance of Germany while Montgomery's 21st Army Group grinds along the Atlantic coast, close enough to smell the salt air. The British general has finally captured Caen, nearby the D-Day beaches Patton left one month ago, and is moving on the vital Belgian port of Antwerp.

Patton is the more aggressive commander in the field, but Montgomery is just as aggressively political. Patton attempts this skill but is too prone to emotion. While the American was fighting his way through France on the front lines, Montgomery was working the room. He is adamant that only one front can be sustained on the drive into Germany—and that front can be only him, acing out Patton completely.

This "full-blooded thrust," in Monty's words, "would be so strong it need fear nothing."

· · ·

Montgomery's audience is the British public, Prime Minister Churchill, and American general Dwight Eisenhower, whom Monty badgers constantly with vainglorious memos.

On August 23, one week before Patton's gas shortage, Ike and Monty met at the British commander's headquarters in the Norman burg of Condé-sur-Noireau. Montgomery showed his plan to Omar Bradley a week ago. Believing the Twelfth Army Group commander agreed with his "full-blooded thrust," Monty felt comfortable detailing his proposed race through the Ardennes Forest with elements of Bradley's Twelfth at his side.

"The American people would never stand for it," Eisenhower fires back at Montgomery's desire to stop Patton cold. The American general's exploits are all over the papers back home. "Public opinion wins wars."

"Victories win wars," Montgomery shoots back. "Give people victory and they won't care who won it."

Ike bends. Patton may be closer to Berlin than any Allied commander, but Dwight Eisenhower is pausing that dash to placate Monty.

The British general has come out on top—and that is still not enough. As always, Monty wants more. After Ike leaves Montgomery's headquarters without giving a yes or no answer about Monty's role following Antwerp, the general confides to other British commanders that Eisenhower is "completely out of touch with the land battle."

· · ·

PACING IN HIS borrowed chateau, George S. Patton ponders the problems of his own making:

Paris. Winning. Montgomery.

He has done everything right. Germany is so close.

"It is a terrible mistake," the general writes in his diary. "We got no gas."

16

Ike likes to be liked. That's his way. Yet General Dwight Eisenhower is about to burn bridges.

A lot of bridges.

Thursday. Outside, a clear blue flying day. Inside his headquarters, a tanned and smiling Eisenhower stands before the press. Yellow fingertips, breath of unfiltered cigarettes and twenty cups of coffee. He's the epicenter of today's media briefing—himself, and a soon-to-be-forgotten battle map of Europe emblazoned with red arrows pointing to Allied advances. Ike had nothing to do with those victories, but each is presented as being one and the same with his personal triumphs.

The general's driver not so discreetly stands to one side. Irish-born Kay Summersby, dressed in uniform skirt and blouse, tending to the general's black Scottie. Telek, as the dog is named, wears a collar encrusted with Eisenhower's four stars.* Summersby is thirty-five and available. Eisenhower is fifty-three and four thousand miles from his wife. No one in the room knows for certain whether the general and his lithe young driver are having a thing, but there's talk.†

For security, the British and American press will dateline today's stories "Supreme Allied Headquarters." Before D-Day, this meant London. The main SHAEF—Supreme Headquarters, Allied Expeditionary Force—was located outside the city in Bushy Park. A small secondary command post was also situated near Montgomery's headquarters sixty-five miles south on the coast near Portsmouth. "Sharpener" was slowly enlarged into a tent camp capable of housing four hundred officers and one thousand enlisted men, with the necessary telephone, radio, and teleprinter services to maintain contact with the British War Office in London and US Department of War in Washington. Four scheduled daily flights between Sharpener and London allowed Ike and his staff easy transit back and forth.

On July 7, "Supreme Allied Headquarters" assumed a new location as Eisenhower formally arrived in France one day after George Patton, landing on the same type of Advanced Landing Grounds airstrip just off Omaha Beach, although with a much bigger fighter escort. It is typical for Eisenhower's personal B-25 fast medium bomber to have as many as eighteen P-51 Mustangs or Canadian Royal Air Force Spitfire escorts. His custom plane features cloth passenger seats like an airliner

---

* Telek was presented to Eisenhower as a birthday gift in 1942. His name was a combination of "Telegraph Cottage"—Eisenhower's wartime retreat outside London—and Kay Summersby's first initial. Some sources suggest the dog was a gift for Summersby, using the birthday gift to Ike as a ruse to deflect any suggestion the two were a couple.

† John "Beaver" Thompson of the *Chicago Tribune* will remark of the Eisenhower-Summersby rumors: "I have never before seen a chauffeur get out of a car and kiss the general good morning when he comes from his office."

and a fold-down map table. A bed is laid in the bomb bay. Eisenhower continues to shuttle back and forth to London with Summersby and his dog, but the slow transition to life in France has begun.

"Shellburst," as the utilitarian headquarters in a Tournières apple orchard was known, constituted a small collection of tents and trailers. The organized rows of trees provided a breeze, shade, and camouflage should the reeling Luftwaffe find a way to rebound and penetrate overhead airspace. This was Eisenhower's beachhead of sorts, a first arrival on the continent to establish presence before larger quarters could be found.

Indeed, the new SHAEF will soon be a castle. Beginning on September 20, Ike will move to the grand Trianon Palace Hotel, twelve miles south of Paris in Versailles. Eisenhower has strictly demanded that the location be outside the city to avoid "temptations to go night clubbing." The general is immune to those whims, spending insomniac nights with dime-store novels and a carton of Camels. On a practical note, the former residence of Louis XIV will also place Ike closer to the fighting as the front extends into Germany.

But for now, Supreme Allied Headquarters is the Norman town of Jullouville, just inland from the green summer sea and a long strip of scenic sandy beach. La colonie scolaire de St-Ouen, a former boarding school, has been transformed into a command post. Located on the outskirts of town, the towering three-story facility built of gray Norman granite features a forbidding design inspired by industrial architecture. The main building looks like the gateway to a penitentiary. The facility contains a war room, mess, and communications center. There aren't phones yet. All communication with the front lines is done by radio. Dormitories in back provide quarters for female staffers. In all, 750 officers and 2,500 enlisted personnel crowd into this small village, now the epicenter of the global fight against Nazi tyranny.*

---

* Jullouville erected a monument in Eisenhower's honor in 2013.

There's more. Senior commanders of the Allied Expeditionary Air Force, the Navy, and the French fighting forces are headquartered seven miles north in the fishing village of Granville, with their own prefabricated huts, signal units, supply depots, and hundreds upon hundreds of jeeps and trucks. Eisenhower maintains a chateau there, along the rocky coast looking out upon the sea. One month ago, Patton's Third Army rumbled through Granville's *centre ville* on its way into battle, his long armored column shaking the ground so hard that metal signs fell off houses and shops.*

Since then, this charming and otherwise remote corner of France, known for its shellfish, cod, and healing waters, has become a bustling Allied metropolis. Visiting English-speakers outnumber French locals. Best or worst duty in the army, depending upon personal preference for tranquility or the after-dark prowl of a Parisian night.

Hardly a secret location.

Yet a pretense is a pretense, and for the sake of drill—because this is war, after all, and it's good to be in the habit of keeping secrets, and not having their press passes yanked—the assembled war correspondents in the room today will begin each story with "Supreme Allied Headquarters" followed by the date—a fact also subject to whimsy depending upon how long SHAEF wants to delay a telltale nugget of information.

The press likes Ike. Today, they are flattered to be in such close proximity to the great general. Even the German press likes Eisenhower. *Neueste Nachrichten*, based in Munich, has previously written that he "has an athletic appearance, full of health and strength, a well-formed jaw and head showing great will, and is a man whom his countrymen would call a he-man. He is a man who has great abilities as an organizer and who has demonstrated great good sense in leadership and tactics."

---

* Incredibly, the German Army reoccupied Granville as late as March 1945.

A serialized biography titled "The Life of Eisenhower," now running nationwide in American newspapers, deifies the simple man born in Texas and raised in Kansas as being "invested with the greatest authority in history, greater than that of old Roman generals. Commanding all Allied land, sea, and air forces, the joint American-British governments have given him control never before placed in the hands of one man."

Hagiographic but true. Knowing they are in the presence of such power on this August afternoon, all too eager to file their stories and while away the evening in an oceanfront café, the media tread lightly during the press conference. They chuckle appreciatively when Ike pretends to forget the name of the vaunted Siegfried Line on the border of Germany and France, Hitler's last line of defense against Allied invasion. Their stories will laud Eisenhower's authority, using strong words like "declares" and "predicts" in describing his comments on the coming end of the war.

Yet the search for an eye-catching headline is ingrained. So even as the journalists nod their heads in agreement when Eisenhower says the war will be over in 1944 "if everyone on the battlefront and at home did their duty," that's old news. Ike said the same thing last Christmas, when transferring from Tangiers to England to assume Overlord command.

They like his rhetoric about the German Army "scraping the bottom of the barrel" to find good soldiers these days.

Also old news.

Then Eisenhower throws them a bone. At first, the press thinks this is why he's holding a press conference: Effective tomorrow, Ike is realigning his command. He will no longer cede control of ground forces in Europe to General Montgomery. Eisenhower is here to stay and will personally dictate strategy until the war ends. The breakout from the beaches is complete, and the time has come for a new command structure.

This has been expected for some time, having been agreed upon long before Overlord. Yet news to most readers. Good stuff.

What comes next is what rocks the room.

General Omar Bradley will no longer be subordinate to General Montgomery.

The British general is a four-star, while Bradley wears just three. But the generals will now command as equals. As George Patton prayed in his diary one month ago, Bradley's Twelfth Army Group will be peeled away from Monty's command.

"Bradley Made Monty's Equal," the Associated Press headline will read.

Eisenhower is not done.

The many months living in England have made him well aware of the mood of a British population who believe their wartime struggles are overshadowed. Britain has fought longer and in far more battles than the Americans, having entered the war in September 1939 and then fighting on alone since France fell in 1940. The nation is exhausted from too many funerals and being flat-out poor. Her resilient people are traumatized by bombing and hardship, her soldiers weary after too many battles on too many fronts. Montgomery is their hero, Daniel striding unafraid into the lion's den. It is good and right in the eyes of Britons that Monty knows the glory of entering Germany first—and also winning the race to Berlin.

And the British people know that Patton is not Montgomery's only competition. The Russians are coming. Operation Bagration is a stunning success. The Soviet advance through Nazi-held territory has been punishing and quick. Nearly two million Red Army soldiers are recapturing territory lost to the Germans early in the war—then keeping right on going, moving beyond prewar Soviet borders, advancing into Poland and Romania en route to the German capital. Few foresee that the Russians are not planning on liberating these lands but keeping them forever.

Eisenhower knows some American publications are buying into the hype about Monty, represented right now by journalists in this very room: "Hawk-eyed, didactic General Sir Bernard Law Montgomery is the darling of the British public," proclaims *Time* magazine.

Yet Ike, a seemingly simple man with a card shark's poker face, plays the political game like a pro. Even Montgomery isn't this good.

Eisenhower is a friend to Winston Churchill, spending weekends at Prime Minister's official country residence, Chequers. He knows that the prescient Churchill is struggling to assure Great Britain remains a dominant power when the war is over, not a weak sister to the Americans and Soviets.

Eisenhower knows that in the eyes of Britain, America is late to the conflict, declaring war in 1941 but really flexing its military muscle only in the last year with major campaigns in Sicily and Italy. The United States plays the role of rich uncle, massive industrial might manufacturing the guns, tanks, ships, and planes so vital to crushing Hitler—which says nothing at all about the millions of American soldiers flooding into British ports, there to spend their pay in British pubs and steal the girlfriends of British soldiers absent on duty, the Brits already years into the hard job of war to which these callow, untested, and entirely too eager Americans are just now squaring their shoulders.

So, before the British press can react with outrage to Monty's loss of status, citing El-Alamein and Montgomery's many other triumphs to appease their readership, Ike softens the blow.

"This is not a demotion," states the SHAEF commander. The assembled media turn on him ever so slightly. Ike reacts with defiance. He reminds the press that he has "lived Allied for two years," as a personal call for British-American unity. Eisenhower professes he and Monty are "warm and close friends."

Then this, certain to win Ike many friends on the British side:

"Montgomery is one of the greatest generals of this or any other war."

Borderline insincerity. Eisenhower well knows Montgomery and Britain's other top generals hold him in low regard, finding him ambivalent, more politician than general. Ike has been described by Sir Alan Brooke of the Imperial General Staff as having a "very, very limited brain from a strategic point of view." So, for Eisenhower to shrug off those insults smacks of pandering. It is most certainly a political half-truth. Whether planned or impulsive, "greatest" is a description Ike can never walk back.

But on this day, that's what he needs to say.

London's *Daily Mail* will write of being "warmed" by Eisenhower's lofty compliment.

King George VI goes one better. At the urging of Winston Churchill, the sovereign promotes Montgomery to field marshal. This is a rank higher than even Eisenhower's, equivalent to that of a five-star general in the United States Army. Monty now outranks his own boss. The British are showing their steel.

Reporting from London, the Associated Press will note: "The announcement of the appointment effective today came only a few hours after General Eisenhower revealed that Lt. Gen. Omar N. Bradley had been given equal status with Montgomery as field commander of an army group. However, unofficial sources emphasized the Montgomery appointment had no connection with this and had been planned for some time as recognition of 'valuable service to the empire.'"

• • •

GENERAL GEORGE PATTON hears the news while listening to the radio with Omar Bradley. He has flown back to the Breton coast to lead a charm offensive, hoping to reopen the flow of gasoline to Third Army. The two men are old friends with a complicated history. Patton disagrees strongly with Bradley's oft-passive approach to war but enjoys the company of his former subordinate.

Both men are also longtime friends of Dwight Eisenhower. They came of age as West Pointers, then as forgotten young officers, fording the juncture between two wars as so many peers abandoned the service for the civilian world in search of greener pastures. With that personal familiarity comes candid judgment.

Bradley, as always, is diplomatic. Patton finds fault with all his contemporaries, his scathing criticisms all over the emotional road map. When it comes to Ike, Patton leans on sarcasm. He openly refers to Eisenhower as "Britain's best general" for his tendency to align with Montgomery and Winston Churchill.

That remark now feels more true than ever.

"At 0800 we heard on the radio that Ike said Monty was the greatest living soldier and is now a Field Marshal," a disgusted Patton journals.*

"The Field Marshal thing made us sick."

.   .   .

"MAYBE THERE ARE five thousand, maybe ten thousand, Nazi bastards in their concrete foxholes before the Third Army," Patton comments a few days later during his weekly press briefing. He thwacks the tip of a pointer into a battlefront map. Ever cavalier, the general swears the press to secrecy.

Whatever that means. Despite a history of leaked remarks, Patton can't help himself.

He feels like he deserves a loose word or two. Patton knows his history. No general has enjoyed a hot August like Patton's. The general believes himself omnipotent. Untouchable.

No longer a secret in any sense of the word.

Patton now offers the press his uniquely candid view on how the Allies can and will win the war.

---

* Though Patton is not specific in naming which radio broadcast, it was most likely the US Army's American Forces Network. The British Broadcasting Corporation in London allowed use of their facilities. Another possible outfit would be the Canadian Broadcasting Corporation, also based in London. After D-Day, AFN used mobile stations in France to broadcast to the troops.

"If Ike stops holding Monty's hand and gives me the supplies," he brags to the assembled British and American media, much to their delight. He speaks to them like soldiers in shopworn phrases known to inspire affection.

"I'll go through the Siegfried Line like shit through a goose."

17

Adolf Hitler is sick of losing the war.

And the Führer is doing something about it.

Cloudless Friday evening. Waning light. Pre-autumn blossoms turning cherry trees gold and bronze. Pubs open for business as thirsty men spill in from work, busier than before the war as the weekend begins.*

In the west London village of Chiswick, three-year-old Rosemary Clarke sleeps on a cot in a small bedroom at No. 1 Staveley Road. Her parents tend to six-year-old brother John as he splashes in the bath

---

* "The local," as a neighborhood pub is known in Britain, was a term born during World War II. As noted in *The Local: A History of the British Pub* by Paul Jennings, public drinking and socializing were considered harmful to war efforts during the First World War. But during the Second World War, pubs were seen as good for morale. Instead of air raid shelters, many chose to go to their local during German bombings.

with a small toy boat. Rosemary is blond. Chubby arms. Cute fat baby fingers. A happy child.

Next door at No. 3, Ada and William Harrison, both in their sixties, enjoy a restful afternoon away from Bonanza, the newspaper shop near Chiswick Station where they also sell sweets. Their house is brick, two stories tall, Tudor windows, and a sloping tiled roof, just like every home on Staveley. William is bald with a broad mustache and the mischievous smile of a lucky man.

Ada is the sensible one. A half decade older than her husband. Doubting eyes. Pursed lips. Dowdy.

Sapper Bernard Browning, a Royal Army engineer home on leave, walks Glenwood Road to the station. Twenty-eight. Toothy grin. Lively eyes. Garrison cap cocked jauntily to the right. Middle name: Hammerton. Parents are Robert James Browning and Phoebe Gertrude Browning, in whose home he now spends his short time away from the war.

Sapper Browning is taking the train to meet his girl: Hounslow Loop Line from Chiswick to Barnes Bridge, then on to the Waterloo-Reading Line.

All are unafraid. England no longer has anything to fear from Nazi Germany—or so its citizens believe. The Luftwaffe is incapable of bombing British cities. Unmanned aerial attacks from V-1 terror rockets have been stopped. Just three days ago, Home Secretary Herbert Morrison stated that "the enemy is unlikely to be able to launch rockets or flying bombs against London on any appreciable scale."

"Appreciable scale" doesn't mean *no* rockets, as Home Secretary means the public to believe.

Just not a lot of rockets.

But all it takes is one if it's aimed right at you.

· · ·

IN BERLIN, THE German people are being asked to sacrifice. Reich Minister Joseph Goebbels has issued a mandate to its 2.8 million residents closing schools and theaters. A sixty-hour workweek is introduced and holidays abolished. Small shops are closed. Productivity in factories must increase, even as men from all walks of life and all ages are mobilized for war.

· · ·

IN LONDON, THE sacrifice is of a more ultimate nature.

Five minutes ago, and two hundred miles across the English Channel in the prosperous Dutch town of Wassenaar, one of Hitler's ruthless new weapons of war shot into the sky. At forty-six feet long and over five feet wide, the *Vergeltungswaffe* 2—"Retribution Weapon 2"— is the world's first ballistic missile. The rocket carries a one-ton explosive package of the component Amatol. This mixture of dynamite and ammonium nitrate is stable, allowing it to be packed inside the rocket's nose cone, then withstand supersonic flight without detonation. The rocket reaches fifty miles of altitude minutes after liftoff. The engines then shut down automatically for the free fall to earth, depending upon trajectory and a complicated system of internal gyroscopes to aim the rocket toward whatever it will land upon and blow to hell.

Force will cause the Amatol to combust when the V-2 descends and strikes the earth at 1,790 miles per hour. The explosion will be so powerful that it will form a crater sixty feet wide and twenty-five deep. Three thousand tons of whatever it strikes will be displaced: streets, homes, turning cherry trees of Chiswick—even little Rosemary Clarke.

Everything.

Best of all in the mind of Adolf Hitler, no one will hear it coming. Germany's first attempt at rocketry, the V-1, was a gadfly in comparison to the V-2, half the size and not supersonic. That missile made so much noise its loud buzzing gave the rocket an English nickname: "doodlebug." London was struck by 2,340 V-1s, killing 5,475 citizens. Yet the tragedy could have been far worse. Flying straight and level, more than 3,900 of those simple German bombs were easily shot down by Spitfires and 40mm Bofors antiaircraft guns before reaching British targets.

But the V-2 is impervious to defense. The retribution weapon becomes completely silent as it punches through the sound barrier, traveling so fast that its booming thunder trails far behind. No air raid siren will wail its approach. Nobody in its random path will scramble into an air raid shelter.

And the path *is* random. Tens of thousands of slave laborers are building Hitler's *Wunderwaffe*—"wonder weapons"—in secret underground German factories. The rocket's internal guidance system is imperfect. These men and women risk their lives to defeat the Nazi cause by committing sabotage. This can result in a dummy warhead or compromised gyroscopes. The Führer authorized the launching of V-2s on August 29. Since then, the first three *Vergeltungswaffe* to be fired bear witness to vulnerability.

The initial wave was aimed at Paris. Hitler's first two rockets crashed shortly after takeoff, barely rising above the launchpad. The third struck the city's outskirts, its explosion nowhere near as powerful as it should have been—perhaps due to sabotage—causing little damage.

Today's is the first V-2 aimed at London. It targets the emotional heart of the city—Piccadilly Circus, Westminster Abbey, Big Ben. Army Air Corps and Royal Air Force bombers now humiliate the Nazi regime, pummeling Berlin day and night (Americans in sunshine, Brits in the dark). A German rocket strike at the epicenter of all things British will remind the Allies that Adolf Hitler and Nazi Germany are still the superior race.

But as Rosemary Clarke sleeps in the front bedroom of her parent's home, Ada Harrison enjoys an afternoon without newspaper ink staining her fingertips, and Sapper Browning rushes to meet the woman he loves, all are about to become victim to a nameless rocket, imagined by a despot and constructed by innocent Europeans torn from their homes by war and sentenced to starvation and forced labor as slaves, completely missing its target by six miles.

The V-2 plummets to earth at the junction of Burlington Lane and Staveley Road. The ground buckles in a detonation so enormous that Londoners miles away wonder if a local munitions dump has suffered a direct hit. Eruption. Earthquake. Thick black column of smoke. Bricks and tiles shooting skyward, then falling down like rain. The inevitable crater. Eleven houses demolished instantly. Almost 550 more severely damaged. All those Tudor windows shooting spikes of glass into the evening.

"It sounded as though every thunderstorm in England had gathered and released its energy over Chiswick," local Tony Simpson will remember. He is riding his bicycle to a swimming workout on this seventy-degree evening when the bomb hits. "Following the explosion and aftershock there was such a silence, the only thing I could hear was the roaring in my ears. The hole extended across the road, the adjoining verges and pavements, demolished the front of many houses on both sides of the road and damaged many more. It was not long before the occupants of surviving properties joined me at the terrible scene of devastation."

Little Rosemary Clarke is whisked to West Middlesex County Hospital, but it is far too late. She dies as the detonation and smoke suck oxygen from the blast, her tiny lungs destroyed. The technical term is blast lung injury. Though there is not a mark on her body, Rosemary is torn, bruised, and swollen on the inside, her lungs no longer capable of drawing breath.

Caretaker Robert Stubbs of the nearby Staveley Road School is thrown twenty feet. Like everyone in the blast radius, Stubbs is temporarily unable to hear. But though her cries are not audible, Stubbs catches sight of Ada Harrison crawling from the wreckage of No. 3, face white in plaster dust. Stubbs rushes to her assistance—only to have the shopkeeper die in his arms.*

William Harrison is still somewhere inside that collapsed house as his wife breathes her last. Rescue crews will find him in the rubble and take him to the hospital, where he survives for a time, then dies later from his wounds.

Sapper Bernard Browning is the only military casualty. One second he walks down Glenwood Road: uniform creased, train to catch, fanciful thoughts of what tonight might bring.

Flash. Shadow. Whoosh. Then, the biggest explosion London has ever seen. Browning never hears it. His skull is fractured and eardrums ruptured and all the air in the world sucked right out of his chest. Corpse tossed like a rag doll. Nothing to do but fly through the air and slam to the ground, dead before the young man with so much to live for knows Britain is under attack.

Browning's girlfriend will not know of his death for a very long time. British authorities will keep the V-2 attack a secret, denying Adolf Hitler the pleasure of knowing that the bombing is a success. She will wonder what's keeping him, destined to reluctantly move on and marry another, like so many brokenhearted lovers of soldiers lost in war.

As what remains of Sapper Browning lies at odd angles on Glenwood Road, British officials blame a faulty gas main for the explosion. When V-2 attacks on London become common for many months to come, citizens will refer to the rockets as "flying gas pipes."

Home Secretary Morrison is wrong: Adolf Hitler still possesses the ability to launch rockets at England in significant numbers. Today is just the beginning. Thirty thousand will die before the program

---

* Ada Harrison's name was placed on the "Civilian War Dead Roll of Honour 1939–1945," compiled by the Imperial War Graves Commission. This list was later placed in Westminster Abbey, where it can be found in the nave, near the grave of African explorer David Livingstone.

comes to an end. At a time when the rest of the world feels this war winding down, the long-suffering citizens of Great Britain once again brace for attacks on their homeland that come without warning.

And without a sound.

The only defense against the V-2 is a good offense. This means capturing the launch sites before Retribution Weapons can take flight. Operational range is two hundred miles. Most of these locations must be across the Channel in German-occupied Holland. Liberating that nation is suddenly imperative.

Quite coincidentally, invading the Netherlands is a vital part of Field Marshal Bernard Law Montgomery's "full-blooded thrust."

18

General Dwight Eisenhower is in extreme pain.

And Field Marshal Bernard Law Montgomery is only a small part of the problem.

Sunday. Long story. The short version is that Ike's personal B-25 broke during a recent rough landing. Now his knee is in a cast from a fluke injury involving a sandy beach and a much smaller plane. The same sprained ligaments cost him his football career at West Point. Yet despite his suffering, it is Eisenhower who flew to meet his most persistent general—not the other way around.

Ike now sits with Monty inside a C-47 at a former German airfield outside the Brussels city center. The general is in too much pain to climb down onto the tarmac, giving Monty a most captive audience for the enormous request he is about to make.

The field marshal first orders Eisenhower's staff to leave the plane. It is insubordinate of Monty to make this rash demand, just like demanding that Eisenhower fly here to meet on his terms. A less tactful man than Eisenhower would have said no, but in truth, he likes to fly. Time away from headquarters clears his head.

Montgomery is emboldened more than ever by the need to halt V-2 attacks. Ike's view of the war's main goal, which he will formally put in a communiqué to Monty and other top commanders five days from now, is already well known by the field marshal—and thus cause for elation: "Berlin is the main prize, and the prize in defense of which the enemy is likely to concentrate the bulk of his force," Eisenhower will write Monty, feeling the need to show his tactical awareness. "There is no doubt whatsoever in my mind that we should concentrate all our energies and resources on a rapid thrust to Berlin . . .

"Simply stated, it is my desire to move on Berlin by the most direct and expeditious route."

Montgomery is certain *his* route fits that definition.

He has a point. Since taking Caen, Montgomery's columns have raced north into Belgium. "The British Army has kept going like a cat on its way to heaven," one American broadcaster tells his audience. "Already it's so far from this transmitter that we almost have to cover its movements by crystal ball."

German troops are retreating by any means possible. The world's most feared fighting force is proving to be anything but. There is no motorized component to their getaway. Horses pull carts and wagons with tall wooden wheels, loaded with hay and sleeping soldiers.

But most of all, bikes.

"No one who hasn't seen a German infantry column on the move can understand how unlike a modern army it is," Robert Barr of the BBC describes the enemy withdrawal. "There were soldiers on bicycles: all kinds of bicycles, ladies' bicycles, men's bicycles, racing bicycles, tall upright bicycles. There were soldiers on foot loaded down with equipment like soldiers of the last war."

Montgomery's new plan is known as "Operation Market Garden."

Leading the British advance will be Monty's top commander, Lieutenant General Brian Horrocks. He is tasked with getting tanks to the Dutch town of Eindhoven within three hours of setting out from the Belgian border. The bridge at Arnhem is to be attained in three days. Operation Market Garden—"Market" for the airborne and "Garden" for the armored ground force—depends completely on speed. Horrocks has shown quite recently that he is the man for such a job.

The veteran of El-Alamein and Tunisia has only recently returned to action. On D-Day he was still convalescing from a year-old wound, arriving in France to take command of the armored 30 Corps only in August. The British were still stuck at the time, but Horrocks saw opportunity. "It was quite obvious that the *Boche* was beginning to crack," he will remember, invoking French slang for the Germans. "There were the same signs we had seen when he began to crack in Tunisia. But when the enemy begins to crack you have to attack all the harder. You have to accelerate the defeat before he can rally."

Horrocks concludes: "What the men had to have was victory. They had to see German prisoners coming with their hands up."

Horrocks has lived a remarkable life: born in India to a Royal Army doctor, taken prisoner twice in the First World War, competed in modern pentathlon in the 1924 Olympics, speaks fluent Russian. Horrocks was so exhilarated about his release from a World War I German prisoner of war camp after four years in captivity—a time in which his salary accumulated in his absence—that he ran through all his back pay in a six-week London binge.

Thin, jaunty, a man known for speaking man-to-man with every soldier, from private to general. Forty-nine just three days ago, Horrocks transformed himself from one of the poorest students in his class at the Royal Military Academy at Sandhurst into a brilliant officer. No less than Dwight Eisenhower considers him Montgomery's top general.

Horrocks is a man known for battlefield intuition. Nowhere was this more obvious than two weeks ago, outside the French town of Amiens. His armor was halted by enemy resistance in what the general considers "good tank country."

"The Germans intended to hold their strong line on the Somme," Horrocks will remember fondly. "Our problem was to get there before they could blow the bridges. So at four o'clock that day, forty-five miles outside Amiens, I went to see the commander of one of the armored divisions. I said to him exactly what I'd said to him one day in Tunisia. I said: there's moonlight tonight."

Horrocks will describe what he meant: "Sometimes you sniff the air and it doesn't smell quite right. But this time it smelled right."

Attacking through the night in driving rain on country roads and farmland, Horrocks and the British armor advance sixty miles in twenty-four hours, not only capturing Amiens but crossing the Seine before the bridges could be blown.

This is Montgomery's inspiration for Market Garden. If General Horrocks can do it in France, there's no reason he can't do the same in Holland.

.   .   .

FIELD MARSHAL BERNARD Law Montgomery talks down to Dwight Eisenhower, treating his commander like a slow schoolboy. As they sit inside the C-47 here outside Brussels, Ike reaches across and pats Monty on the knee, reminding him who's boss. Montgomery catches himself, then presses on, determined to sell his plan.

Eisenhower is listening.

Three times, Eisenhower has already said no to Montgomery's attack. But with the Germans in full retreat and British armor flashing overdue confidence, Ike is now more willing to listen. As much as the wisdom of great generals and the training of elite soldiers, weather and logistics now shape Eisenhower's strategic mindset. He can either stay put for the winter, knowing that vital ports like Antwerp will be open to the Allies by spring—well aware the Germans will use that time to regroup. Or he can attack now, while the enemy is in chaos. The supply issues won't be ideal, but now might be a time for good enough.

Monty adds an intriguing twist: paratroops on the most massive scale in history. Not just the relatively small squads he has mentioned in previous versions of his thrust but thousands upon thousands of men dropping from the sky to work hand in glove with British armor.

Airborne units are the Allies' favorite new toy, an elite fighting force capable of dropping into any combat zone. Yet troops trained to jump out of perfectly good airplanes are so new to warfare that proper tactical use is still a question mark. This leaves them underutilized. More than thirty airborne operations were planned for the month of August. Not one was executed. Airborne troops remain at their bases in England, eager to fight but overlooked.

Montgomery's new plan will be quite the opposite, the greatest test of airborne fighting forces in their short military history. American, British, and Polish units will drop behind German lines, some as far back as a bold—and perhaps overconfident—sixty-four miles.

They must then capture intact five key bridges spanning Highway 69, the main road from the Belgian border. They will travel through Holland, then cross the Rhine at the German border. The final crossing is Arnhem, placing Allied troops in the Fatherland for the first time. Meanwhile, Montgomery's armor and infantry will advance from the border of Belgium up that lone stretch of two-lane road. Along the way, the tankers will link up with the airborne units, preventing the lightly armed paratroopers from being surrounded and cut off—in effect, rescuing the airborne soldiers before the shortcomings of being a lightly armed force can be exposed.

Monty's entire 21st Army Group will then drive north to Berlin.

War over by Christmas.

Cakewalk.

Montgomery's top paratroop commander, Lieutenant General Frederick "Boy" Browning, is not so sure. Dapper. Slim. Olympic bobsledder. Married to a celebrated novelist.*

Browning is the expert on all things airborne. Looking at a map showing that single stretch of highway linking five bridges over five major waterways, he is particularly troubled by the final span—the lower Rhine bridge at Arnhem. The sixty-four miles 30 Corps tanks must travel to reach this bridge looks . . .

. . . well . . .

. . . ambitious.

Perhaps too much so.

"We can hold it for four," Browning hems to Montgomery, referring to the number of days his paratroopers can make a stand so far away from help.

"But, sir," Browning adds, in words that will follow him the rest of his life.

"I think we may be going a bridge too far."†

Montgomery doesn't listen. This is the Rhine, after all. Gateway to Berlin.

And by the time Browning gives his opinion, it's already too late.

A fascinated Eisenhower has flown back to Jullouville in his C-47, painful knee and all.

"I'll tell you what I'll do," he informed Montgomery as their

---

* Browning's wife was bestselling writer Daphne Du Maurier, who wrote historical romance and suspense. Her short stories "The Birds" and "Don't Look Now" were both adapted into films. The couple lived in Cornwall and had three children. General Browning is no relation to the deceased Sapper Browning from the Chiswick V-2 attack.

† Some believe this quote was contrived after the fact. Nonetheless, Browning will forever be known for this remark.

meeting ended. "I'll give you whatever you ask to get over the Rhine, because I want a bridgehead."

The supreme Allied commander doesn't just give his blessing to Montgomery's brazen Market Garden.

He also wants the job done right away.

HOLLAND

———◆———

19

General James Gavin drives from London at top speed.

He's late. Can't be helped. The briefing is starting without him.

Boy Browning stands at the front of a grand hall fit for a king, preaching to more than two dozen senior officers. It is three hours and a Channel crossing since Monty's arm-twisting in Ike's C-47. Browning flew straight from Brussels to explain the plan.

Sunninghill, as this country estate is normally known, indeed fetes royalty. William the Conqueror hunted in the local woods eight centuries ago. The property has been a British constant in the thirty-eight royal coronations since. Ascot racecourse lies dormant one driveway over, horse racing suspended for the duration. When the war finally ends, Sunninghill will revert to its royal footing, destined to be purchased as a marital residence for Princess Elizabeth and Prince Philip, Duke of Edinburgh.*

But while this great room has long spoken of wealth and will soon again, right now it's all war. "Gangway," not Sunninghill. Situation maps line the walls. Senior officers slouch in armchairs and sofas. The less accomplished stand. Cigars, cigarettes, pipes.

Browning enthusiastically explains Monty's race to the Rhine, despite his personal "bridge too far" doubts. General Lewis H. Brereton, commander of Ninth Air Force, which includes all Allied airborne troops, appears calm as Browning delivers details. Yet the accomplished general chain-smokes, insides churning.†

James Gavin steps quietly into the haze. No one begrudges his tardiness. He only got the call an hour ago, making the thirty-five-mile drive from the blacked-out streets of London as fast as he could.

Gavin knew the way. England is once again home to 82nd Airborne. They flew back more than a month ago after "thirty-three days of action without relief, without replacements. Every mission accomplished. No ground gained was ever relinquished," in the words of the division battle report. Each soldier was given a short furlough before Gavin put them to work. Having suffered almost five thousand casualties in horrific firefights, forever placing tactically vital but otherwise insignificant villages like Ste-Mère-Église and La Fière on the

---

* The couple will never move in. Sunninghill burns down shortly before their wedding in November 1947. Princess Elizabeth will ascend to the throne and be crowned queen of England on June 2, 1953.

† A pioneer in military aviation and staunch advocate of airborne troops, the controversial Brereton kept this framed quotation on his desk: "Where is the prince who can afford so to cover his country with troops for its defense, as that 10,000 men descending from the clouds, might not, in many places, do an infinite deal of mischief before a force could be brought together to repel them?" The quotation is from Benjamin Franklin, written January 16, 1784.

historical map, the unit needed time to heal, train replacements, gin up for what's next.*

If there's a next. Despite losing so many best friends and fellow warriors, the 82nd is impatient to fight again, yet unsure that will happen.

Gavin scans the briefing room. The usual mix of gray hair, posturing, and mild impatience—every man too powerful to be summoned on a Sunday night, so this better be good. He's youngest by years. Maybe the tallest. Certainly the most well-conditioned. The general knows the faces, particularly forty-three-year-old General Maxwell Taylor of the US 101st Airborne and General Roy Urquhart of the British 1st Airborne—a six-foot, two-hundred-pound Scot just months younger than Taylor. Though he transferred to airborne only a year ago after ground tours in North Africa and Sicily, Urquhart's work ethic and discipline inspires respect. One British glider pilot will fondly call him "a bloody general who didn't mind doing the job of a sergeant."

As Browning lays out Market Garden, it becomes clear that Gavin, Taylor, and Urquhart will be pivotal. Each will command one of the three airborne divisions vital to success.

"General Browning continued to outline the plan for the proposed operation," Gavin will remember. "It envisioned seizing bridges over five major waterways, as well as a number of other tactical objectives."

Gavin's oversimplification downplays Market Garden's enormous scale and the haste with which it must be executed. Parachute operations over Sicily and Normandy needed five months to plan, yet the drop on Holland happens next week.

Next week.

---

* The modern coat of arms for Ste-Mère-Église bears the image of two parachutes descending on the town.

More than thirty-five thousand troops will either parachute or be flown in by glider. This means five thousand planes and a thousand more escorts.*

Most dangerous of all, the moon is dark. Pilots and paratroopers can't possibly locate drop zones.

So, Market Garden, an airborne operation dwarfing the D-Day drops by an exponential figure, will take place in broad daylight.

"The object," Browning concludes in an optimistic tone, "is to lay a carpet of airborne troops down over which our ground forces can pass."†

Browning cedes the floor to Brereton, his immediate superior. In contrast to the dapper British general, the American has a palpable edge. The Pittsburgh native and Naval Academy graduate is a drinker and a bully with a fondness for luxury, such as this estate where he chooses to make his headquarters. The general is one of the few officers from any nation to fight in the European and Pacific theaters, "unique among sky chiefs in his practical experiences on all our main fronts against all enemies in this global war," *Collier's* will write of Brereton. "He is widely acclaimed the foremost tactician of modern airpower."

---

* The Horsa glider was a basic all-wood aircraft featuring two pilots and a hinged cockpit that opened the entire front of the aircraft, allowing instant access to the loading compartment. Wingspan was eighty-eight feet, length sixty-seven, and glide speed one hundred miles per hour. The Horsa was capable of carrying an infantry platoon, jeep, or artillery piece. The aircraft was towed into combat before unhooking the rope to glide onto a target. A typical landing required one hundred yards of ground. Although the Horsa was highly effective during airborne operations, the aircraft was susceptible to cargo coming loose and sliding toward the nose in flight, interrupting the gliding process with fatal results.

† William Goldman, in the screenplay for the 1977 film *A Bridge Too Far*, will have one character compare the Market Garden plan with a western: The Germans are the bad guys, the paratroopers the besieged settlers, and British armor the cavalry riding to the rescue.

Yet the veteran general has no experience in airborne operations. Taking the room this Sunday evening, wire-framed glasses high on the bridge of his nose, the general is already deconstructing the outlandish plan that landed in his lap one hour ago. The hazards of dropping paratroopers into combat are obvious: enemy ground fire, soldiers landing miles from drop zones, shaky reconnaissance. Yet right now, logistics singular to airborne present a far bigger problem. Finding enough bullets, maps, and reconnaissance photographs, as well as transporting paratroopers from their training bases to their departure airfields here in England, is dwarfed by an even greater reality:

Brereton needs more planes. Lots more.

Nothing happens until he solves that problem.

And though the general assures the room that "advantages far outweigh the risks" of this quixotic plan, Brereton's words are irrelevant. Ike and Monty don't care if these officers think Market Garden will work. It's approved. A time for persuasion is past. The men in this room need to make it happen.

It does not matter that five thousand C-47s do not exist. Nor that it is within the realm of fantasy to believe a column of British armor will travel sixty-four miles from the Belgian border to Arnhem Bridge in four days—particularly when Monty's tanks took a very un-Patton-like two months to conquer Caen.

The fifty-four-year-old Brereton realizes his limitations, particularly when it comes to an operation that could decide whether the war ends by Christmas. Success or failure of the drop will reflect on his leadership. As an airborne virgin with a black mark against his record due to a fiasco in the Pacific, he cannot afford another setback. So the veteran commander makes a savvy decision that is all the more brilliant for appearing magnanimous.

Since General Brereton took command of airborne operations thirty-three days ago, he has clashed repeatedly with Boy Browning.

The Englishman is considered one of the great minds of airborne operations, while Brereton has never commanded paratroopers in combat. He got the job because he was American. Browning felt slighted and said so, recently offering his resignation.

Then came the flight to Brussels. The talk with Monty. The mandate to be British, above all else. Browning knows that his angry letter needs to be ripped in two.

This is made clear when Brereton concludes his talk by announcing he will be commanding Market Garden from luxurious Gangway. The general will fly alongside the drop to witness the majestic sight, then return here to follow the action from afar.

But he will not lead the fight. It is Browning who will drop into Holland with the troops. The Brit will be in charge from there on out.

9:00 P.M.

MEETING BREAKS UP. Officers cluster in smaller groups to talk the night away, hammering out details. It is agreed that the British 1st will take the most dangerous assignment, capturing the Rhine bridge at Arnhem, holding that vital crossing into Germany until Monty's armor rescues them. The US 101st will capture the other end of the invasion, taking control of crossings and highways linking the Belgian border with the first few miles into Holland. Gavin and the 82nd will conquer the middle, from the penultimate bridge at Nijmegen in the north and a ten-mile corridor of Highway 69 leading south to the Grave bridge over the Maas River. Gavin's men will later become unsettled about the spelling of their objective—G-R-A-V-E—believing it might portend bad luck. Yet otherwise, the 82nd will conclude the plan is solid.

And complex.

Every water crossing in succession must be taken by the 101st, then the 82nd, and finally the 1st. Monty's armor will dash up the highway, cross the Rhine, then race to Berlin.

But . . .

But if those dominoes do not fall, British armor's race to Arnhem will fail. General Urquhart's 1st will be stranded, surrounded by Nazis, with no way of escape.

And Field Marshal Montgomery's dash to Berlin will be over before it starts.

. . .

BY DAWN, ESTIMATES of aircraft availability are confirmed. Good news, bad news.

Good news is the attack can launch as soon as September 17, just six days from now. But lack of gliders and transports means airborne troops must take off in waves, one day apart, rather than in a single massive drop. The element of surprise will not be completely lost, but the initial attack won't be the overwhelming force Monty envisions.

Ever so slightly, Market Garden unravels.

20

General James Gavin plans every possible scenario.

Two hours north of London. 82nd Airborne Division's rural headquarters. Gavin's war room open for business twenty-four hours. Rows of prefabricated metal Nissen huts house his men. Local farms growing wheat and barley, vital commodities in wartime. Legendary local ghosts: the scorned groom often seen hanging by the neck from a farmhouse beam, that sad young boy in Victorian dress, the midnight carriages drawn by black horses that vanish in an instant, and that pretty girl dressed all in white walking the corridors of stately Braunstone Hall.

Gavin ignores the ghost stories. He's got enough scary thoughts of his own.

"My memory of the next three days is a blur of checking troop units, re-examining details of our tactical plans, flying a light plane to various units to check their planning, and then every evening poring over the aerial photographs over the territory over which we were to land and fight, searching for signs of enemy activity," he will remember.

"I thoroughly studied the intelligence reports."

The findings cause concern. Enemy defenses are stiffening as Germans prepare to defend the Fatherland for the first time. Allied bomber crews returning from missions over Berlin report massive antiaircraft fire at the Rhine. British intelligence suspects at least one, perhaps two panzer divisions are concealed in the thick forests outside Nijmegen.

Market Garden has been sold as a pell-mell sprint down a long, flat, extremely straight highway. Yet the countryside is much more than a road and five bridges. There are farms and towns and people and forests rising in sudden thick clusters right next to carefully plowed fields of rich black soil and country lanes lined with towering oaks and maples and limes specially planted to stop the wind. Here and there, old-fashioned windmills with broad wooden blades remind everyone they're in Holland.

Highway 69 is not the only route through Dutch countryside. And the path is anything but straight. The road is a serpent, a twist, a random turn, an invitation to get unforgettably lost between Belgium and Arnhem.

Yet weird roads can't stop Market Garden. No one worries—at least no one who can modify the operation. Gavin himself is concerned, but his men are eager to jump, regardless of the risk.

The term "party" is used by officers and troops to describe what will, hopefully, be an enormous breakthrough. When Major Brian Urquhart, chief intelligence officer of the British 1st Airborne who bears the same last name but no relation to his division commander, produces reconnaissance photos showing the presence of the 9th and 10th SS Panzer Divisions in Arnhem and Nijmegen, he is ordered to take sick leave for treatment of "nervous strain and exhaustion."*

. . .

FRIDAY, SEPTEMBER 15, two days before launch.

General Gavin orders his paratroopers driven to their takeoff bases. Transport vehicles drop them after dark. The men shuffle into barracks for hot showers and their last good night of sleep for the next week.

Meanwhile, Gavin assembles his battalion commanders. The subject is proper bridge-capturing technique.

"First of all, cut all wires leading to the bridge, whether they were obviously connected to demolitions or not," he tells his leaders. "Next, whenever possible, bridges must be attacked at both ends simultaneously. While a movement to reach the far end of any bridge might be costly, it is very likely not nearly so costly as piling up casualties at one end of the bridge where all the enemy fire power could be brought to bear in a small area, after which the enemy would blow up the bridge."

Bridge fighting was a footnote to the airborne training syllabus back at Fort Bragg, North Carolina. An occasional exercise. Long forgotten.

Yet the obscure tactics must be executed with precision.

No matter the epoch, no matter the conflict, no matter the combatants, one constant through history is that every battlefield presents unique puzzles—and demands they be solved through improvised skill sets. As Gavin refreshes his commanders on this warm September start to the weekend, crossing from one side of a broad black river to the other seems like the most extraordinary challenge his troops will face.

---

* In the movie *A Bridge Too Far* his name will be changed to "Major Fuller" to avoid confusion.

And it will be.

Though hardly in the way Gavin imagines.

. . .

SATURDAY PASSES IN a flurry of cleaning weapons, sorting ammunition, performing last checks on maps and reconnaissance, and going down each commander's checklist of which unit is responsible for which aspect of the battle plan. Gloomy drizzle falls on the barracks, weather not conducive to jumping—or hope. Each man is issued a gas mask, and a life vest in case of a watery landing. The "escape kit" containing Dutch guilders is for thanking locals willing to hide them.

The general is concerned he is asking too much of the veteran troops making their second or third jump—like himself, "fugitives from the law of averages." Gavin ponders what traits allow them to remain unscathed despite the enormous casualty rate.

He thinks of the firefights, the wounded, the dead.

And he worries.

"To ask them once again to jump into combat more than fifty miles behind the German lines in broad daylight was just asking a great deal," he will write. Gavin will later describe this concern by quoting a line from Lord Moran's classic study on bravery, that "courage, for every man, is like a bank account—it can be overdrawn."*

As the sun sets on Saturday, September 16, Gavin speaks to those men, individually and in groups. Their average age is twenty-two. "The troops of the 82nd Airborne Division look like tough boys, and they are," journalist Martha Gellhorn will write. "They are good at their trade, too, and they know it, and they walk as if they know it. This trade is war: most of them are too young to have learned any other profession."

---

* Lord Moran was Winston Churchill's personal physician. *The Anatomy of Courage* was one of the first books written about the psychology of war, published in 1945. Gavin quotes that line in his own memoir, written in 1978.

It is James Gavin who has instilled these traits through rigorous training and personal example. He now talks to them about the battle plan, assuring the veterans of superior Allied airpower. A daylight jump, their general tells them, seeking to allay their fears and at the same time his own, is going to work out just fine.

Gavin concludes every one-on-one in the same fashion. "Finally, I assured [each soldier] that we had adequate troops and weapons to deal with the Germans on the ground."

The general does not say so, but men and guns are not enough.

It is also vital that the bank account of courage remains in good standing.

. . .

GAVIN DOESN'T SLEEP much on a good night. Less before a drop. Sunday morning's flights won't launch until chaplains say Mass, yet the general is up long before dawn. Rare is the trooper who isn't.

So it is, after seven short days of intense preparation, James Gavin and his staff brief the men one last time after breakfast, letting them see for themselves the flat, soggy Dutch terrain on sand tables, providing up-to-the-minute drop zone status based on aerial photographs taken this very morning by some brave young Spitfire pilot who got up in the dead of night to skim low over German guns that would turn him into vapor with a direct hit, then zoomed back to base in time for an English breakfast.

Here in the British Midlands, the countryside airfield is green with a nip of autumn chill. Men walk to their assigned planes with the swagger of star quarterbacks striding out of a stadium tunnel. "Long files of the fighting skymen are waddling in their grotesque clothes, and with packs and weapons of all sizes carried on their shoulders, out to the planes," writes journalist W. B. Courtney, who will observe the drop as an airborne guest of General Lewis Brereton. "You are not prepared for their happy-go-lucky mood at such a moment, so unlike the quiet grimness of land infantry. They shout and wise crack and catcall. They see a handful of US nurses, trim in blue fatigue coveralls, watching them from beside the control tower, and immediately there is an outburst of whistling all over the field."

General Gavin is driven by jeep to the C-47 with his departure number chalked on the fuselage. Jump door already open. Waiting. Gavin dons gear in the shadow of the left wing. No fawning aides. No pretense. He ignores a photographer kneeling to snap a photo of the handsome young general buckling into his kit.

Swagger without trying. Lanky, haircut high and tight, doesn't need the star on his helmet to let every one of the beloved animals he commands know who's in charge.

Gavin checks his watch, already synchronized with his officers'. It's time. The general climbs into the belly and awaits the telltale belch of Pratt & Whitneys sputtering to life—as always, his cue that there is no turning back.

Engines cough. Catch. Three big blades per wing eat the delicious, moist British air. Wheel chocks tugged away. C-47s roll forward in a long line searching for a runway. Ground crews wonder if this is the last time they'll see the planes whose every rivet and cowling they know as well as the contour of their faraway girlfriends' breasts.

The general is alone. Marriage back home in shambles. Thoughts tending toward the detailed. He runs a mental checklist of all the things that need to go right today—and the potential ghosts that might haunt Market Garden.

"The die was cast," Gavin will remember of his plane powering toward Nijmegen.

No matter what else happens on this Sunday morning, General James Gavin will be the first 82nd Airborne paratrooper leaping out of the first 82nd Airborne plane.

Third time's the charm.

What happens after the drop is anyone's guess.

21

General Norman "Dutch" Cota is overwhelmed with grief.

Three weeks and more than two hundred miles since the march through Paris. One mile inside the German frontier. No more thoughts of the war ending by Christmas. So much death.

Commanding the 28th came easily at first. Cota led the unit through a triumphant ten-day dash from Paris, chasing the German Army back inside their borders. The Pennsylvania unit captured all of Luxembourg single-handedly, then became the first American unit to touch German soil. But there the party ended. Dense minefields, rolls of barbed wire, anti-tank defenses, and concrete pillboxes are arrayed along the border.

Just days ago, the Germans were beaten. No doubt about it. Exhausted, scared, uninterested in anything but going home. What a difference German soil makes.

Now the enemy punishes every move the 28th makes. Four days ago, Cota launched two attacks against German positions. Both failed.

And it wasn't just that the enemy fought harder. Since taking over the National Guard unit, Cota has struggled to replace an entrenched officer corps, some of whom have served in the same role since World War I. Cota has doubts about the chief of staff and operations officer he inherited. Both appear incompetent.

The troubled division seems snakebit, its leadership problems tracing back to before Cota. Just three weeks after landing in France on July 22, one division commander was relieved of duty, only to have his replacement shot by an enemy sniper. The disciplined Cota has been brought in to make changes. After the most recent failed attack in these muddy autumn conditions, Cota fired regimental commander Colonel William Blanton for withdrawing his men from action without permission.

Over the last four days, however, the 28th has slowly gained ground. Every attack is met by a German counterattack. SS infantry and flame-throwing half-tracks terrorized the division. One line of three American tank destroyers was incinerated by direct enemy fire, the men inside cooked alive in a crushing blow to morale for all who witnessed it. "One minute I looked and they were there, firing," one officer will remember. "The next they were burning like hell."

Yet this morning the high ground above Üttfeld, this hilly collective of farms and forests crisscrossed with winding country roads, was finally taken.

General Norman Cota wants to finish the job. As Cota prepares to lay waste to the town itself, he receives a call from his boss, Major General Leonard Gerow of Fifth Corps. The attack is off. The 28th's advance has led to a salient—a peninsula poking from the American lines into the Germans'—whose flanks cannot be protected. Cota must stand down.

The general is not surprised. He finds Gerow to have a controlling personality and very little character.

Not only that, but the 28th is being pulled off the line for a short rest. Cota finally has the time to address the leadership issues, perhaps replacing men like Blanton who don't always go with the program. He is also tasked with training replacement troops, then integrating them with the veterans.

The more glaring issue is death. Between September 13 and 17, the 28th has taken 1,500 casualties. Even the Germans are appalled by how many members of the 28th have perished in five days of fighting. Noting the red keystone emblem each soldier wears on his left shoulder, the enemy compares the shape with a bucket. And not just any kind of bucket: *der blutiger Eimer.*

"The Bloody Bucket."

This is not the reputation General Norman Cota hoped to achieve with his first major command.

Sadly, that reputation will only get worse.

22

Airplanes. Everywhere, airplanes.

Sunshine on Sunday. Somewhere over the Channel. The cramped fuselage smells of aircraft fuel, army-issue cigarettes, and the damp aroma of distant green countryside. Gavin's C-47 is half-full, soldiers and personal staff. Everyone's jumping.

General James Gavin stands mid-flight in the open doorway—alone, pensive, prisoner to detail. Air-sea rescue launches dash into position on the whitecapped water below, ready to pick up aircrews ditching now or on the way home.

Everywhere else, airplanes. The general knew today's armada would be enormous, but the sight of so many aircraft above, behind, and below his own plane is astounding. A total of 1,545 C-47s and 478 gliders departed from twenty-four British airfields just after eleven. "The sky is so full and solid with planes that you have the illusion it is only we that are motionless and substantial, and the earth that is transitory," journalist W. B. Courtney will write.

143

The American writer is not the only one in awe. Unlike the midnight Normandy launch, daylight allows dazzled British citizens to bear witness.

"Thousands of people on England's coast," the London *Daily Express* will report, "saw the great glider armada streaming out to sea toward Holland. For an hour and a half, from 11 A.M. to 12:30 P.M., the fleet filled the skies. So great was the roar that no one on the coast could use the telephone until the planes had passed."

The Dutch coast nears. Gavin looks down from his 1,500-foot altitude. Fighter escorts bristle with cannon and machine guns. The pilots are creatures of intention and impulse, flitting in and out of formation to cut and wheel through the blue sky, always searching for something to kill. They are British Spitfires and Typhoons; American Mustangs, Thunderbolts, and Lightnings—1,130 in all.

Pewter sea replaced by coastal Dutch sand dunes replaced by flat farmland crisscrossed with elevated roadways and canals. People on the ground stop what they are doing to look up at the sky.

Gavin checks his watch. Less than an hour to red light. The 82nd will utilize three separate drop areas and an additional landing zone capable of handling fifty Waco gliders. Gavin has contrived to parachute field artillery pieces into Holland. The 105mm howitzers have a range of nearly nine miles, more than enough to slow—but not stop—a charging SS panzer division.

Paratroopers remove their yellow Mae West life belts now that the Channel is behind them. Same for gas masks. Now unnecessary, they get shoved into the seat webbing.

Gavin orders everyone to stand. The men rise more slowly than normal, physically weighed down by learned lessons from Normandy. There weren't enough mines for that jump. Now almost everyone carries a circular ten-pound M1 anti-tank explosive device should panzers be hidden in the hilly Groesbeek forest near the Nijmegen drop zone. This is the only high ground for miles around. The German

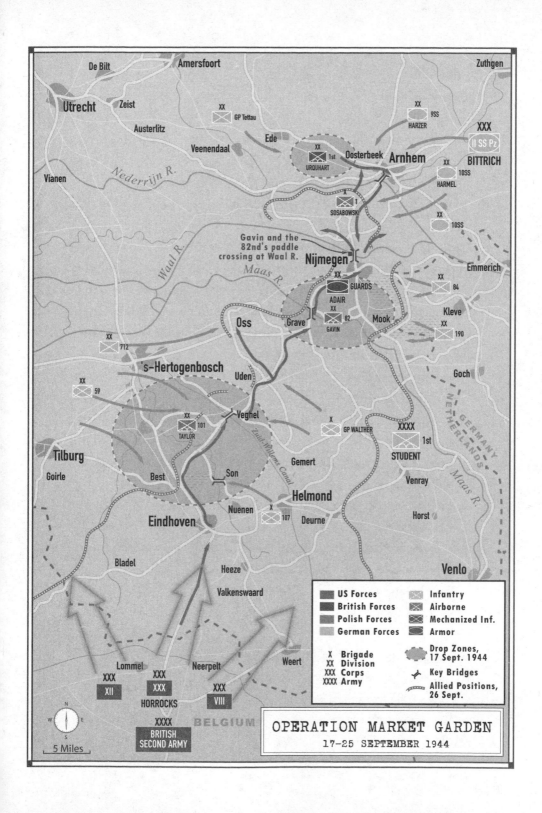

De Bilt · Amersfoort · Zuthgen

Utrecht · Zeist

Austerlitz

Veenendaal · Ede · Oosterbeek · **Arnhem**

Vianen

Nederrijn R.

GP Tettau (XX)

9SS (XX) HARZER

XXX (II SS Pz) BITTRICH

1st URQUHART (XX)

10SS (XX) HARMEL

1 SOSABOWSKI (X)

10SS (XX)

Waal R.

Gavin and the 82nd's paddle crossing at Waal R.

Maas R. · **Nijmegen**

Emmerich

GUARDS (XX) ADAIR

84 (XX)

82 GAVIN (XX) · Mook

Kleve

190 (XX)

Oss · Grave

712 (XX)

's-Hertogenbosch · Uden

Goch

59 (XX)

GERMANY NETHERLANDS

101 TAYLOR (XX) · Veghel

GP WALTHER (X)

XXXX 1st STUDENT

Tilburg · Gemert

Goirle

Best · Son · *Zuid-Willems Canal*

Venray · *Maas R.*

Nuenen · **Helmond**

107 (X) · Deurne

Horst

Eindhoven

Bladel · Heeze

Venlo

Valkenswaard

Lommel · Neerpelt · Weert

XXX XII · XXX HORROCKS · XXX VIII

XXXX BRITISH SECOND ARMY

5 Miles

BELGIUM

Legend

US Forces	Infantry
British Forces	Airborne
Polish Forces	Mechanized Inf.
German Forces	Armor

X Brigade
XX Division
XXX Corps
XXXX Army

Drop Zones, 17 Sept. 1944
Key Bridges
Allied Positions, 26 Sept.

OPERATION MARKET GARDEN
17–25 SEPTEMBER 1944

border is just on the other side, in a second wooded area named the Reichswald—"imperial forest." A panzer division emerging from either tree line to open fire would be the worst sort of surprise.

Another new addition to each man's arsenal is a pistol. Firing a rifle at targets on the ground is difficult while descending in a parachute. The M1911A1 .45 ACP pistol—just ".45"—ensures that one arm is constantly ready to fire. Gavin's handgun is holstered on his right hip, just below the sling of his parachute harness and above the oversize pants pocket stuffed with bullets and grenades. During the D-Day drop over Ste-Mère-Église, Hitler's troops fired automatic weapons at the descending 82nd paratroopers. White phosphorous parachute flares launched by the Germans floated to earth alongside Gavin's men, mingling with fires from burning buildings to illuminate everything in the night sky. Many an American was machine-gunned before touching the ground.

Thus, pistols.

A collective *snap* of metal on metal as paratroopers clip into the static jump line.

The red light flashes like Rudolph's nose above the open doorway. No one panics.

Except General James Gavin. Suddenly, a wave of C-47s crosses directly below the general's aircraft, a diagonal flight path close enough he can see paratroops standing in the doorway, poised to leap.

This is not the drop zone.

Then it gets worse.

Men pour out of the planes. "Parachutes began to blossom," Gavin will recall.

Colossal mistake. Horrific. Monumental. Irreversible. Charlie Foxtrot. Nothing about the terrain corresponds with 82nd's landing sites. Not one single thing.

The pilots Gavin trusts so completely are making a catastrophic error. The entire tightly wound Market Garden operation is in tatters. Thousands will die because of this simple fuckup.

Yet good paratroopers already jumped. There is nothing the general can do to fix this.

Then Gavin feels a whoosh of relief. He's got the wrong stick:

"As it turned out, it was the 101st."

The young general watches his American counterparts float to earth, flush in the belief that the Market Garden plan is still working—for now.

·   ·   ·

NAZI GERMANY KNOWS what's coming. General Kurt Student of the Luftwaffe's First Parachute Division watches the incoming planes, hears "the crash of bombs and fire from aircraft armaments and anti-aircraft guns in my immediate vicinity."

This is followed by "the endless stream of enemy transport and cargo planes, as far as the eye could see."

Yet it is one thing to see an invasion, quite another to fight back. Committing forces to battle without knowing the enemy's objective could be sending his men into a trap.

So, General Student waits for orders—and prays his antiaircraft batteries do their job.

·   ·   ·

GENERAL JAMES GAVIN is impatient for green. Checks his watch. Checks the light above the door. Still red.

Gavin sees what he needs to see: low steel girders of the bridge at Grave, thick hilly Groesbeek woods, then the mighty Nijmegen Bridge itself, almost two thousand feet long and easily recognized by massive arches topping the span like three steel rainbows.

This belongs to the 82nd.

Every paratrooper looks out the small cabin window corresponding with his place in line. They see Kansas: haystacks, wheat, long broad

147

fields with plenty of room for gliders to slide their splendidly curved undercarriages against the earth in a one-hundred-yard landing.

As each target looms closer, aircrews in each cockpit don bullet- and fragment-resistant flak suits. Some pilots slap a steel helmet over their headset. After the jump, crews will put the C-47s into a wide left turn while remaining in tight formation, standing one wing on its end, then returning home over a hundred miles of enemy territory and the broad width of the Channel. These pilots will do it again to- morrow and every day until Market Garden is over, at first carrying a new wave of troops, then dropping supplies of food and ammunition.

That is to come. First, today's drop. The C-47 pilots descend and slow airspeed to 110 knots. Jump altitude is 680 feet. Like the para- troopers, many aircrews are veterans of Sicily, Italy, and Normandy. They also fly Gavin's airborne practice jumps, giving each pilot and copilot a wealth of knowledge about the precise methodology of nail- ing a perfect drop.

"As the ground rose," General Gavin will write of his aircraft's descent, "it seemed to be very close to us, and everything I had memo- rized was coming into sight. The triangular patch of woods near where I was to jump appeared under us just as the jump light went on. Although we seemed quite close to the ground we went out without a second's delay."

German tracer rounds rise from the ground to meet the plane.

"One," Gavin yells as he leaps, denoting his place in the stick. Be- hind him, though he cannot hear, each paratrooper in sequence calls out their jump number: "Two. Three. Four . . ."

Then they hang in the air after their parachutes blossom, "like lit- tle brown dolls hanging under a green lampshade," in the words of CBS correspondent Edward R. Murrow.

First to leap, first to land. Gavin hits the ground hard, breaking his back in two places. In the sky above, C-47 crews "pour the coal" to the Pratt & Whitneys of their empty planes, racing to avoid the antiaircraft fire now pocking the sky in yellow-gray bursts. Lying on the ground, finding it difficult to stand, Gavin places his pistol within easy reach as he unclips his billowing parachute and shrugs out of his harness. Nothing to be done about the pain but push through. The general then holsters his .45 and hefts his M1 rifle, all the while coming under small-arms fire from the woods. The terrain is rural and green. Broad pastures, country roads lined by evenly spaced elms, houses with tall, steep roofs and red shingles. Every now and then a church.

Parachutes settle to earth everywhere around Gavin. The sun is momentarily blocked. Determined troopers fire down on suspected German antiaircraft positions with their new pistols, later laughing they were just as likely to shoot themselves while twisting beneath their canopies. Yet the ploy works. Young enemy soldiers run off in fear, racing back toward Germany. "We were all pleased with the ability of the troopers to jump in daylight on antiaircraft positions and destroy them," Gavin will write.

"Early indications were that the drop had been unusually successful. Unit after unit reported in on-schedule, and with few exceptions, all were in their pre-planned locations."

A good start. But still a lot to accomplish. General Gavin's mission involves three primary objectives: capturing the bridge over the River Maas at Grave; taking control of the ten miles of Highway 69 and several miles of territory on either side; and capturing the Nijmegen Bridge intact.*

None of that will be sustainable without capturing the high ground of the Groesbeek woods. The general witnessed rows of enemy trenches filled with soldiers as he dropped to earth. In the chaos of parachutes landing, gunfire, and units assembling, he surveys the next tactical maneuver. Amazingly, as the battlefield reveals itself, a P-47 Thunderbolt in the sky above is hit by enemy fire and begins to crack in two,

---

* The Maas is known as the Meuse in France.

but the pilot manages to land in a nearby field and slide out of the cockpit very much alive.

Within eighteen minutes, 4,511 soldiers of the 82nd are on the ground, out of their chutes, organizing into units, and rushing into position. By night, the division will land 7,467 men, among them Market Garden's overall commander, British general Frederick "Boy" Browning. He will set up his operational headquarters here in Gavin's rural sector—though not before attending to a most important piece of business.

Upon landing, Browning steps out of the glider that carried him to the drop zone and quickly sprints toward the German border. He soon walks back, a study in triumph.

"I wanted to be the first British officer to pee in Germany," Browning explains to his staff.

.   .   .

THE BRIDGE. NOTHING matters if Gavin can't capture Nijmegen Bridge. Only then can the armored column of the British 30 Corps pass over and continue twelve miles up the road to the final span in Arnhem. Reports confirm that Urquhart and the British 1st's drop on that sector has been successful. Now the Scot and his men must hold the Rhine crossing for four long days.

That countdown also applies to the 82nd.

Gavin estimates British armor must battle their way into his sector within *three* days. Any longer and the Germans will regroup. The same catastrophe—encirclement, capture, and most likely death— predicted for General Urquhart and the British 1st in Arnhem might befall his men.

General Gavin sets up headquarters nine miles outside Nijmegen, impatient for news from the city.

"I personally directed Colonel Roy E. Lindquist, commanding the 508th Parachute Infantry," the general will recall, "to commit his first battalion against the Nijmegen bridge without delay after landing but to keep a very close watch on it in the event he needed it to protect himself against the Reichswald."

By late afternoon, Lindquist and his men probe the southern end of the Nijmegen Bridge. This is not wide-open countryside but densely packed city. Citizens spent the morning outdoors, enjoying the late-summer warmth. The afternoon was for watching parachutes land in and around their city—many Dutch from their rooftops—then taking shelter in their cellars to await the fighting.

All is quiet as the 508th makes their way toward the hulking gray bridge.

Not for long.

. . .

JAMES GAVIN IS eager for news.

He tries to sleep. It's been hours. No moon and thick woods. Dutch night the color of jump boot shoe polish. The general stretches out beneath a copse of pines, stressful day behind him and many more to come. So much on his mind. Units reported in all afternoon, confirming the jump's success and noting that they have begun accomplishing their assigned tasks—in particular, expanding the Allied position by capturing minor bridges over the Maas-Waal Canal near Honinghutje, Hatert, Malden, and Heumen. Everything is going right so far.

Gavin dozes, tossing and turning on the damp pine straw.

Elements of the 82nd also captured the vital bridge at Grave, overwhelming the defenders in a precise aerial drop and surprise attack. More good news for the general, but a successful landing is just the start.

Finally, it's no use.

"I awakened," writes Gavin. "I had slept rather fitfully. I was very much concerned about what our combat units would be doing during the night and what the tactical situation would be like at first light. I tried to get up, but my back was giving me considerable difficulty. I held onto a nearby pine tree and pulled myself to my feet . . . having pulled myself to my feet, I went to the operations center."

There, Gavin passes the dark hours.

The news from Nijmegen is a sharp blow to the solar plexus: The Germans were waiting. Impossible as it seems, they knew precisely when and where the Americans would strike. Colonel Lindquist and his men were devastated by 88mm artillery and mortar, caught out in a mundane urban traffic circle. Five paratroopers are dead.

Neither side is retreating. Nijmegen Bridge is still not taken, but Lindquist's 508th is close to the southern entrance. Captured German prisoners are brought in for interrogation, their boastful dispositions a much different attitude than the Americans expect.

"This encounter," Gavin will write, "was the first indication to us that something had been amiss in the intelligence briefings given us before we left England. This was not a broken German army in full retreat."

In fact, the Americans are fighting none other than the battle-hardened 10th SS Panzer Division.

"Those we captured were tough and confident. The Germans were in far better condition to fight than we had realized."

. . .

BUT THE GERMANS also had help.

By an amazing stroke of luck for German general Kurt Student, an American glider was shot down near the German First Parachute Division's command post.

German forces searched the wreckage and found a complete copy of the Market Garden plan. An unknown Allied officer erroneously neglected to leave those precious documents in England.

Two hours after Gavin breaks his back landing in Holland, those battle maps are already on the desk of German general Student.

Nothing that happens next will surprise the German Army.

Almost nothing.

23

The British are here.

A euphoric General James Gavin watches tanks of the British 30 Corps roll across the Grave bridge. Gray skies. Two days since the drop. "Grave, a clean cozy little market town in the middle of dairy farming and orchard country," in the words of the BBC.

Orange Dutch flags announcing liberation. Schoolchildren flashing orange hair ribbons and bow ties. Netherlands' Boy Scout band on the side of the road greeting British armor with trumpet fanfare. A local father, new child born just this morning, boasts to a reporter that the boy will be named Tommy, in honor of the British troops.

All Gavin cares about are the rumble and clank of oncoming tanks, a welcome noise so loud he hears Shermans and Churchills before seeing them. The 82nd can breathe easy.

Yet there is no time to waste. The clock is ticking for the British 1st in Arnhem. Fighting there is intense; General Urquhart's paratroopers are taking heavy losses but holding their positions. They're doomed if this British armor doesn't reach them in forty-eight hours.

Still, the success of the mission does not rest on the shoulders of General Brian Horrocks, commander of 30 Corps. Not yet.

Because the British tankers cannot do their job until General James Gavin does his.

"It seemed to me the hour was getting desperate," Gavin will admit. "I still did not have the big Nijmegen bridge."

Yet the ticking clock means this is not a simple military problem. "If I did nothing but pour infantry and British armor into the battle at our end of the bridge, we could be fighting there for days," Gavin will remember. "Urquhart would be lost."

So the bridge must be taken with lightning speed.

But even a quick conquest will not be enough.

Crossing will not be a simple matter of British tanks rumbling the 1,982 feet from one side of the Nijmegen Bridge to the other, then racing up Highway 69 to Arnhem. Everyone on both sides of the battle knows the span is already wired for demolition. "The Germans in control of the other end of the bridge," Gavin well knows, "would blow it up as they withdrew."

This is the scenario Gavin predicts: the eight-year-old bridge buckling as explosives detonate, a once-graceful span instantly transformed into a twisted mangle of steel and concrete, no longer needed by the retreating Nazis and of absolutely no further use to the liberators. This is straight out of his pre-jump refresher meeting on capturing bridges.

More devastating, the thirty-ton Allied tanks will plunge one hundred feet into the swift and muddy Waal, never to be seen again. The five-man crews will drown but the Germans will live on, retreating toward their homeland to fight another day.

General Gavin believes there is another way. The important part of capturing any bridge is getting men to the other side. That does not necessarily mean driving or walking.

Gavin calls an audible: boats.

There is nothing amphibious about paratrooping. Gavin's men are trained to jump on a target, not sail toward it—they're airborne after all, not United States Marines. His troops have such disinterest in all things aquatic that many didn't stash their life belts in the C-47 seat webbing—they actually kicked the yellow Mae Wests out the door.

But Nijmegen Bridge must be taken. "I could not conceive of sitting on the southern bank with a regiment of infantry and the Guards Armored Division while Urquhart was destroyed eleven miles away," Gavin broods.

The general proposes to paddle the Waal—all four hundred yards wide.

Ideally, the crossing should take place in darkness, preceded by a massive bombardment of the enemy shore. As Gavin hastily imagines a plan, he foresees "every artillery piece, every tank gun, and every weapon we had would pour fire into the German positions on the far side."

The big guns will fire smoke canisters to lay down a protective screen at water level, "as much smoke as we could get our hands on to cover the crossing," in Gavin's estimation.

The general well knows the historical heft of what he is attempting. There is every chance this seat-of-the-pants attack will be a failure. Down through history, sending an army across water has been considered extremely perilous.

"Since the time of Julius Caesar, a crossing of the Rhine," Gavin will write metaphorically, "was considered a major military feat, to be attempted only after thorough preparation."

.   .   .

YET GAVIN DOESN'T have that kind of time.

He doesn't even have boats.

Ideally, the 82nd would own M2 assault craft. Those American-made vessels are relatively sturdy and easy to navigate. But the American general did not foresee the need, despite his hours of thorough preinvasion planning. The logistics of finding enough planes to carry enough boats, then wrangling them in and out of the cargo door of a C-47 and parachuting them to earth are considerable. Even if gliders were used as transport, a nimble fighting force like the 82nd has no means of hauling a flotilla of M2s once they land in a drop zone.

So General Gavin shares his crazy tactic with the British, wondering if it is at all possible that they might have something his paratroopers could paddle across the Waal. To his delight, General Brian Horrocks and 30 Corps not only brought along boats; they've also used them before.

That crossing came three weeks ago, as the British advanced on Brussels. The Germans held the Senne, using the river as a defensive obstacle. At dusk, Horrocks ordered a twenty-minute barrage of "every gun we could bear" on the enemy shore. Boats went into the water next. Some got stuck on submerged sandbars. Many British lives were lost. But the daring sunset assault succeeded. Horrocks's men made it across and kept right on going.

So the British general agrees to loan Gavin a few boats. Now they just need to find them. At the very rear of the long thin column of British armor advancing into Holland is truck after truck filled with all manner of supplies. Somewhere, "well down the road in the train somewhere," is a stack of battle-tested collapsibles. "The discussion on this point quickly spread among the staff. They finally agreed that they should have about twenty-eight folding canvas boats in trucks somewhere farther to the rear."

Gavin is stuck on the word "canvas." But there's more cause for concern. The British boats are lightweight, flimsy and collapsible, made with a thin deck and those fabric sides.

Gavin will write, adding a note of apprehension: "American boats, with which I was familiar, were plywood.

"But at that moment boats were boats and I had to have them."

24

G o."

As one, General Gavin's paratroopers hoist borrowed boats onto their shoulders and climb the steep grassy berm concealing them from the Waal. Twenty-six wobbly and unstable vessels. Nineteen feet long. Ten men per. The Americans struggle up and over the steep rise, grunting that the fragile boats are heavier than they look. Reaching the top, the 260 soldiers begin the long walk down a broad exposed stretch of short green grass to the fast-flowing water.

On the far shore, the enemy awaits. Estimates range from four hundred to six hundred enemy soldiers dug into foxholes. They shouldn't be there. This was supposed to be a surprise. Not even a lengthy salvo of tank shelling and aerial bombardment by RAF Typhoons dislodged them. Gavin's paratroopers must do the job themselves.

It took the British more than a day to find the boats. While they waited, Gavin's men took cover in the swale one hundred yards from the Waal. For a time, the Germans didn't know they were there. Gavin's plan seemed to be working.

But then a couple paratroopers got curious.

"Late in the morning, the impossible happened. Two men showed themselves on the river bank and were fired at by the enemy," Bill Downs of CBS News will report. "A few hours later, machine guns were dug into the marshes on the far side—the plan has been discovered . . . Several hundred Germans with machine guns were sitting on the far bank, waiting for the crossing."

Those Wehrmacht soldiers take aim now, watching the Americans carry their heavy boats to the shoreline. "The weight of our boat seemed imponderable," one American soldier will write of the 330-pound British boats. To a man, the paratroopers do not trust the canvas vessels. "Our feet sank deep into the sand."

The Germans watch the paratroopers struggle in the fine pale brown sand. Then the boats being placed into the water—the broad, muddy gray Waal flowing downstream at a brisk eight knots.

Behind them, concealed British tanks open fire once again, taking aim at German positions, "giving our little fleet as much cover as possible," in the words of CBS's Downs. Mortars and artillery also take aim. One eyewitness will describe the noise as "earth-shattering."

As Gavin requested, the armor launches a smoke screen over the water, perfectly concealing the Americans from enemy guns. Once again, the plan is working.

Then the smoke vanishes, carried away on the afternoon wind.

· · ·

GENERAL JAMES GAVIN holds his breath as the desperate crossing begins. Downs and a handful of other journalists and officers stand nearby, huddled in the protective cover of a large power plant two hundred yards left of the berm where the boats were assembled. Nijmegen Bridge and the heart of the city are one mile to his right. On the far shore lies the flat sandy bank and a long field of marshy grass hiding the German Army.

Time is running out for the stranded Allied paratroopers in Arnhem. It is more than twenty-four hours since Gavin proposed the risky crossing. The besieged British and Polish warriors have now been cut off for three days. Their initial strength of 10,000 is down to just 2,500.

The wait for the boats to arrive has gone on all day. Gavin grew so impatient he seriously considered having his men swim the Waal. But he decided that was too risky. "It was broad daylight. What were we going to do? There were two and a half thousand of the British left out of their combat division of ten thousand. Two and a half thousand left to be killed and sacrificed and we could not cross the river," Gavin will write. "We could not expect the people to swim the river."

Finally, less than an hour ago, the British watercraft arrived. Official name: Goatley Boat, designed to carry bridge-building engineers, not an assault force. Wooden slats for a deck, three rows of one-inch horizontal ribbing. The paratroopers hurried to offload and assemble, complaining all the while about the lack of outboard motors and the impossibility of rowing such pathetic craft into the teeth of thick German fire. And just like everything when it comes to Market Garden, there weren't enough. First it was planes, then boats. As with the airborne drop, paddling the Waal must take place in two waves. Three men per canvas dinghy are tasked with rowing back to pick up the second group, making the suicidal crossing twice—an act of courage with few equals.

Yet as the German defenses tighten, the notion of one crossing seems impossible, let alone two.

. . .

EACH AMERICAN BATTLES to pull himself from the river and into the small cloth boat he wouldn't trust for a country picnic back home.

Climbing up and over the gunwales is a clumsy process in wet boots, while laden with weapons and ammunition. The two-foot-high walls of the flimsy Goatleys are held up by six thin vertical wooden slats, but there is little to grip for leverage. And yet the men still make jokes, sarcastic gripes about being in the "airborne navy" and about "airborne submarines." There is no decorum. Some kneel to paddle once they get onboard. Others sit.

Then they leave shore behind. It's already agreed: only men who know how to row get a paddle. That doesn't matter. Some boats come with as many as eight oars while some are equipped with just two. The solution is rifle butts. At 43.5 inches long, an M1 is shorter than a fifty-inch canoe-style paddle, but not by much. Some men even use their hands, which does little but make them feel like they're contributing. The need to get across is that desperate.

Whether oars, wooden stock, or cupped palms, every man is in agreement: now that the smoke screen is gone, the 82nd is so defenseless they might as well be standing downrange at target practice during a live-fire drill.

The first yards across the Waal are a fiasco, boats spinning in circles as the paratroopers get the hang of paddling. Gavin can do nothing but watch the impending catastrophe as his men search for a proper paddling rhythm. A wooden tiller at the rear of each boat does little good. "On-the-job training," one grim American officer watching from shore says to no one. Then crews get in sync. The race across the Waal commences in earnest.

At first, there's little enemy fire. Small arms rounds from the German side—rapid-fire Maschinengewehr 34 machine guns, Sturmgewehr 44 assault rifles, Karabiner 43 rifles—peck at the Americans. Enemy tracer bullets whiz past. The Germans are lousy shots.

But the lazy gunning ends as Gavin's boats draw closer to the north shore.

"All of a sudden, hell broke loose," one trooper will write. "Jerry opened up with all he had . . . as if in a rage at our trying anything so drastic, he was pouring everything he possessed at us."

. . . .

THE PARATROOPERS PADDLE on. Their battalion commander is Major Julian Cook, a twenty-seven-year-old West Point graduate. He knows what's on the other side. Should his men reach the far bank they must first contend with the men and machine guns in German foxholes. From there it is a three-hundred-yard sprint across flat ground to an elevated stretch of road. "We could see all along the Kraut side," one of his officers will write home, having performed reconnaissance with Cook this morning, "strong defensive positions, a formidable line both in length as well as in depth pillboxes, machine gun emplacements."

Major Cook is the rare paratrooper who has commanded a river crossing, leading a training exercise back at Fort Bragg. But it is the big guns that soon start sinking boats—artillery and mortar rounds.

"Men slumped in their seats," Downs will report. "Other men could be seen shifting a body to take over the paddling. One man rose up in his seat and fell overboard."

"There was no thought of turning back."

One by one, boats sink, shot through with holes. Men who cannot swim drown when their craft goes down. The water is so roiled by bullets, 20mm explosive shells, and mortar rounds—such a fury of lead—that men will describe the river's frothing surface as "a school of piranha in a feeding frenzy."*

Cook demands more, yelling for the men to row faster if they want to keep on living. Bullets riddle the canvas, killing or wounding every

---

* The Flak 30 and Flak 38 (Flugzeugabwehrkanone 30 and 38) were particularly terrifying weapons to fire at human beings. Designed as antiaircraft weapons, their four-foot barrels fired bullet-shaped projectiles that were 7.98 inches long and 1 inch wide at a rate of 120 rounds per minute. The effect upon striking the skull, in particular, was horrific.

other man. Troopers stuff handkerchiefs into the openings. Dead and dying sprawl on the plywood decks as their buddies bail river water with their steel helmets. German bullets and explosive shells never stop, the air alive with the snap and crack brought on by supersonic flight. The enemy does not fire at the boats but at a position two or three feet above the waterline to hit Americans in the chest—or the head. More than one skull is blown clean off. Dead American bodies bob in the water, pushed downstream by the current. To a man, Gavin's paratroopers are in awe—this is the most intense fire they've ever endured.

Yet this is not the awe of admiration but the numb humiliation of being utterly powerless.

Trapped in a sinking boat, completely exposed, half-kneeling in water made red by the blood of cohorts they might have one day invited to their wedding or set up with their sister, this elite fighting force is being shredded alive. Half the 260 who formed the first wave are dead or wounded. There is nothing the living can do but survive this boat trip from hell.

Then there will be vengeance.

Until that moment, Cook and his men can only keep paddling.

And in this way, against unbelievable odds, the 82nd Airborne crosses the River Waal.

. . .

"To THOSE WATCHING the crossing, it seemed forever before the first boats touched down on the northern bank," Gavin will recall. "Men struggled out of the boats, waded, and made their way through the mud, running forward. Some of them said later that they were so glad to be alive that they had only one thought: to kill the Germans."

And they do.

. . .

PARATROOPERS LEAP OUT the instant the bullet-riddled canvas finally kisses the muddy bank of the north shore. Those chosen to go back for the second wave immediately push off and turn around. Of the initial twenty-six collapsibles, only thirteen are still afloat.

There is no hesitation, no moment to catch a breath. Paratroopers sprint away from the river, racing across the flat bare earth to the elevated road. Every step is marked by a palpable fury. Soldiers run toward the Germans until they are shot. Those that don't get hit never stop. "Many times I have seen troops who are driven to a fever pitch—troops who, for a brief interval of combat, are lifted out of themselves, fanatics rendered crazy by rage and the lust for killing—men who temporarily forget the meaning of fear," one American officer will remember.

"I have never witnessed this human metamorphosis so acutely displayed as on this day.

"The men were beside themselves."

Back on the south bank, frustrated troopers from the second wave grow tired of waiting for a ride. Men strip off packs, strap rifles across their backs, and swim. They come out of the water fighting when they reach the far side, canvas bandoliers slung over their shoulders.

The brutal fighting goes on for two hours, rifle shots replaced by grenades, then bayonets, as the Americans come closer and closer and finally overrun German trenches. Surrender is not allowed. Enemy soldiers raising their hands are shot dead. German bodies are placed on the lips of their former foxholes as the Americans climb inside the defensive positions for a brief rest. The corpses provide extra protection from incoming fire.

By 5:00 P.M., the 82nd is moving from their crossing location to capture the northern end of the bridge. German soldiers prepared to fight to the death are strapped into the girders. These men are shot, their limp bodies dangling from the high steel. Other Germans dive from the bridge, their faint hope of escape most often ending in suicide. Simultaneously, the southern end is captured by Gavin's paratroopers fighting from rooftops, going building to building, blowing holes in adjacent walls to move from one house to the next.

Then comes the moment everyone is waiting for.

British tanks rumble out onto the bridge. They pour across the span, desperate to reach the north shore. Each man in each tank wonders if the bridge will blow before they get there. The drop down into the Waal seems impossibly far. The bridge is going to be detonated. It's just a matter of when.

From the southern shore, Gavin and everyone around him hold their breath. The armor reaches halfway.

Still no explosion.

Two hundred yards to go.

German general Heinz Harmel watches the procession from an outpost on the northern bank. "Let it blow," he orders a combat engineer. The soldier stands next to him, hands on the detonation plunger. Nijmegen Bridge is packed with explosives, all painted the same color of the stone supports and girders to camouflage their location.

The engineer pushes down.

But there's no explosion. The British tanks keep rolling forward.

"Again," Harmel commands.

Once more, the detonation fails. "They moved relentlessly forward," Harmel will remember of the advancing armor. "Getting bigger and bigger, closer and closer."

Harmel and the engineer run for their lives.

General James Gavin has his bridge.

Arnhem and the "bridge too far" over the Rhine are still eleven miles away. And Urquhart's 1st Airborne can't hold out much longer. Autumn rain and clouds are making aerial resupply impossible. The road between Nijmegen and Arnhem is now bristling with German tanks and artillery. No longer is the route known as Highway 69 but "Hell's Highway."

Gavin and the 82nd have done all they can. Their job is done.

But so is the British 1st.

. . .

"There remained the last lap to Arnhem, where bad weather had hampered the fly-in of reinforcements, food, and ammunition," Winston Churchill will write in his memoirs. "Every possible effort was made from the southern bank to rescue them, but the enemy were too strong."

On September 25—not four but *eight* days and nights since the opening wave of Market Garden—Field Marshal Bernard Law Montgomery orders General Urquhart to find a way home. Because he has awaited help twice as long as promised, there is no disgrace in falling back. Under cover of darkness, the surviving 2,400 paratroopers float down the Rhine in small boats to safety. The 1st is too depleted to fight anymore. Their war is over.

So is Montgomery's single-thrust strategy. For the first time since D-Day, the Germans hold the line.

The road to Berlin is closed.*

---

* Forty-eight paratroopers from the 82nd Airborne died during the paddle across the Waal. A bridge has since been built across the river at that location. These fallen men are commemorated by the forty-eight streetlamps atop that span. Each day at sunset these streetlights are lit up pair by pair at the pace of a slow march—requiring twelve minutes to light the entire bridge. In addition, the Waal crossing is reenacted every year at Fort Bragg, North Carolina, home of the 82nd.

AUTUMN

25

Winston Churchill brings his nation up to speed.

A pensive prime minister rises to address the House of Commons. Chalk-striped black suit, waistcoat, impossibly white handkerchief floating up from his breast pocket. German bombs destroyed the Commons chamber at the start of the war, so today's session is held in the House of Lords. Crowded benches. American and Soviet ambassadors seated to the side, ready to scrutinize each syllable. This is politics but also theater. Churchill has delivered more than four hundred speeches this year, almost all forgettable. But when the renowned orator speaks, there is anticipation of a perhaps memorable performance. The audience leans in.

Churchill's voice is low and steady as he explains Market Garden. The setback is in all the papers. All of Britain knows about it, particularly the men in this room. Prime Minister is offering perspective.

Yet there are no dramatic pauses. No thundering histrionics. That's for later. Instead, the prime minister opens with humility and an olive branch by appealing to the collective good.

"Here I must pay a tribute, which the House will consider due, to the superb feat of arms performed by our First Airborne Division," Churchill begins. That faint hint of a lisp. Words projecting so naturally after a lifetime of public speaking, filling the chamber with syllables and vowels and consonants, all arranged just so.

"Full and deeply moving accounts have already been given to the country and to the world of this glorious and fruitful operation, which will take a lasting place in our military annals and will, in succeeding generations, inspire our youth with the highest ideals of duty and of daring."*

Platitudes before reality. Always. Make people happy before hitting them with truth. It has been this way since Churchill's great speeches early in the war, the "never surrender" and "never in the field of human conflict was so much owed by so many to so few" and "we shall fight on the beaches."

Builds trust.†

"The cost has been heavy; the casualties in a single division have been grievous," Churchill admits. "But for those who mourn there is

---

* Churchill will remain steadfast in his appreciation for the gallantry of the 1st Airborne. However, when it is suggested in Parliament that they be given a special award for their stand, the prime minister will argue against it. "I do not think that the award of a special medal would be appropriate. Indeed, were such special distinction to be considered for this very gallant episode it would have to be considered with many other noble and memorable battles and actions that have taken place and may yet take place, at sea and in the air, as well as on land."

† Churchill is thought to have borrowed one of his most famous lines from Rudyard Kipling's *The Jungle Book*. His speech reads: "We shall fight on the beaches, we shall fight on the landing grounds, we shall fight in the fields and in the streets, we shall fight in the hills." Kipling, as commonly presented in Chapter Four, "The White Seal," writes: "They fought in the breakers, they fought in the sand, and they fought on the smooth-worn basalt rocks of the nurseries."

at least the consolation that the sacrifice was not needlessly demanded nor given without results. The delay caused to the enemy's advance upon Nijmegen enabled their British and American comrades in the other two airborne divisions, and the British Second Army, to secure intact the vitally important bridges and to form a strong bridgehead over the main stream of the Rhine at Nijmegen.

"'Not in vain' may be the pride of those who have survived and the epitaph of those who fell."

. . .

CHURCHILL MOVES ON. Today's speech focuses on the current state of the war. He frames the British struggles in Arnhem and Burma as victories. The prime minister tells with relish of successful fighting in Italy. British and American forces are moving into the northern portion of that nation along a route he personally believes to be the fastest path to Berlin. Churchill speaks of the second front in France, opened with an American invasion of the southern Riviera actively assisted by "a British airborne brigade, a British Air Force and the Royal Navy."

And Winston Churchill proudly boasts that more than two million Allied soldiers now stand on French soil—and that the British are fighting in great numbers and at the same enormous cost as their American counterparts. "I am glad to say that after one hundred and twenty days of fighting we still bear, in the cross-Channel troops, a proportion of two to three in personnel and of four to five-and-a-half in fighting divisions in France. Casualties have followed very closely the proportions of the numbers. In fact, these troops fight so level that the casualties almost exactly follow the numbers engaged. We have, I regret to say, lost upwards of ninety thousand men, killed, wounded and missing, and the United States . . . over one hundred and forty-five thousand. Such is the price in blood paid by the English-speaking democracies for the actual liberation of the soil of France."

Then Churchill turns his attention to the Soviet Union. For

members of Parliament, the next chunk of today's speech means little. But for the diplomats in this House, soon to transmit these words to their superiors in Washington and Moscow, Britain's attitude toward the Soviet Union speaks volumes about Europe's postwar shape.

"In thus trying to do justice to the British and American achievements, we must never forget . . . the measureless services which Russia has rendered to the common cause, through long years of suffering, by tearing out the life of the German military monster," Churchill begins.

The prime minister spoke by phone with Joseph Stalin just yesterday.

"The terms in which Marshal Stalin recently, in conversation, has referred to our efforts in the West have been of such a generous and admiring character that I feel, in my turn, bound to point out that Russia is holding and beating far larger hostile forces than those which face the Allies in the West, and has through long years, at enormous loss, borne the brunt of the struggle on land."

That's for Stalin. Making nice. Yet the coming passage is perhaps the most subtle rebuke of the Soviet ambitions possible. Churchill makes it clear that Britain is a vital partner—and will be for years to come.

"There is honor for all. It is a matter of rejoicing that we, for our part and in our turn, have struck resounding blows, and it is right that they should be recorded among the other feats of arms so loyally performed throughout the Grand Alliance."

· · ·

PRIME MINISTER IS already looking ahead to the end of the war. Adolf Hitler was once his great antagonist, but Churchill now spends much more time dwelling on Joseph Stalin and the Soviet Union as their alliance grows increasingly fragile.

"Winston never talks of Hitler these days," Churchill's physician, Lord Moran, wrote in his personal diary a few days ago. "He is always harping on the dangers of communism. He dreams of the Red Army spreading like a cancer from one country to the other. It has become an obsession, and he seems to think of nothing else."

Moran has spent considerable time with Churchill lately. The doctor is deeply concerned about his patient's health. Moran will see Churchill through a "heart attack . . . three attacks of pneumonia . . . two strokes . . . two operations . . . senile pruritus . . . conjunctivitis," through their many years as physician and patient. The king is often so alarmed at his prime minister's refusal to accept physical weakness, writing him to "beg of you to take care of yourself & get as much rest as you possibly can."

But the recent trip to North America was the worst of times. The sixty-nine-year-old prime minister appeared to be dying. Instead of steeling himself through intense study and discussion for meetings with President Roosevelt at what will become known as the Quebec Conference, Churchill lacked energy, holding his head in his hands to induce concentration. The Atlantic journey on board the *Queen Mary* found Moran quietly predicting that a heart attack or stroke would kill Churchill soon. "He looked old, unwell, and depressed," Field Marshal Alan Brooke will recall.

Churchill has long enjoyed the *Queen Mary*, sleeping in a massive suite paneled with rare tropical hardwood procured from throughout the United Kingdom. A series of successful encounters with Roosevelt to discuss the shape of postwar Europe and a restful weeklong return crossing have brought back ruddy good health. No sooner does he arrive in London than Prime Minister makes plans to leave again, this time to Moscow. The Soviets are advancing on Berlin at a far greater pace than the Americans and British, sweeping aside German opposition.

Unlike President Roosevelt, now running for reelection at a most pivotal time in the war, Churchill does not trust their eastern ally.

"As the victory of the Grand Alliance became only a matter of time, it was natural that Russian ambitions should grow. Communism raised its head behind the thundering Russian battlefront. Russia was the deliverer and Communism the gospel she brought," Prime Minister believes.

"Hitler and Hitlerism were doomed, but after Hitler what?"

. . .

BACK IN PARLIAMENT, a break for lunch. Such a long speech requires fortification. Prime Minister resumes his briefing to Parliament at promptly 2:00 P.M., stomach full and mind charged from the meal and a helpful bottle of Pol Roger champagne.

Churchill already discussed the contents of today's message with King George two days ago. There was much to talk about. Churchill's extensive September travels put a monthlong halt to their weekly lunches. The liberation of Paris, conquest of Caen, and partial success and horrific losses of Market Garden were open for discussion.

This speech is a recap of Churchill's report to the king. It is not one of his most stirring oratories—nor is it intended to be. But the sheer volume of detail about what lies beyond the war years is remarkable in itself. Now, looking ahead to the end of the fighting, Churchill tells Parliament of the need for another summit with Allied leadership to discuss the transition.

"The fact that the President and I have been so closely brought together at the Quebec Conference and have been able to discuss so many matters bearing upon the course of the war and on the measures to be taken after the Germans surrender and also for the broad future, makes it all the more necessary that our third partner, Marshal Stalin, who has, of course, been kept informed, should join with us in a tripartite conference as soon as the military situation renders this possible," Churchill states.

There is a sense that he is alone in this desire. President Roosevelt is too wrapped up in his reelection to leave America. Chairman Stalin is focused on his armies massing outside the Polish capital of Warsaw, still in Nazi hands. Churchill is troubled that the Soviet armies are not passing through Warsaw on their way to Berlin but settling in to establish a permanent communist state. Churchill is equally concerned that Roosevelt, a man known for political intuition, does not believe Stalin is a threat.

Prime Minister brings today's speech toward the end with a minor flourish.

"The future of the whole world, and certainly the future of Europe, perhaps for several generations, depends upon the cordial, trustful and comprehending association of the British Empire, the United States and Soviet Russia, and no pains must be spared and no patience grudged which are necessary to bring that supreme hope to fruition."

Winston Churchill sits down, his mind made up: He's going back to Russia.

As soon as possible.

Roosevelt won't leave Washington. Stalin won't leave Moscow.

Winston Churchill saved Europe four years ago.

Prime Minister now seeks to save the world.

26

artha Gellhorn is about to be detained.

Again.

"I have no idea what Nijmegen used to look like," the journalist will write of her latest wartime adventures, this time in Holland. She is not allowed to be here. Nijmegen has long been taken. General James Gavin and the 82nd remain in garrison duty, enduring the occasional artillery barrage and sending out night patrols to stay sharp. Not a lovely place to be stuck.

Winter is coming. Rains all the time.

"Heartbreak rain," Gellhorn calls it, "that washes away men's hope of peace and home, and it is the rain that warns you of the ugly winter ahead, another ugly winter of war."

The bridge across the Waal was taken days ago, yet the Germans still drop occasional rounds on the city. Gellhorn was content to travel here at the rumor of war, leaving Brussels and catching rides in the long train of British vehicles snaking down Highway 69, leapfrogging to the front. The trip was ambitious. She arrived after the shooting was done but remains in town until the next great battle calls her name.

Gellhorn still writes for *Collier's*, even elevated on the masthead to "invasion correspondent" in the same font size as her husband. Yet military officials have stripped Gellhorn of all credentials—press pass, ration card, military ID—because of her being a D-Day stowaway. These documents are gold in her world. Without them, travel through war zones is impossible.

For most reporters.

Lack of credentials is just another inconvenience to Martha Gellhorn, like being a woman in a male-dominated profession. Like her famous husband and his too-willing mistress. Or like finding a way to bypass military handlers who forbid female journalists from visiting the front lines. She was not given the chance to fly alongside General Brereton in a B-17 to witness the Market Garden drop like her breathless *Collier's* colleague W. B. Courtney. Nor did she have a front-row seat for the courageous paddling of the Waal like Bill Downs of CBS News. But Gellhorn still has a job to do. And so she now finds herself in heavily bombarded Nijmegen, looking for a story to tell *Collier's* 2.5 million readers.

Of course, *Collier's* has no idea their rising star has been stripped of her credentials.

If she is caught, there is a very good chance Gellhorn will be sent home. Not to Paris or London, but to America. So the journalist gives wide berth to any individual resembling an authority figure—in particular, military police.

Gellhorn tries to keep a low profile. Yet she can't help but stand out. The journalist is known for being fastidious in her personal appearance. As she wanders the destruction of this Dutch city under a slate-gray sky, she hardly looks like a woman who has spent a week on the battlefield or hunkered down in a root cellar during an artillery bombardment from those enormous German guns on the other side of the bridge connecting Nijmegen and Arnhem. Hair neatly combed. Face washed. Perfect smile.

And American. The accent is unmistakable. Hardly a "careful Dutch . . . housewife" or one of the Nijmegen women who collaborated with the Nazi cause, now being held prisoner by their Dutch neighbors: "dreary looking young women, ill, lying in bed with very small babies."

Cheerful, flirtatious, industrious in her note-taking.

A lot of note-taking. No other way to write a vivid depiction of all she sees and hears.

"There was probably quite a sweet old part to the city, judging from some of the ruins, some remnants of roofs and a carved doorway here and there. Also, I imagine the curve of houses on the bluff by the Waal River was charming, but as the houses are all burned out it is hard to tell."

Despite her lack of credentials, the journalist has covered the war on many fronts since Omaha Beach. She witnessed the fighting in Northern Italy, where Allied troops are still facing solid German opposition. Near the Foglia River, traveling with a Canadian brigade, Gellhorn came across the remnants of a tank battle.

"The Sherman had received an 88 shell through its turret. Inside the turret were plastered pieces of flesh and much blood. Outside the Tiger the body of a German lay, with straw covering everything except his two black clawlike hands, the swollen blood-caked head, and the twisted feet. He did not smell too much yet," she reported for *Collier's*.

Then Paris, where Gellhorn avoided Hemingway and toured Gestapo torture chambers. "You will find it impossible to imagine that in a sordid little brick hut, and in cheap and carelessly made cages, human beings could scream with pain and find no other human being who would release them from such torment," she will describe her visits. "There will be a little box of a room with four round steel eyelets cemented into the wall. A man or a woman was tied hand and foot to

General George S. Patton
Bettmann

Prime Minister Winston Churchill   *Central Press*

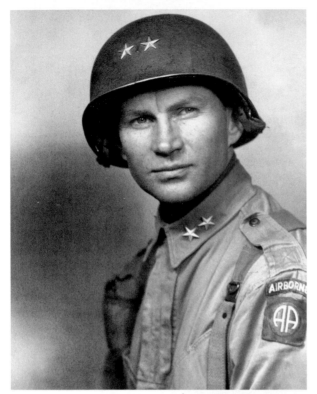

General James Gavin   *MPI*

Writer Martha Gellhorn, the lifelong journalist and wife of Ernest Hemingway who had no fear of placing herself in harm's way   *FPG*

General Norman Cota, the hero of D-Day who would endure much harsh criticism the last year of the war   *National Archives*

General George S. Patton, General Omar Bradley, and Field Marshal Bernard Law Montgomery. Forced by Alliance to work together, the ongoing rivalry between Patton and Montgomery dictated Allied operations in Europe.   *PhotoQuest*

General George S. Patton and General Dwight
D. Eisenhower, whose longtime friendship was
sorely tested in the last months of the war

Bettmann

General James Gavin
putting on his gear
before the parachute
drop at Market
Garden   *AKG Images*

Young victims of Soviet atrocity at the Nemmersdorf massacre

Picture Alliance

Martha Gellhorn
interviewing soldiers
Keystone

The Big Three: Winston Churchill, Franklin Roosevelt, and Joseph Stalin at Yalta.
Roosevelt would die two months later. *DEA Picture Library*

The bridge at Torgau, site of the meeting point between Soviet and
American soldiers, and one of the few places Martha Gellhorn was not
allowed the journalistic access she so often achieved   *AFP*

the wall, the body unbearably stretched. After that came the long, the repeated, the scientific beating."

And on to Brussels, a city that stayed drunk for a week in celebration of their freedom, assisted by the discovery of eighty thousand hidden bottles of claret left by the Nazis.

None of this was done with permission. Gellhorn travels by her wiles, convincing military pilots to give her a lift, sweet-talking front-line commanders into embedding her with their units, and touring cities like Nijmegen by hitching a ride in any jeep with an empty passenger seat.

Unlike Paris and Brussels, there are no celebrations in Nijmegen, "a town where people sleep in cellars and walk with care on the streets, listening hard for incoming shells. The Dutch sweep up broken glass every morning in a despairingly tidy way, but there is no transport to carry glass away, so under the dripping autumn trees and along the shell-marked streets there are neat mounds of rubble and glass."

Gellhorn spends a night in the destroyed riverfront town, blackout curtains drawn. She finds it interesting that the city has no bars, cafés, or movie theaters but feels lively. In daylight, she watches three Spitfires engage a lone Messerschmitt in aerial combat with detached fascination, as if it is entertainment rather than a duel to the death. Gellhorn witnesses a nun arrested for collaborating, "looking frozen and unforgiving, and alongside her two stupid homely girls who worked in the Germans' kitchens and were soldiers' delights as a sideline."

So many sidebars. So many dramas being played out between the front lines, by average people unlucky enough to be caught in the fighting, in the midst of artillery concussion and small-arms fire. So many sketches drawing out details of life during wartime. "We gave a lift to a thin dark worried-looking woman who worked in the Dutch Red Cross. She did not seem an especially inspiring woman and she seemed unusually nervous (which, in perilous places, is always unpleasant, because the proper manner under such circumstances is a real or assumed calm)."

Gellhorn editorializes, a danger for any journalist, one she blithely ignores. "The Dutch suffered as everyone has suffered under the Germans, from the outrage and humiliation of the Nazi regime. Free people cannot learn to live without disgust under that domination, and these were terrible years in which each man alone found each day that this tyranny, this stupidity, this corruption was unendurable, and yet there would always be tomorrow and tomorrow, and the tyranny had to be accepted since there was nothing to do but wait."

Then, the arrest. Military police from the American 82nd Airborne confront Gellhorn as she roams. Demand credentials. The journalist can only shrug and say she has none, hoping moxie, good looks, and feigned fearlessness will once again get her out of a tight jam.

Not this time.

The MPs call her a spy, leafing through her notebook filled with detailed descriptions.

Running would do no good. Gellhorn is ordered into a jeep, where she is driven down a sunken dirt road lined with pine trees. The jeep crosses over a paved road and then railroad tracks before arriving at the Division Command Post in the Groesbeek woods, east of town. Gellhorn curses her stupidity: too comfortable, too sure no one noticed her. This could very well be her last day in Europe.

Yet none of the military police know what to do with this woman without credentials or uniform—a journalist, she claims—possessing a notebook showing she has seen some very sensitive tactical situations, everything from artillery positions to troop emplacements. If she *is* a spy, what next? Interrogation is the obvious answer. Initially, here in Nijmegen, then a flight to the UK for a proper questioning. But it's one thing to capture a German spy, yet another to arrest an American woman on the same charges. Spies get shot. That's headline news.

Not wanting to mishandle the potentially volatile situation—and certainly not wishing to make the wrong sort of headlines—military police take Gellhorn directly to their commanding officer:

General James Gavin.

Gellhorn has already decided to tell the whole truth. She freely admits her lack of credentials. The journalist details her travels through Holland with the British Army, and how she came to be in Nijmegen after days of finding food and sleep where she could.

The general laughs.

Not a derisive "Look what you've gotten yourself into, little lady" chuckle. Not a sneer.

Sympathetic, like a kindred spirit.

Gellhorn will long remember this encounter. They are almost the same age, Gavin older by a year. Both want out of strained marriages to writers. She will recall Gavin's charisma, height, and the way his eyes focused upon her—a sensation so intense she feels as if he is actually placing a hand on her cheek.

The young general tells Gellhorn that her talent for living off the land is like that of a top guerrilla fighter. If she's dumb enough to wander into a combat zone, then he's just dumb enough to let her go. Gavin's plan is to pretend he's never seen her.

That should be the end of it.

But Gavin has one last question, wondering where Gellhorn does her writing when she's not on the front lines.

"Paris," she says to her new friend.

"The Lincoln Hotel."

27

Field Marshal Erwin Rommel writes to an old friend.

Their relationship is precarious. Rommel has a special request and chooses his words wisely. His friend's answer is a matter of life and death.

Autumn has arrived—that of Rommel's life and of the forest behind his home. Leaves of spruce, beech, and oak turning red and gold. Towering evergreens. It is ten weeks of deep thought since he was thrown from his staff car, an eternity of ruminating in his study, dressed in his new daily uniform of brown civilian jacket worn over riding breeches.

This remote home in the "Swabian Alps" was his hideaway long before the crash, a world away from the politics of Berlin and so far off the beaten path the Allies will exhaust themselves hunting for him when they enter Germany. But now the walls are closing in. The British and Americans might never find Rommel, yet the Gestapo know Herrlingen well enough to walk the streets without asking directions.

The field marshal now puts pen to paper.

"Mein Fuehrer!" the letter begins. "Unfortunately, my health is not yet as I could have wished. The four fractures of the skull, the unfavorable development of the situation in the west since I was wounded, and not least the removal from his post and arrest of my former Chief of Staff, Lt. Gen. Speidel—of which I learnt only by chance—have made demands on my nerves far beyond my endurance. I no longer feel myself equal to further trials."

Speidel is forty-six, a career soldier and fellow Swabian. Studious face, receding hairline, wire-rimmed glasses. His *New York Times* obituary will describe the general as "an amiable and worldly man who dedicated most of his life to the profession of arms." Despite his high rank, Speidel followed Rommel's lead and never joined the Nazi party.

This tendency toward not following the rules also manifests itself in other ways. It was Speidel who answered the phone on August 26, 1944, in German headquarters for the Western Front. He listened as the German High Command, at the behest of the Führer, ordered the complete destruction of Paris by V-2 rockets.

"Is Paris burning?" Adolf Hitler is said to have repeatedly demanded of his staff in the hours that followed.

It was not. All because General Speidel ignored the launch order. The city was liberated with very little damage.

But it was one month earlier, during his tenure as Rommel's chief of staff, that Speidel showed the depth of his insurrection. He arrived in the job by accident, Lucia Rommel demanding that the previous chief be fired after she got into a nasty fight with his wife. Ever faithful, Rommel complied.

Speidel proved to be an ideal replacement. Their shared Swabian heritage is a relief for two men who have long endured the uptight, formal ways of the Prussian officer class controlling the German Army. Speidel believes that the Soviets are winning the war on the Eastern

Front because of "too many Russians and one German too many"—
that German being the Austrian-born Hitler. He and Rommel also
have quiet talks about saving their country by granting the Allies an
uncontested path to Berlin once they cross the border. When that day
comes, Allied leadership will be approached about a separate peace.

And they also talk about murdering Adolf Hitler.

Not in conversational terms, but in code. Before Rommel's crash,
Speidel was specifically tasked by the men who tried to kill Hitler on
July 20. Their aim was to recruit Rommel into joining their cause. It is
well known in military circles that Erwin Rommel's experiences in
North Africa turned him against Hitler as far back as 1942, "when he
found out he did not get the support he asked for or the support that
was promised to him," as Speidel describes. Thus, convincing the field
marshal to join the plot does not take much effort. There is ample time
for Speidel to build an argument in favor of assassination, for the two
men spend hours together each day.

If the assassination plan succeeded, the next step was overthrow-
ing the Nazi regime, the arrest of Nazi officials loyal to Hitler, return
to the rule of law, and negotiating peace with the Allies. It was the
plotters' hope that Germany remain a European power, her people
and cities still standing. Rommel was among those being considered
as Hitler's replacement to lead Germany.

But Rommel resisted taking an active role in the bombing. "In the
end," Speidel will state, "he was one of the very few field marshals
who said 'I am against [Hitler] and I am willing to do something
against him.'"

But Rommel does not want Hitler killed. He prefers the Führer defend his actions in a court of law and be given a prison sentence once
peace is brokered. Speidel considers this "unrealistic."

"He knew about it," Speidel says of Rommel and the plot to kill
Hitler. "He didn't say yes, but he knew about it."

And as thousands of Germans have already learned, *knowing* about the July 20 plot can get you killed.

Among them Hans Speidel.

The lifelong officer remains locked in an undisclosed location, where he has been detained more than three weeks, in the throes of Gestapo torture, awaiting Hitler's meat hook. His wife will become a "traitor widow," ineligible for the wartime pension all women receive when their husbands fall in the line of duty.

And Speidel's beloved Ruth will not know the time or place of his death. A courier will simply show up on her doorstep with his wedding ring in a small box.

After delivering her husband's band, the messenger will then present Ruth with a bill for her husband's execution.

Erwin Rommel is trying to prevent that moment from taking place.

. . .

THE FIELD MARSHAL's desperate attempt to save Hans Speidel's life continues.

"Shortly before taking up office with the Army Group he had been awarded the Knight's Cross by you, and had been promoted to Lt. General," Rommel writes the Führer, reminding Hitler of Speidel's résumé. "Speidel showed himself to be an outstandingly efficient and diligent Chief of Staff. He took firm control of the staff, showed great understanding for the troops and helped me to create the defenses of the Atlantic Wall as quickly as possible with the available means."

Rommel continues with a litany of Speidel's accomplishments, many which mirror his own: construction of the Atlantic Wall, attempting to defeat the Normandy invasion, loyalty to Germany. But Rommel missteps when he gets around to the purpose of the letter: freeing Hans Speidel. Hitler knows Rommel to be candid, so it is out of character when the field marshal's words turn disingenuous.

"I cannot imagine what can have led to Lt. General Speidel's removal and arrest," Rommel lies.

And Adolf Hitler knows this is a lie. More than a few conspirators have already confessed that Rommel knew of the bomb plot. There is already a covert file known as "The Rommel Case," and the field marshal's name has been mentioned before the Army Court of Honor. For the field marshal to feign innocence is an insult, as if the Führer is dumb or even gullible. It is understood that Rommel is showing his courage by sticking up for a man most likely to be executed. A man less courageous than the field marshal would never stick out his neck this way, fearing the association might also get himself killed.

And yet, Speidel's arrest on September 7 was quite long ago. By now, he has most likely cracked under torture. Everyone cracks. It's always just a matter of time. The general is surely being asked about Rommel's involvement. The smart move for Rommel is to get out in front of any damning words Speidel might tell his interrogators. Because in his heart of hearts, Erwin Rommel doesn't just want to avoid prosecution; he also wants another chance to command an army in battle.

So, Rommel reminds the Führer of all he has done for Nazi Germany—and for his good friend Adolf Hitler.

"You, mein Fuehrer, know I have exerted my whole strength and capacity, be it in the Western Campaign 1940 or in Africa 1941–43 or in Italy 1943 or again in the West 1944.

"One thought only possesses me constantly, to fight and win for your new Germany.

"Heil, mein Fuehrer!*

"E. Rommel."

---

* Führer, meaning "leader," can be spelled "Führer" or, as Erwin Rommel prefers, "Fuehrer."

· · ·

ADOLF HITLER NEVER responds.

On October 7, one week after writing the Führer, Erwin Rommel receives a dispatch from Field Marshal Wilhelm Keitel. The head of the German High Command is requesting Rommel's attendance at a special conference in Berlin. Keitel's unquestioning loyalty to Hitler is well known among other top officers. In his six years at the top of OKW, as the high command is known, the field marshal has consistently been placed in roles of the highest authority. Currently, Keitel sits on the Army Board of Honor overseeing the prosecution of the seven thousand Germans suspected of playing a role in the July 20 assassination plot.

Keitel showed his willingness to prosecute high-ranking officers when Field Marshal Erwin von Witzleben was convicted of playing a role. After the guilty verdict, von Witzleben berated the court: "You can turn us over to the executioner. In three months, the outraged and tormented people will call you to account and drag you through the filth and streets alive."

Those words were so ferocious that Nazi propaganda minister Joseph Goebbels refused to show film of that moment to the public, fearing it would sway opinion toward the conspirators.

That same day, von Witzleben was executed at Berlin's Plötzensee Prison. His body was lifted up on a meat hook, because Adolf Hitler decreed that his plotters should die like animals. A thin rope around his throat strangled von Witzleben slowly, not snapping his neck instantly like a noose.

Now, Keitel is inviting Field Marshal Rommel to Berlin. He is sending a special train so the Desert Fox can travel without pain.

Rommel reads the invitation and turns to Manfred. Though the teenager has returned to work at his Luftwaffe gun battery, he comes home often. Time together has strengthened their relationship. He feels the boy capable of grasping the reality of what is taking place. "I'm not that much of a fool," Rommel confides. "We know these people now . . .

"I would not be afraid to be tried in public, for I can defend everything I have done. But I know that I should never reach Berlin alive."

So it is that Erwin Rommel refuses the German High Command's summons.

The man with very few days to live knows the end is coming.

He's just not sure how it will happen.

28

Winston Churchill has many years to live—long enough to rue the mistake he is making tonight.

Prime Minister is an exhausted traveler. Thirty-three hours in the air. London to Naples to Cairo to Moscow—taking the long way around to avoid the war. His personal Avro York, nicknamed *Ascalon*, stayed below eight thousand feet the whole way on orders of Lord Moran, who feared that any higher might compromise Churchill's heart. He now sits with a wide-awake Soviet leader Joseph Stalin here in the Kremlin. Their respective foreign ministers— Anthony Eden and Vyacheslav Molotov—are in attendance. Two interpreters. A table.*

---

* The Avro York was a British transport aircraft. The design was based on that of the Avro Lancaster bomber. The aircraft was not pressurized. Above eight thousand feet, the oxygen would be too thin for Churchill. Efforts were made to build a sarcophagus-like pressurized aluminum "pod" in which the prime minister could sleep and even smoke, all the while experiencing an air pressure equivalent to five thousand feet.

Stalin smokes his curved Dunhill pipe. A single large star on Stalin's uniform epaulets. His left arm is shorter than his right from a childhood accident involving a horse-drawn carriage. In moments of anger, sparks and smoke leap from the large bowl. When in a thoughtful good mood, he often lets the flame go out. Right now, there is no sign of smoke.

Churchill's right hand is devoted to his cigar, and tonight he wears a simple four-button uniform, matching Stalin's military fixation. His Romeo y Julieta is very much lit.

The Americans are not here. They should be. But Franklin Roosevelt faces yet another reelection next month, setting himself up for a record fourth term in office. The New Yorker is reluctant to risk his presidency on tonight's tawdry discussion. It is the natural order of things for a colonial power and an authoritarian state to divide the world, but not so the leader of a democracy built on personal freedoms and inalienable rights.

So while Churchill has previously briefed his American counterpart on what will transpire tonight, the president has already distanced himself. In a message to Stalin, Roosevelt made it clear that Churchill does not speak for the United States. The president is the youngest of the Allied leaders but, at sixty-two, closest to death. He is also the most politically obsessed, capable of finding intrigue and influence in a breakfast menu. But this forewarning to Stalin is an act of naivete, signaling a weakness in the Anglo-American partnership the Soviet leader is only too happy to exploit—and will continue to do so until his dying day.

Churchill is eager to make a deal. He plans to be in Moscow for several days, which includes entertainment such as a public visit to the Bolshoi Theater. As Soviet troops advance closer to Berlin, the German

---

However, the pod was too large to fit inside *Ascalon* without dismantling the aircraft. Despite later claims that Churchill flew inside the pod, it was never used.

threat is no more. Leningrad just turned on its streetlights for the first time in three years, and Moscow wants to be entertained. Stalin's mistress, prima ballerina Olga Lepeshinskaya, is to dance *Giselle*. Just as it has been important for Churchill to make public appearances back in London, taking Clementine to see stage productions of Shaw's *Arms and the Man* and Shakespeare's *Richard III* on consecutive nights before flying to Moscow, he understands the galvanizing role Stalin's attendance at the Bolshoi will have on Muscovites.

And that sense of shared understanding is what drives tonight's business at hand. "Let us settle about our affairs in the Balkans," Churchill demands of Stalin. "We have interests, missions, and agents there. Don't let us get at cross purposes in small ways."

Stalin does not speak English and Churchill does not speak Russian. Churchill's opening remarks are translated to Stalin. As this takes place, Prime Minister writes down nations and percentages on a half sheet of paper: Romania—90/10; Greece—90/10; Yugoslavia—50/50; Hungary—50/50; Bulgaria—75/25.

No translation necessary. Churchill passes the paper to Stalin, who studies each nation. Taking up a blue pencil, the dictator makes a large check mark across the top of the page in a show of approval that will tarnish the prime minister like a scarlet letter.

Churchill and Stalin have just decided the fate of millions. The percentages determine how much of each postwar nation belongs to the Soviets, and how much belongs to Great Britain (written as "the others" in deference to America). That half sheet of paper must never see the light of day.

"They would be considered crude and even callous if they were exposed to the scrutiny of the Foreign Offices and diplomats all over the world," Churchill will write to Stalin of the secret percentages. "Therefore, they could not be the basis of any public document, certainly not at the present time."

Knowing history will judge him harshly for this desperate desire to maintain Britain's prominent place on the world stage, Churchill adds: "If we manage these affairs we shall perhaps prevent several civil wars and some bloodshed and strife in the small countries concerned."

Stalin places the paper with the blue tick on the table. No one touches it.

"At length I said, might it not be thought rather cynical if it seemed we had disposed of these issues, so fateful to millions of people, in such an offhand manner. Let us burn the paper," Churchill suggests delicately.

Stalin has no intention of honoring the percentages. He does not believe Churchill's suggestion constitutes a formal agreement. The dictator plans on taking full possession of Romania, Greece, Yugoslavia, Hungary, and Bulgaria. For though the British prime minister believes the war will end by Christmas with Hitler's defeat, the Soviet dictator will not consider it over until these pieces of Europe are in Russian possession.

"No," the Soviet dictator tells Winston Churchill. The silly scrap of paper means nothing.

"You keep it."

World War II is not over.

And already, the Cold War has begun.

29

E rwin Rommel keeps his thoughts to himself.

For now.

Morning coffee in a quiet house. Cook preparing breakfast in the kitchen. Lucia remains in bed. The dachshund puppy he brought back from France, normally so playful, sleeps.

Rommel wears his everyday brown jacket and tie with riding breeches. Face almost healed. The field marshal is subdued, alone, pondering what are perhaps the final hours of his life. Nothing in his countenance shows sweat or fear. The anticipation is like the hours before battle, when anything might happen. From somewhere in the house, the puppy suddenly barks.

A door to the house opens and shuts. The now-familiar clatter of a rucksack being dropped to the floor. Manfred Rommel, dressed in full Luftwaffe uniform, returns home from his gun battery. Seeing that his father is already taking breakfast, the young soldier steps into the kitchen for a coffee of his own, then sits with his father. The two men breakfast together. Quiet morning small talk. Afterward, a thoughtful field marshal leads his son outside for a walk in the garden.

Just days ago, Rommel had a discussion with a longtime friend who was days away from being arrested by the Gestapo. "Hitler will never dare do anything to you," Oskar Farny told the field marshal. "You're too popular. It would attract too much attention."

Eyes wide open after the Führer's lack of response to his letter two weeks ago, as well as by the recent invitation to come to Berlin, Rommel responds with brutal honesty. "You're wrong," he tells Farny, a longtime politician and army reservist. "Hitler wants to get rid of me, and he'll leave no stone unturned to do it."

Rommel is not being paranoid. The list of German field marshals and generals implicated in the assassination plot continues to grow. Field Marshal Gerd von Rundstedt, who once sat with Rommel and Hitler at Soissons—and then again two weeks later at Hitler's Berchtesgaden retreat in Bavaria—was replaced in France by Field Marshal Günther von Kluge. The regal Prussian officer—sixty-one, shaved head, veteran of the Russian Front—was soon implicated in the Hitler assassination. While making the long drive from his Paris headquarters to meet with the Führer, von Kluge committed suicide with potassium cyanide, biting into the poisonous vial rather than endure torture.*

So on this autumn morning, three days after his discussion with Oskar Farny, Field Marshal Erwin Rommel knows what might happen when the big staff car comes for him.

Walking in the garden with his son, Erwin Rommel undertakes the most difficult discussion of his life. It is a talk that will always stay

---

* Von Kluge's suicide note was a plea for sanity: "My Fuehrer, make up your mind to end the war. The German people have undergone such untold suffering that it is time to put an end to this frightfulness . . . You have fought an honorable and great fight. History will prove that for you. Show yourself also great enough to put an end to a hopeless struggle when necessary." As history will show, those words were ignored.

with Manfred. "At twelve o'clock today, two generals are coming to see me to discuss my future employment," he tells his son. "So today will decide what is planned for me. Whether a People's Court or a new command in the East."

Their months of political discussion give Manfred pause. His father has made his opinions on the futility of the war very clear—in particular, fighting with the Soviets. "Would you accept such a command?"

"My dear boy," the field marshal says, aggressively grabbing his son's arm. Erwin Rommel is fifty-two, a full life already lived, but with the chance to add to his many accomplishments. Even if he were defeated by the Soviet Army, the German people would still call him a hero—perhaps even more so than ever before.

"Our enemy in the east is so terrible that every other consideration has to give way before it. If he succeeds in overrunning Europe, even only temporarily, it will be the end of everything which has made life appear worth living. Of course I would go."

. . .

THREE DREADFUL HOURS waiting for Hitler's henchmen. The Rommels retreat to their separate spaces: father, son, and wife, Lucia—who remains in her bedroom. Manfred, a boy no longer, smokes. Lumps in throats and knots in stomachs. Living a nightmare. The coming visitors might as well walk through the door carrying broadswords. Even in the best-case scenario that they are offering Rommel a command on the Eastern Front, such a posting is almost certainly a death sentence.

Erwin Rommel changes from civilian clothing into his famous Afrika Korps uniform just before noon. He affixes his Iron Cross medals around his neck, wearing both at the same time having become a common part of his attire during those famous years in Egypt and Libya. Rommel's field marshal's baton is close at hand, but he does not wield it.

Then they are here.

An Opel sedan pulls up the drive off the main public road in front of Rommel's white mansion.

"A dark green car with a Berlin number stopped in front of our garden gate," Manfred will long remember. "Burgdorf, a powerful florid man, and Maisel, small and slender, alighted from the car and entered the house. They were respectful and courteous and asked to speak to my father alone."

General Wilhelm Burgdorf is fifty, an officer of Prussian ancestry who was first commissioned at the age of twelve, now working as Adolf Hitler's chief adjutant and head of the Army Personnel Office. Despite short experiences in command, Burgdorf is known mostly for his bureaucratic skills instead of frontline fighting. Despite his high rank and position at this current time, his war will not end well.

Not so his companion. General Ernst Maisel is another bureaucrat, head of Officers' Education and Welfare for the Army Personnel Group. The general, as Manfred Rommel notes, appears less intimidating than the ruddy, broad-shouldered drinker standing with him in the Rommel living room. And his professional title now takes on an air of irony, for there is no amount of education he can pass on to Erwin Rommel that the field marshal does not already know. And if it is welfare that brings Maisel here this midday, it is certainly his own. The general will live to the age of eighty-two, his life forever identified by the incident that will take place within the next hour. At first that legend will be honor in the eyes of Adolf Hitler, then denial when confronted by the Allies after the war. Then something shameful that must never be talked about for the rest of his days.

. . .

MANFRED ROMMEL IS so taken with the courtesy shown by Burgdorf and Maisel that he retreats to his upstairs bedroom to read. It seems there is nothing to fear. Lucia Rommel remains in her bedroom. Like Manfred, Rommel staff member Captain Hermann Aldinger is asked by the visitors to allow them a private moment with the field marshal.

"They are not going to arrest him," Manfred comforts himself as he opens a book.

The teenager does not read long. After what seems like just a few minutes, though in truth it is nearly an hour, he hears his father's footsteps walking up the stairs to where Lucia waits. Manfred suddenly fears the worst. He walks quickly into his mother's bedroom. Erwin Rommel has already given her the news. He stands pale and visibly upset.

"Come outside with me," Manfred will write of his father's next words. The field marshal's voice is unusual—pinched and nervous, not at all the calm, knowing demeanor the son has come to know.

The two men leave Lucia's bedroom.

"I have just had to tell your mother that I shall be dead in a quarter of an hour," Erwin Rommel breaks the news to his son. "The house is surrounded and Hitler is charging me with high treason.

"In view of my services in Africa"—and here the field marshal's voice grows calm and sarcastic, as if it is not enough just to be the most famous German general—"I am to have the chance of dying by poison."

Manfred does not speak. Cannot. What is there to say?

His father continues: "The two generals have brought it with them. It's fatal in three seconds. If I accept, none of the usual steps will be taken against my family—that is, against you."

And so it comes out: The Gestapo spies watching the Rommel home so carefully have learned that the best way to get at the father is through the son. It is for the two visiting paper pushers to carry out this threat. Manfred Rommel is a member of the military, subject to military discipline, which could very well mean standing before a People's Court in Berlin. There, forced to don the shabby clothes required of all defendants, in a cavernous room whose high walls are decorated with massive swastikas, Manfred will not know standard courtroom discourse. More typically, Judge-President Roland Freisler will angrily berate him and seek a confession. A defense attorney will be present but will say nothing in the young Rommel's defense as Freisler passes sentence. If the death penalty is invoked, Manfred will be taken immediately to Plötzensee Prison for hanging. If the sentence is not death, Manfred will be taken by train to a concentration camp. With the winter months soon to come, surviving in such a facility will mean harsh cold, starvation, and forced labor. Like many who have already suffered the same fate, the teenager will wish he is already dead.

Manfred Rommel knows all this. He does not care.

"Can't we defend ourselves," the boy pleads to his father. There are guns in the house. They know the local trails from many hours of hunting.

"There's no point," says the field marshal, foreseeing the fatal gun battle that will befall his home. "We've practically no ammunition."

Captain Aldinger is summoned. Like Manfred, he wants to fight. Erwin Rommel takes command for the last time in his legendary life. "It's all been prepared," he tells his distraught audience. "I'm to be given a state funeral . . . in a quarter of an hour, you, Aldinger, will receive a telephone call from the Wagnerschule reserve hospital in Ulm to say that I've had a brain seizure on my way to a conference."

Rommel looks at his watch. "I must go."

The happy dachshund bounds into the room barking as the field marshal walks down the stairs. "Shut the dog in the study, Manfred," he orders. The field marshal dons his long leather coat, removes his wallet, and begins to give a batch of marks to Aldinger, knowing they will be useless to himself within a few minutes. The captain refuses to take the money.

Rommel picks up his field marshal baton on the way out the door. Manfred returns from his chore and walks his father down the gravel path to the waiting Opel. He offers his hand to Aldinger and Manfred, who help him into the back of the car and slam the door.

Field Marshal Erwin Rommel takes one last look at his son. The car drives away. Rommel never looks back.

Twenty minutes later, as young Manfred lights a cigarette, the phone rings.

. . .

"To FRAU LUCIE Rommel—

"Accept my sincerest sympathy for the heavy loss you have suffered with the death of your husband. The name of Field Marshal Rommel will forever be linked with the heroic battles of North Africa.

"Adolf Hitler"

. . .

"To GIVE THE last dying realism to the farce," a bitter Manfred will write, "thousands of German soldiers were dying in the north, south, east, and west, with little hope, but with belief in the integrity of their command."*

---

* Adolf Hitler's attempts to convince the public that Erwin Rommel died accidentally were immediately in doubt. On October 19, 1944, Pierre J. Huss, former manager of the Berlin bureau of the International News Service, reported that "Sunday night's bald announcement of Rommel's death was merely confirmation of what every talkative German prisoner or French table waiter reported since July. They differed somewhat on the version of how the fatal injuries were inflicted but no one doubted the death." Huss, writing from the Moselle River while traveling with General George Patton's Third Army, concluded: "On the whole, Rommel's death bears familiar earmarks to all of those dying suddenly after Hitler's kiss of death."

30

I t's not just German soldiers dying.

A little village on a winding river. Protestant church made of stone, sacristy facing east but now missing its bell tower. Population was once 653. Farmers, mostly. Women and children. A small inn. The propaganda machine is on its way to take pictures of what has happened, then splash them around the globe. Film crews will turn their lenses on the tragedy, perfect for Nazi newsreels.

Five days ago, the Russians took Nemmersdorf. They're gone now, beaten back by a Nazi counterattack. Troops of the German Fourth Army have seen much during the war, some soldiers having served through the fight for France, then the invasion of Russia. They now hold the far borders of Germany, a region of ethnic Germans known as East Prussia. In their travels, these men have seen those shocking things soldiers see but rarely talk about when the war is over. And despite knowing full well the atrocities committed by their countrymen during the ill-fated advance on Moscow, the sights greeting them today are beyond horrific.

At Roter Krug, that local inn, a naked woman is crucified against the barn doors. She has been raped. Throughout the village, other rape victims are similarly stripped and nailed to any piece of wood that the Soviets could find, including wagon wheels.

A farmer "whose throat had been drilled through with a pitchfork so that his entire body is hanging on a barn door," one German soldier will write in his diary. "It is impossible for me to describe all the terrible sights we have witnessed in Nemmersdorf."

Corpses flattened by Soviet tanks are pressed into the soil. A root cellar contains the corpses of citizens machine-gunned while taking cover from the fighting.

Fifty French prisoners of war assigned to work at a local farm are machine-gunned, their bodies left where they fell. Too late, they discovered that their Russian "allies" have not come to liberate them.

Homes did not offer sanctuary. "In the dwellings we found a total of seventy-two women, including children, and one old man, seventy-four in all," one German soldier will write. "All murdered in a bestial fashion, except only for a few who had bullet holes in their heads. Some babies had their heads bashed in."

Some atrocities are exaggerated by the Nazis for propaganda purposes. Yet the evidence here is very real: this is what the Soviets do to people—and theirs is the nation with which Winston Churchill is casually dividing the world, Joseph Stalin's little blue check mark indicating his approval for the brutal methods needed to grant people everywhere membership in his proletariat.

As each soldier in the Fourth Army well knows, this orgy of savagery will not be confined to this remote village.

Berlin is five hundred miles west.

Should the Russians get there first, the violence will be unspeakable.

31

General George Patton is 412 miles from Berlin.

And Field Marshal Erwin Rommel helps him prepare for the morning attack.

A restless Patton awakens hours before this morning's first salvos. Dark and gloomy night. Not time to get up. Not yet. He lies in bed. Reaches for the book on his nightstand. Driving rain pounds the windows of his headquarters chateau. November. Rain comes with the autumn package. But not rain like *this*. Downpour means no air cover—and Patton *needs* air cover. Fighting without that layer of protection could spell defeat.

Right now, the general needs inspiration—and hope. He turns to his former counterpart, whom he knows so well through the written word.

Patton opens *Infantry Attacks* and looks for words of solace, a believer poring through the Bible. This seminal book caught Adolf Hitler's attention years ago, before the war as Germany was building its army, leading to Rommel's swift rise through the ranks.

It takes a while but Rommel talks to Patton. "It was most helpful as he described all the rains he had in September 1914. And also the fact that, despite the heavy rains, the Germans got along," Patton will write in his journal tonight.

This focus on minor details—controlling what he can, doing his best with what he can't—drives Patton, keeping his army ready for anything. Some call it nitpicking. Patton prefers "readiness."

Third Army will attack this morning, rain or shine. Patton's force will number ten divisions, the first time he is sending so many men into battle at the same time. Today's objective is a sixty-mile push across the border into Germany and a place known as the Siegfried Line. This line of anti-tank obstacles and pillboxes stretches the length of the German frontier, four hundred miles from the Atlantic coast to the Swiss border. Thousands of bunkers and more than one hundred concrete barriers line what the Germans call the "Westwall." First built in 1938, these strongpoints were reinforced by the Wehrmacht, beginning with a direct order from Adolf Hitler on August 29, 1944. Slave labor and German locals worked tirelessly to ensure the defense of their homeland. Montgomery's failure to capture the Arnhem Bridge and push into Germany ensured that Hitler had time to finish before winter. Now, deteriorating weather conditions brought on by seasonal change ensure a war of attrition in the coming months. Patton's fondness for mobility and speed must be set aside.

Yet the general likes his chances.

"I can't see how we can loose," he wrote home to Beatrice, not worrying about his spelling.

This attack has been two months in coming. Since Montgomery launched Market Garden, Third Army has moved forward into Germany, but not by much. Patton long ago predicted his attack on the fortress city of Metz (422 miles since Normandy, a distance equal to London to Edinburgh) would be a slog—and he was correct. As his intelligence officer, Colonel Oscar Koch, informed Patton months ago, the Germans "will continue to fight until destroyed or captured."

And those two months have proven Koch correct. Metz is the opposite of Patton's aggressive fighting style, a prolonged siege engagement that feels almost like a defensive maneuver. General Dwight Eisenhower is returning to his "broad front" strategy after Market Garden. This successful tactic has carried the day for centuries, from Hannibal back in 216 BC to General Ulysses S. Grant in 1865.

Now, as Field Marshal Montgomery is pinned down in the Low Countries, finally focused on clearing the German Army from the vital eighty-mile Scheldt estuary connecting the English Channel and the port of Antwerp, it is Patton launching a major offensive into Germany.*

Patton was once angry at being stopped by Eisenhower. That passed. In addition to the fighting at Metz, Patton used the downtime to focus on the next great fight. Patton once again became the all-obsessed commander for whom no detail is too small to be managed. He worried that his men were not getting sleep and hot food, visited field hospitals to pay his respects to the wounded, and fretted that rain will lead to an outbreak of trench foot—something as minor as wet feet can destroy an infantry on the move.

Patton even reverted to his practice of pep talks while waiting to invade Germany's Saar region. And it wasn't just new replacements who got a fire in their belly. The general was surprised and pleased

---

* Antwerp was liberated by the Allies on September 4, 1944. The port should have been a crucial method of fixing supply problems, capable of handling one thousand ships weighing up to nineteen thousand tons at a time. With its ten square miles of docks, twenty miles of waterfront, and six hundred cranes, Antwerp's position eighty miles from the ocean also saved time shipping supplies to units at the front. However, although the city and port were liberated, the long Scheldt estuary remained in German hands. The water itself was mined. Until those enemy forces and their explosives were removed, Antwerp was useless to the Allies.

when two veteran outfits—the 4th and 6th Armored Divisions—were upset because he didn't speak to them. "There is nothing about war I can tell them," he noted in confusion, believing such veterans would not care to hear his thoughts on combat. A flattered Patton then made a point to address them for the sake of morale.

And Patton isn't just tightening the bond with his soldiers.

Only a few days ago, Patton broke the cardinal rule of wartime secrecy by actually telling the media about this morning's attack.

"Some time ago," he confided to members of the press attached to Third Army. Patton knows most reporters well enough to call them by name. "I told you we were going to be stopped for awhile. Now, we are going to start again."

That was the general's sly method of announcing the Saar operations—and also letting the writers know he trusted them. Patton continued the conversation by imploring the journalists not to reveal his army's movements. "You all do some lying and say this is simply what we called in the last war 'correcting a line.' In other words, I do not want the Germans to start moving reserves until they have to."

A reporter raised his hand. "Is the objective unlimited?"

"I don't know anything beyond Berlin," Patton responded.

The general chose his words carefully. He knows better than to step into a political mess. The Knutsford incident was only six months ago, recent enough that the near loss of his command is still fresh on his mind. The Soviets are prickly about American intentions in Europe and parse any comments that might suggest a lesser Russian role in a postwar world.

Patton believes the opposite—that it is the Soviets who are untrustworthy. He is in favor of being first to Berlin, then keeping right on going, pushing back the Russians as far as possible—or at least to within their prewar borders. It now appears the Soviet Union is occupying countries such as Poland and Latvia as they drive west toward

Berlin. Because these countries have a long history of being invaded, the Soviets appear to be cultivating more "buffer states" to expand their empire and make it difficult for a foreign army to invade. In many ways, this is the essence of that territory now known as the Soviet Union—a collective of territories designed to surround and protect Mother Russia, where all roads lead to Moscow.

But for George S. Patton, fighting the Russians will have to wait. The Germans come first.

Patton places Rommel on the nightstand. Lying flat on his back, Patton calms himself for another hour of sleep.

· · ·

0515. ARTILLERY BOOMING. Power and death. Patton opens his eyes. Listens for rain but hears nothing. He walks to the window and looks at the sky, seeing only stars. An elated Patton knows nothing can now halt his attack. His thoughts turn to the Germans on the receiving end of those deadly rounds hurtling their way.

"The discharge of 400 guns sounded like the slamming of doors in an empty house—very many doors all slamming at once," he will journal. "The eastern sky glowed and trembled with the flashes of guns, and I thought how the enemy must feel, knowing at last that the attack he has dreaded has come."

Anticipation. Exhilaration. Patton is so excited he has trouble breathing—"my usual reaction to an impending fight or match."

· · ·

0745. AIR COVER is still a question mark. General Omar Bradley calls and asks if Patton still plans on launching his offensive. The normally cautious Bradley is elated when the general replies in the affirmative.

To Patton's surprise, General Eisenhower is the next call: "I expect a lot of you," Ike tells Patton. "Carry the ball all the way."

Patton does not ask Eisenhower if he said the same thing to Montgomery before Market Garden.

. . .

1000. Finally, the welcome rumble and buzz of air cover. "Our fighter bombers appeared in force and attacked the known enemy command posts. The day was the brightest and the best we have had in two months . . . Thank God."

. . .

1700 hours. Raining again, this time a storm of biblical proportions. Rivers are overflowing their banks, locals telling Patton that the Moselle and Meurthe are at the highest flood stage in twenty-five years. Bridges are out. "Many trucks, airplanes, and one hospital platoon are in the water or marooned," he writes in his journal.

Yet Patton is thrilled as Third Army continues moving forward. Nothing bothers him today.

"We are doing fine," he tells Beatrice.

Two days into the attack, Patton celebrates turning fifty-nine. "I celebrated my birthday by getting up where the dead were still warm. Then I visited the wounded and made quite a hit when I removed my helmet in the presence of a man who had killed a German with a grenade and been wounded by the same weapon," he writes his wife once more, mixing harsh battlefield reality with romance and strategy. "I love you and wish you were here to hold my hand till the river goes down and I get some guns over."

. . .

Patton's mercurial personality comes back to earth. He is attending Sunday church services on what he calls the most "crutial [sic] day of the battle." No anticipation or exhilaration. No shortness of breath. Just frustration that the job is still not done. Stuck in the mud somewhere in the swamps of Germany.

The general chooses not to blame the Almighty for allowing Third Army to remain stuck in the mud, but the general feels quite comfortable focusing his anger on a heavenly intermediary.

"Went to church where I heard the worst service yet," he writes in his journal on November 12. "Sent for the Chief of Chaplains to have the offender removed and get a new chaplain."

General George S. Patton is still racing for Berlin.

It may take all winter, but he will get there.

Or so he thinks.

32

General Norman Cota doesn't like the plan.

He never did. And he said so. Right from the start. Just like D-Day. Now, once again, the general is proven correct. Yet again, this is a horrible way to be right.

Generals Dwight Eisenhower and Omar Bradley step into Cota's command post. Wednesday. A small inn twenty miles from the front. Snowing, though weather is just the beginning of the story. These are the worst conditions Cota has ever seen. His offensive is now six days old. In that time, a trench foot epidemic on the front line has soldiers stripping fresh boots from the dead.

He explains all this to the SHAEF commander. The time for telling Eisenhower how he would have done things differently is past, but Cota alludes to that, too. He is an emotional man, and losing so many soldiers makes him want to weep.

"Well, Dutch," Eisenhower says dismissively, "it looks like you've got a bloody nose."

Short of insubordination, Cota knows of no good response. He's suffered six thousand casualties. He glares—but agrees. The sleep-deprived Cota has lost all control—of the battlefield, his men, and his own temper. Vaunted military reputation in tatters, he is on the verge of being relieved for incompetence.

The Germans call this wooded morass of one-lane muddy roads the Hürtgenwald. Americans say Hürtgen Forest.

Same place. In truth, there is no such place. There is the town of Hürtgen and there is forest all around, carefully planted in neat rows by men, other places growing naturally, covering the steep hillsides. Trees grow together so thick they blot out the sun. So many that a walk in the woods can mean squeezing between one tree and then another. "The Hürtgen Forest is a seemingly impenetrable mass," the *U.S. Army History* will describe it. "A vast, undulating, blackish-green ocean stretching as far as the eye can see. Upon entering the forest, you want to drop things behind to mark your path, as Hansel and Gretel did with their bread crumbs."

Twenty miles from top to bottom. Ten miles wide. Steep hills, valleys, crags, rugged creek beds. Europe was once a vast swath of primeval forest. This rugged region is part of what's left.

No less than General James Gavin will call the forest "a monster, an ice-coated Moloch, with an insatiable capacity for humans."

The Germans have turned the Hürtgen into a defensive marvel, using the Roer River on the far east as one barrier, the Siegfried Line running down the center as another, and then adding barbed wire. Signs in German warning the locals *Eintritt Verboten* foretell of mines sown one pace apart, camouflaged wooden pillboxes where every machine gun has an interlocking field of fire, and trees cut back so gunners can zero in on every speck of the forest with superior artillery emplacement. Snipers take aim from woods, haystacks, and the belfries in small towns within the region's open spaces.

The 28th's objective is a town called Schmidt. This fight will be

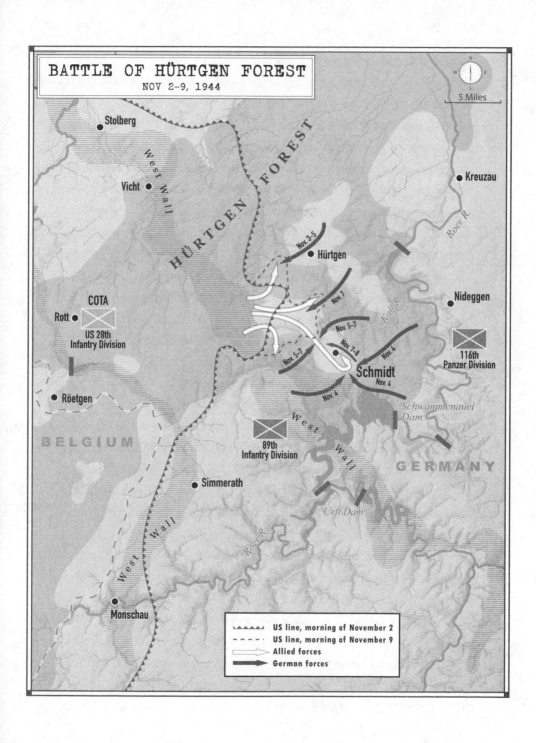

BATTLE OF HÜRTGEN FOREST
NOV 2-9, 1944

5 Miles

Stolberg

West Wall

Vicht

HÜRTGEN FOREST

Kreuzau

Roer R.

Nov. 3-5

Hürtgen

Nideggen

COTA

Rott

US 28th
Infantry Division

Nov. 7

Nov. 5-7

Kall R.

116th
Panzer Division

Nov. 7-8

Nov. 5-7

Nov. 4

Schmidt
Nov. 4

Röetgen

Nov. 4

Schwammenauel
Dam

BELGIUM

West Wall

89th
Infantry Division

GERMANY

Simmerath

Urft Dam

Roer R.

West Wall

Monschau

US line, morning of November 2
US line, morning of November 9
Allied forces
German forces

remembered as the *Allerseelenschlacht*—"All Souls Day Battle"—for the day it was launched.

The American is much simpler and not as poetic: The Battle for Schmidt.

In a remarkable coincidence, on the morning of November 2, as the American artillery barrage ended and the 28th stepped out of their foxholes to attack, German generals were at Schlenderhan castle west of nearby Cologne, war-gaming the possible scenario of American troops launching an offensive in the Hürtgen Forest. To say Germany was ready would be one of the more enormous understatements of autumn 1944.

The weather does not help either side. Soldiers will long remember the Hürtgen as some of the most miserable fighting of the war, the rain turning narrow roads and trails into sucking mud ten inches deep. Exposed on a bare ridge separating the towns of Schmidt and Vossenack, the Americans are relentlessly pounded by German artillery.

By the time the Battle for the Hürtgen Forest ends, it will be the longest single offensive in American history, beginning September 12, 1944, and ending on February 8, 1945. Cota, the 28th, and their fight for Schmidt fall somewhere in the middle, in what will be remembered as the bloodiest of the fighting.

The plan Norman Cota dislikes so much requires that he split his division into three separate regiments instead of one unified force to capture Schmidt. By Day Two, Cota's men had taken the village church. There, the big German guns found them. German 89th Infantry Division and 272nd "People's Grenadier" Division dropped round after round on American positions.

Cota is not helping his cause. He decided the mud is too much for tanks, so at first he fought with very little armored support. This renders the mud-drenched battlefield a throwback to the trench warfare of the First World War, but instead of trenches, the 28th lives in foxholes, cannon fodder all the same.

Another Cota mistake was a lack of prebattle advance patrols to gauge enemy strength and positions. Although he was told the enemy force consisted of boys and World War I veterans, Cota never knew this for sure. Indeed, the 28th is facing three entrenched German divisions consisting of combat veterans.

Those numbers only describe the horror of the Hürtgen in the abstract. The 28th is being slaughtered. German artillery pins men in their foxholes, where they stand in water up to their ankles and defecate in empty C-ration cans as the rounds land closer. There are so many head wounds that soldiers wonder if snipers are using the Bloody Bucket patch as an aiming point. Jewish soldiers terrified of being taken prisoner flatten down the "H" religious designation on their dog tags. Soldiers up and down the line abandon their positions to run for their lives, a feral pack of once-proud warriors pissing themselves at the sound of German gunfire surrounding them on all sides.*

Some even run the wrong way in the confusing woodland terrain, straight into the German guns. One group of one hundred such men sees only three survivors.

In one section of the fighting near the Kall River, the 2,200 Americans beginning the fight will be reduced to 300.

By 3:00 P.M. on November 8, long after Eisenhower and Bradley left, soon to be replaced by an irate First Army commander General Courtney Hodges, General Norman Cota receives the order to pull his men off the line. In the dead of night, having destroyed all tanks, vehicles, and artillery rather than leave them for the enemy, then abandoned any metal on their persons that might make a clattering sound and give away their position, the 28th crawls away from their foxholes. Mess kits littering the forest floor, they form a long line, hand on the shoulder of the next man up, then navigate the eerie total darkness of the Kall Valley on their flight to safety.

---

* An estimated fifty thousand American soldiers deserted their units in World War II.

"Like blind cattle the men thrashed through the underbrush. Any hope of maintaining formation was dispelled quickly by the blackness of the night and by German shelling. All through the night and into the next day, frightened, fatigued men made their way across the icy Kall in small irregular groups, or alone," the official army history will read.

Hundreds of GIs remain behind, lost in the forest. The body of one American soldier will not be discovered for fifty-six years.* The survivors reach safety, where they ride by truck to nearby Roetgen and dine on hot pancakes and cold beer. Their week in the Hürtgen has changed them. From here on out, they will fight the Nazis with a new respect— and brutality. The division band assembles nearby, playing their Paris marching song, "Khaki Bill," now a dirge after the Hürtgen—"Goodbye you boys of liberty, we sing farewell, farewell to thee."

The sixty-piece band also plays the 28th's new fight song, commissioned in a contest of General Cota's making. "Roll On" is the unit's battle cry.

> Let the Keystone shine
> Right down the line
> For all the world to see.
> When we meet the foe
> We'll let them know
> We're Iron Infantry,
> So, Roll On, 28th, Roll On!

"Roll on" is a favorite term of Cota's, sometimes used to sign off correspondence. He is not losing his job, although that is because the

---

* PFC Robert Cahow of the 78th Infantry Division was killed while attacking a German bunker on December 13, five weeks after the 28th pulled out. The Germans buried him next to the bunker. His body was discovered by a mine-clearing detail in 2000. Cahow's remains were sent back to the United States, but a memorial cairn marks his original burial site atop a hill known as Ochsenkopf.

high casualty rate means a paucity of qualified leaders. Cota will now once again lead his men to a quiet corner of the war to train new replacements.

General Bradley feels he knows just the place—another forest, but one where there is very little chance of the 28th seeing any action until they're good and ready.

It's a town called Clervaux, in a region known as the Ardennes.

And right now, though Bradley's intelligence officers have not discovered it so far, that is very near the precise location where Adolf Hitler is secretly massing the full weight of his western army for a surprise attack.

Roll on.

33

One hundred miles southwest of General Norman Cota, the 442nd Regimental Combat Team stands at parade rest, staring straight ahead. Shitty day for a review but perfect weather for wearing a scarf—which is not the case with any man in this elite fighting unit. Snow mixed with freezing rain lashes exposed faces. Arctic gusts so strong the color guard keeps the US flag and regimental colors furled. Officers in tightly belted trench coats stand ready to award medals. The men would rather sleep. They've seen nothing but combat and killing since arriving in France a month ago.

Two-star general John Dahlquist, irritated by the weather and an obvious attempt by the 442nd leadership to ignore his commands, scrutinizes the very small band of soldiers. It's obvious to the burly general that a large portion of the regiment is, indeed, enjoying a warm barracks somewhere.

"You disobeyed my orders," he accuses Colonel Virgil Miller. "I told you to have the whole regiment."

216

"General, this *is* the regiment," Miller replies coolly. "The rest are either dead or in the hospital."

. . .

FIRST MARKET GARDEN.

Then Hürtgen Forest.

Now the "Lost Battalion."

The Wehrmacht shows the Allies why they're considered the most disciplined soldiers on either side of the war. From their northern border on down to Switzerland, the German Army is fighting back—and holding ground. The Westwall is holding strong. The panic once permeating their ranks is forgotten.

The Allies have captured the town of Aachen, moving into Germany with devastating efficiency on October 20—but proceeding not much farther. "The street was shaking with the thunder of reports," Czech journalist Jiří Mucha will report from Aachen for the BBC. "Above our heads, mortar bombs were whining through the air. It was raining. A dead German soldier lay on the pavement in front of me with water streaming down his sallow face."

Mucha will also write of an angry German populace claiming to be sick of Nazi rule, and of hungry German soldiers eager to surrender. Yet that desire to give up seems limited to Aachen. Everywhere else on the Western Front, the Allies face furious opposition. Adolf Hitler has also become suspicious that Great Britain and the US have broken his top secret communications codes—which they have. He has suspended all wireless transmissions for important strategic matters, leaving the Allies blind to his intentions.

So it was, on October 15, when the 442nd was ordered to capture the French town of Bruyères and the four hills overlooking the city, that the exact location and size of German forces in the region was unknown. The battle played out in a series of attacks profane and intimate in the thickly forested Vosges region. Nazi artillery crews fired at the treetops as the 100th Battalion of 442nd advanced, the German shells showering splinters into the air and crushing men to death as severed branches fell to earth. The Americans were still fighting in summer uniforms and became soaked to the skin by cold rains. It was three days of nonstop fighting before Bruyères was taken. So many dead were piled on the roads that it took bulldozers to shove bodies to the shoulder.

On October 20, Staff Sergeant Robert Kuroda sets out to locate the German snipers and machine-gun positions that had taken so many American lives. His men follow behind as Kuroda walks point. The sergeant comes under heavy fire from a wooded hillside. Rather than run or press his body into the ground, the courageous Kuroda somehow remains bulletproof as he carefully creeps alone up to the ridgeline where the German gunners hide in almost total concealment. Kuroda hears the loud report but cannot find the camouflaged nest. Working slowly and cautiously, the sergeant is just ten yards away when he finds the mark. Tossing a hand grenade, he kills three enemy soldiers.

Yet more remain hidden in the position. Sergeant Kuroda fires again and again, using his last bullets to injure three more German soldiers.

Yet even as the sergeant empties the chamber and finally shuts down the German position, more fire comes from a second nearby summit. He rushes over under heavy fire. Throwing down his own empty weapon, Kuroda grabs the submachine gun from the corpse of a dead American officer and hoses the second German machine-gun nest.

A lone man on the battlefield does not stay unknown long. German marksmen take note of the one-man killing spree, adjusting their sights as the Hawaiian steps into range. Sergeant Kuroda is killed by a sniper's bullet. He is twenty-one years old.

. . .

AN OFFICIAL DIVISION after-action report will state: "Bruyères will long be remembered, for it was the most viciously fought-for town we had encountered in our long march against the Germans."

Major General Dahlquist is not satisfied. The thickset Minnesota native was once an instructor at the US Army's infantry school and later graduated from the Command and General Staff College. Yet despite his formal book education, Dahlquist's ability to execute tactics in the field is suspect. No sooner does the 100th capture Bruyères than he demands they also take the neighboring village of Biffontaine. The hamlet had no strategic value and the entrenched Germans might easily have been removed with air strikes or artillery. Yet for ten horrific days, the 100th Battalion follows orders—at one point cut off and hiding in cellars as Nazi soldiers demand they come out to surrender.

But once again, the 100th holds the line. And again, casualties defy normal percentages: an average of nine American soldiers per thousand are killed in action, three die by accident or self-inflicted wound, and eighteen are taken off the line with battle exhaustion or nonfatal combat wounds. At Biffontaine, the cost exceeds anything within those percentiles. Twenty-one men die, one hundred twenty-one are wounded, and eighteen are taken prisoner.

Exhausted, the survivors eat their first hot meal in a week and change into fresh uniforms.

But those clean fatigues will not stay new for even three days.

Because the battle that will make legends of the 100th is about to begin.

. . .

THE CALENDAR SAYS November, but this definitely feels like winter. Soldiers from the Texas National Guard march out of Biffontaine. The 275 men of the 1st Battalion slog the four long miles to the summits of two nearby hills. Muddy logging roads. Dense forest, low fog, trees dripping cold rain. The word "hill" does not accurately portray the steep slopes, thick roots, rotting branches, and seemingly endless climb to their summit objective. These columns of Americans, summoned to relieve the exhausted 100th Battalion of the 442nd Regiment, do not see the six thousand German troops hiding on three sides. Nor do they comprehend until it is too late that yet another group of enemy soldiers has settled in behind them.

The Texans have walked into a trap.

Then comes the attack.

The 1st Texas digs in, taking casualties, pressing flat into the cold mud as they endure what will be the first of many German onslaughts. Efforts to escape turn to debacle. A thirty-six-man patrol looking for a way out returns as a party of five.

Because there is no way out. Roads and trails are mined. Well-concealed enemy machine-gun nests and sniper hides are situated for maximum killing efficiency. The Nazi noose grows tighter.

Food, water, medical supplies, and ammunition dwindle. General Dahlquist sends two other battalions associated with his 141st Regiment to the rescue. Neither breaks through. Meanwhile, casualties among the Texans mount. Germans attack the summit in carefully planned waves. Tanks and artillery are not helpful in the thick, steep woods. Any chance of bringing the Texans—already earning the nickname "the Lost Battalion"—out alive must take place through man-to-man fighting.

So Dahlquist once again turns to the 100th.

It is an unusual scenario. Despite their heroics, the unit has long been an untrusted pariah. The 100th is composed entirely of Japanese Americans and Hawaiians long denied the chance to fight for their country. Questions of patriotism have dogged each Nisei since Pearl Harbor. Very often, the men are ridiculed as "Japs" within the army despite their American heritage and citizenship. They are barely tolerated in most of America but in particular the segregated South, of which Texas is a part. And yet, exhausted, bodies aching from two weeks of fighting, mourning the loss of their kindred brothers, maligned at every turn, the 100th immediately goes back into action.

The Nisei have yet to fail in combat. Their motto is "Go for broke."

It might as well read "Something to prove."

Because they do.

. . .

THE MEDAL OF Honor citations record the heroics best.

"On 29 October 1944, in a wooded area in the vicinity of Biffon-taine, France, Private Hajiro initiated an attack up the slope of a hill referred to as 'Suicide Hill' by running forward approximately 100 yards under fire," reads the citation for Private Barney Hajiro. "He then advanced ahead of his comrades about 10 yards, drawing fire and spotting camouflaged machine gun nests. He fearlessly met fire with fire and single-handedly destroyed two machine gun nests and killed two enemy snipers. As a result of Private Hajiro's heroic actions, the attack was successful."

. . .

AND THIS MOH citation, for Private George Sakato: "After his platoon had virtually destroyed two enemy defense lines, during which he personally killed five enemy soldiers and captured four, his unit was pinned down by heavy enemy fire. Disregarding the enemy fire, Private Sakato made a one-man rush that encouraged his platoon to charge and destroy the enemy strongpoint. While his platoon was reorganizing, he proved to be the inspiration of his squad in halting a counter-attack on the left flank during which his squad leader was killed. Taking charge of the squad, he continued his relentless tactics, using an enemy rifle and P-38 pistol to stop an organized enemy attack. During this entire action, he killed 12 and wounded two, personally captured four and assisted his platoon in taking 34 prisoners."

. . .

MEDIC JAMES OKUBO: "On 28 October, under strong enemy fire coming from behind mine fields and roadblocks, Technician Fifth Grade Okubo, a medic, crawled 150 yards to within 40 yards of the enemy lines. Two grenades were thrown at him while he left his last covered position to carry back wounded comrades. Under constant barrages of enemy small arms and machine gun fire, he treated 17 men on 28 October and 8 more men on 29 October. On 4 November, Technician Fifth Grade Okubo ran 75 yards under grazing machine gun fire and, while exposed to hostile fire directed at him, evacuated and treated a seriously wounded crewman from a burning tank, who otherwise would have died."

. . .

A FOURTH: "AFTER three days of unsuccessful attempts by his company to dislodge the enemy from a strongly defended ridge, Private First Class Nishimoto, as acting squad leader, boldly crawled forward through a heavily mined and booby-trapped area. Spotting a machine gun nest, he hurled a grenade and destroyed the emplacement. Then, circling to the rear of another machine gun position, he fired his submachine gun at point-blank range, killing one gunner and wounding another. Pursuing two enemy riflemen, Private First Class Nishimoto killed one, while the other hastily retreated. Continuing his determined assault, he drove another machine gun crew from its position."

. . .

YET ANOTHER MEDAL of Honor will be awarded to men of the 100th. Staff Sergeant Robert Kuroda will earn America's highest military honor for his action in Bruyères.

. . .

COURAGE BEFORE MEDALS; saving lives before glory. The final moment of unit bravery comes on October 29, as the Nisei of the 100th attach bayonets and advance on the German positions in one last charge up.

This is the legendary place known as "Suicide Hill."

At the sight of such fearlessness, the enemy surrenders.

"Patrol from 442nd here," the Lost Battalion radios on October 30, their rescue complete.

"Tell them that we love them!"

. . .

Now, STANDING IN review on this bitter cold November day, the 100th prepares to return to combat. Their month in France has been deadly: 160 men killed and 1,200 wounded. Yet there is no time to pull back from the front lines for a period of rest and training of new troops.

The return to combat will happen tomorrow morning.

In that return to action, they will soon lose one more. Joe Nishimoto, among those chosen to receive the Medal of Honor, will fall just a few miles away in La Houssière.*

"Go for broke!"

Indeed.

---

* Private Nishimoto will receive his Medal of Honor posthumously in 2000.

34

Martha Gellhorn tells the United States of America about the 82nd Airborne.

With only a passing reference to her new lover.

She is long gone from Nijmegen as today's article hits newsstands. But her words, written several weeks ago, shine with admiration. For a woman mired in intense personal conflict, she even sounds happy.

"From the general on down they are all extraordinary characters and each one's story is worth telling," Gellhorn writes for *Collier's*, not mentioning James Gavin by name. "Men who jump out of airplanes onto hostile territory do not have dull lives."

Nor does Gellhorn.

"These rainy days, the 82nd Airborne Division is sweating it out in Holland," she adds. "In this rain, in the flat dreary country of southern Holland, the paratroopers live and now fight a deadly little nibbling campaign which is not their style, and they do not complain, since they are tough boys and not given to complaint."

The writer is quite taken with the paratroopers, marveling over their swagger. "The 82nd is a very proud outfit, having earned the right to this pride. They do not boast when they say that where they fight, they fight without relief or replacements and that they have never relinquished a foot of ground."

In particular, she writes of a Private Theodore Bachenheimer, "twenty-one and tall and solid, with a dark, short mat of hair and bright small eyes and curly mouth." Gellhorn marvels at the risks the German-speaking soldier takes, venturing out alone on patrols behind enemy lines, talking his way past sentries in the darkness. Bachenheimer "is an extremely competent and serious boy, and nothing seemed to shake his modesty." She goes on to casually state that Bachenheimer was recently posted to the Dutch underground by General Gavin. He maintains a headquarters in a Nijmegen schoolhouse, where a "neat, small" arsenal hangs on the wall.

"His previous training for this work consisted of one job in America: he had briefly been press agent for a show that failed," Gellhorn writes, reminding her audience that it takes all kinds to win a war. It is her gift to find human stories like that of Bachenheimer amid the anonymity of military life. Her words all but command readers to wrap the long arms of America around the brave young man born in Germany but raised in California, to protect him from danger.

Gellhorn lingered near Nijmegen long after Market Garden, though the action had moved on. The attractions are Gavin and access. He lets her roam freely among his troops to right a wrong—today's article in *Collier's* is among the first to record the exploits of US paratroopers in Market Garden. The *Washington Post* and the *New York Times* both covered the campaign without mentioning the presence of the 82nd or the 101st. Gavin calls press accounts of Market Garden being a British victory a "myth" and is outraged by lack of coverage for what he considers the best fighting by his unit so far in the war. So, while Gavin quietly revels in the presence of Gellhorn, so quick with a joke or insight, his first priority is his men. Always. Lack of credit for their courage is bad for morale.*

Presented with such access, knowing this story will make for a unique and patriotic byline, Gellhorn observes the 82nd as they continue their garrison duty, preventing the Germans from recapturing Dutch territory lost during Market Garden. Already, the enemy is punishing the local population for supporting the Allies, cutting off all food and fuel to areas of Holland under Nazi control. By winter's end, an estimated twenty thousand Dutch will perish from cold and starvation. Many will be reduced to eating tulip bulbs to survive.

British units finally relieved the "All-American" division, as the 82nd has been known since 1917, on November 11.†

Gellhorn is already back in Paris as her article sees the light of day. Gavin and his men have relocated to "Camp Suippes and Sissonne" near Reims, France. The 82nd's new quarters were once a German barracks. Yet again, it is time for Gavin to rest his veterans and train replacements for the 1,432 casualties suffered in Market Garden. He opens a jump school to turn regular infantry foot soldiers into paratroopers.

"At one time we had six hundred troopers crowding the wards and lining the halls of a Nijmegen hospital," Gavin will write. "We left more than a thousand buried in a cow pasture." The general does not mention that he personally wrote a letter of condolence to the parents of each fallen paratrooper.

But those weeks in Nijmegen are not easily set aside for Gellhorn or Gavin.

---

* "Soldiers like to believe that the people back home learn what they are doing, and when they do well, they want their families to know it," he writes in *On to Berlin*. "Nothing pleased them more, from time to time during the war, than to get a press clipping from back home, in which their outfit was praised for gallantry in action."

† The 82nd was originally formed at Camp Gordon, Georgia, in 1917. The "All-American" nickname can be seen in the custom "AA" uniform patch worn to this day.

For while Gellhorn reveled in her journalistic access to the troops, that privilege took on a whole new level of familiarity in her relationship with General James Gavin.

The date Gavin and Gellhorn became lovers is lost to history. The affair most certainly began before October 22, when the brave Private Theodore Bachenheimer is captured by the Nazis and shot in the back of the head. Gellhorn would have mentioned that in her story.*

And she is still in Holland on November 3, when the journalist writes her husband from Nijmegen, asking for a divorce. "This is a no-good silly arrangement," she tells Ernest Hemingway. "I think it would be best for you to get this finished with me."

The date is not specific, but it is in Nijmegen where Gellhorn and Gavin first meet, beginning an affair that will extend through the war. Against the ugly emotional surface of the greatest conflict in world history, theirs is an unlikely respite from the sights, smells, and daily tragedy of battle both have come to know well.†

Neither is particularly concerned with appearances. This is war: Normal rules don't apply. The general has a staff around him at all times, so little remains secret. He is known for enjoying the company of women. And despite her own protestations that she is awkward in intimate moments, particularly in her lack of physical compatibility with Hemingway, the writer is not above the occasional fling.‡

---

* Bachenheimer was originally buried in Oldebroek General Cemetery in Holland. His remains were later moved to the US Military Cemetery at Neuville-en-Gondroz in Belgium, before being returned to California in 1949, where he was laid to rest at the Beth Olam Cemetery in Hollywood.

† It has been suggested by one Gavin biographer that the general first met Gellhorn in Paris, at a lunch attended by Ernest Hemingway, Mary Welsh, and Marlene Dietrich. This is refuted in Gavin's private journals.

‡ Gellhorn will describe her sexual relations with Hemingway as "wham, bam, thank you, Ma'am, without the thank you."

In each other, they find a true equal—America's up-and-coming general and perhaps the nation's best unsung war correspondent.

Frontline romance is the province of generals and independent women. The only parallel is General Eisenhower and his driver, Kay Summersby. Yet both partners in that relationship will insist the attraction was never consummated. Not so Gavin and Gellhorn. There will be card playing, drinking, furious arguments, and long bouts of lovemaking to the thunder of artillery shells and small-arms fire. The passion is "what I'd guessed, read about, been told about; but not believed, that bodies are something terrific," Gellhorn will write.

Their romance will survive the war, as will most of their letters. "My darling Marty," Gavin will write, before adding gushing paragraphs filled with inside jokes and yearning for her presence, later signing off with "I love you beautiful."

Commas don't matter.

"Dearest Love, dearest Jimmy and darling, I have thought of nothing but you all these days and everyone and everything seems very flat in comparison," she will write. "I love you so much that these are fuzzy dreams and I am living suspended in time, waiting for you to come."

Nijmegen is in the past. Winter is coming. As Gavin and the 82nd await their next orders near Reims, the couple is unsure when they will see one another again.

But they will. This war is staggering in its breadth, yet Gavin and Gellhorn find each other many times.

Reporters and generals always know where to spot the next battlefield.

35

General George S. Patton has big plans for his next battlefield.
Adolf Hitler has other ideas.

Patton's morning intelligence briefing starts on time. Depressing December drizzle outside. Maps outlining Operation Tink line the walls. Willie curled up on the floor near Patton's boots. Junior officers seated around the war room. Everyone's cold.

The general has slept in this chateau for three months, sitting in a green leather chair in his room at nights to read, giving Willie nose drops when the terrier's snoring gets too much. That's eleven weeks more than Patton can bear. France has lost its charm. The Allied offensive in the north is all but over. Nothing but stalemate along the Siegfried Line, thanks to the failure of Market Garden. Three Allied army groups butt up against the German border, but the concrete anti-tank defenses known as "dragon's teeth" for their pyramidal appearance, flood-stage rivers, and lousy weather provide all the protection the Wehrmacht needs.

Farther south, George Patton sees a clear line to Berlin. He is impatient to launch Tink ten days from now. The general has already settled upon the town of Saint-Avold, twenty-five miles east, as his next HQ. Not that it will be much better than drenched Nancy. "I have never seen or imagined such a hell hole of a country," he writes Beatrice. "There is about four inches of liquid mud over everything and it rains all the time. Not hard but steady."

Clad in tailored overcoat and scarf over his uniform, the general sits in an unpadded wooden chair. Gun belt but just one pistol today. This daily morning briefing is the domain of the well-prepared Colonel Oscar Koch, who now stands before highly detailed maps of the Western Front. Each denotes the precise real-time location of not just British, American, Canadian, French, and German positions but also armor, artillery, infantry, and forward air bases.

Koch is thick glasses, preparation, long bouts of analytical thinking.

After the war he will become a spy.

Thirty miles north, Metz celebrates liberation. A "tough nut," Patton calls the city. Weeks of little food and no clean water for the locals as the vital Nazi transportation hub is caught in the cross fire.*

German troops fled Metz yesterday. Patton's conquest was the first time the city had fallen to an invader since 415 AD. Fort Driant, a heavily fortified concrete outpost in the hills above Metz—and Third Army meat grinder, where new troops were "blooded," in Patton's description—finally capitulated, marking the end of the most vicious fighting Patton's army has seen since the Falaise Pocket. Tink is the next step, a full-throttle push past the Siegfried Line into the heart of Nazi Germany. Patton will have his Julius Caesar moment with a

---

* The railway yards at Metz are infamous as the location where French Resistance leader Jean Moulin died after brutal Nazi interrogation while on his way to Berlin for more torture. Today, a plaque at the train station testifies to Moulin's heroism.

crossing of the Rhine River, in which he plans to ceremoniously urinate. Then eastward to the Elbe, which might also receive a christening.

Then Berlin.

No other Allied general has a better chance of standing atop the Reichstag steps come Christmas Day.

Yet Colonel Oscar Koch believes there might be a detour.

Koch has been Patton's G-2—intelligence officer—since 1940. The loyal colonel has been the only member of the general's staff physically present for the awarding of each of Patton's stars. Patton trusts Koch's genius so much he bent rules to bring the colonel here from America. Like a gambler who likes the odds in his favor, Patton can boldly attack when he knows precisely what he's facing. And no one does a better job of providing that information than the colonel.

"Koch." Patton surprised the Milwaukee native after dinner in the United States one night in 1942. The rest of Patton's staff was about to ship out for Africa. Koch was forty-five at the time, restricted from combat due to age, resigned to remaining at home and missing the greatest intelligence-gathering opportunity of his lifetime. "Do you want to go to war?"

"Yes, sir."

"Well, you're going."

Perhaps Patton's highest form of flattery is not just bringing Koch to the war but paying close attention each day as the intelligence officer lays out his findings. In Patton, Koch has an attentive pupil, insatiable in his need to know more about the enemy. Even when Koch is not around, Patton peppers intelligence personnel from other units. SHAEF G-2, British major general Kenneth Strong, notes that Patton possesses "an extraordinary desire for information of all kinds. He invariably came to see me when he was at Supreme Headquarters and would quiz me on details about the enemy, usually to satisfy himself that the risks he intended to undertake were justified."

It is General George S. Patton who leads Third Army, but it is Colonel Oscar Koch's detailed intelligence that allows the general to do so with total awareness of German movements. "I ought to know what I'm doing," Patton will state after being complimented on his prescient battlefield sense. "I have the best damned intelligence officer in any United States command."

Colonel Koch has quietly changed how information is gathered and disseminated. He is rarely wrong. Due to Koch's prodding, every unit in Third Army contains individuals trained in intelligence. Rather than traditional military networks, which send information up the chain of command at a glacial pace, "Third Cavalry" immediately processes new data and sends it directly to Koch. Enemy tactics are studied and order of battle memorized. Prisoners of war are thoroughly questioned, accounting for one-third of all combat intelligence.

Koch war-games two operations in advance of what is happening in real time, meaning that Tink was plotted before Patton even left Normandy. The G-2 knows all aspects of the coming battles, ranging from weather, terrain, towns, and even obstacles like fences to enemy troop strength. Aerial reconnaissance missions flying up to 150 miles in front of Third Army have already given him a bird's-eye view. Koch's intelligence is at an even higher level than normal for Tink—Third Army recently captured a German general who knows everything there is to know about the defenses Patton will soon face, because he personally oversaw their construction.

For these reasons, many Allied commanders believe Tink might win the war.

Germany, the thinking goes, has no reason to keep fighting.

But Colonel Koch has been studying a unique phenomenon north of Patton's position. Since the end of October, the Germans have been withdrawing panzer divisions from the front lines. A large body of enemy troops is massing somewhere near the Ardennes Forest. Analysis of radio reports from First Army advance scouts shows a massive panzer movement taking place in the woods at night. But this is no phantom army: Koch has confirmed the location of multiple German armor and infantry units, as well as ammunition and gasoline dumps.

As Patton listens attentively, Koch points to the map showing these precise locations. He tells Patton about the radio silence of German forces—an ominous indicator of coming attack. Just as worrisome, interrogation of enemy POWs reveals that English-speaking German soldiers are being trained in sabotage, most likely while wearing Allied uniforms taken off captured or dead Americans.

Just to be safe, Koch diverted some of Tink's aerial reconnaissance for a look at the Ardennes. Pilots returned with photographs of unassembled artillery pieces, crates of land mines, and tanks being loaded onto trains in Frankfurt before traveling west. Weeks ago, hundreds of trains were also observed transporting infantry units to the Ardennes.

So, Koch now tells General Patton what might happen.

Might. Just a hunch based on the most comprehensive data possible. But if Koch is right, the consequences could be catastrophic.

Koch tells Patton the Germans have nine divisions secretly arrayed against First Army up north, near the borders of Germany, France, and Luxembourg. The Sixth SS Panzer Army has just finished reequipping in the Ruhr region and has traveled west across the Rhine. Based on current data, the enemy has a two-to-one advantage. A successful attack would drive the Allies out of that region, opening a path to the English Channel. Koch calls it a "large spoiling offensive."

Erring toward caution—for that is another trait of his sleuthing—the colonel also points out there might be no attack at all. Hitler may be hiding those units as reserves for future defense of the Fatherland.

Patton thinks a moment. Those German forces will threaten his left flank as he executes Operation Tink. If the Germans launch an attack before December 19, Tink's "go" date, "our operation will be called off," Patton predicts to his staff, then refers to the First Army. "We'll have to go up there and save their hides."

The general stands. He's made up his mind: Operation Tink will proceed as planned on December 19. Patton adds one caveat. He orders Koch to find the data he needs to place Third Army "in a position to meet whatever happens."

Colonel Oscar Koch gets back to work.

.   .   .

ON THE MORNING of December 16, as George Patton sits down for his morning intel briefing, Koch informs him that "the Germans are going to launch an attack, probably at Luxembourg."

Even as Koch utters those words, the enemy offensive has already begun.

There will be no Operation Tink.

General George S. Patton must find an alternate route to Berlin.

36

General James Gavin gets the shocking news while dressing for Sunday dinner.

Bedroom at his house near headquarters. Nothing fancy. Shave and a shower. Cleaning up after a Sunday of light training for new replacements. Armed Forces Radio Network broadcasting the evening news.

"It sounded ominous," Gavin will write of the sudden bulletin. He is well briefed about American troop strength up and down the Siegfried Line. "Serious German penetrations had been made in the Ardennes area. Knowing our thinness in that area and our paucity of reserves, I was quite concerned."

Yesterday morning at 5:30 A.M., three hours before daylight, Colonel Oscar Koch's prediction came true. German artillery commenced Operation Watch on the Rhine (*Unternehmen Wacht am Rhein*), in a last-ditch effort to push Allied troops out of Germany. The eighty-mile front exploded with the shocking thunder of 1,600 artillery pieces and "Screaming Meemie" rockets. Snow blanketing the ground. Temperature ten degrees.*

Hundreds of panzers and Tiger tanks then rumble forward, the ground shaking as tons of steel churn down normally quiet country roads. Hitler's plan is simple: The German armor has twenty-four hours to break through American lines. Seventy-two to cross the Meuse River.

The Sixth Panzer Division, so recently refitted and shipped back to the Rhine, attacks straight into General Norman Cota and the depleted Pennsylvania 28th.

The enemy also hits the inexperienced US 99th Division. The 99th has been posted to the Ardennes Forest for combat training, the location chosen for relative calm. By the time their battle is over, more than thirty thousand casualties from both sides will bleed into the snow.

Adolf Hitler's objective is capturing the port of Antwerp. He has no desire to go farther. The full might of the German Army on the Western Front will divide the American forces to the south from Montgomery's armies to the north. Wedge complete, Hitler will finally take General Erwin Rommel's advice and sue for peace with the Americans and British. Hitler began planning this bold gambit on September 17, when Rommel was still alive and almost at the same moment American paratroopers dropped into Holland. Success will allow him to cease fighting a two-front war and focus his efforts on defeating the Russians.

Berlin will never fall.[†]

The German Army raced forward in their shocking surprise attack. Panzer divisions overran positions so quickly that American soldiers were cut down as they arrived at their artillery pieces to open fire. German troops fought among themselves for the ample supplies

---

* "Die Wacht am Rhein" is a patriotic German song.

† Planning for Operation Watch on the Rhine was top secret. The original launch date was late November but was pushed for logistical purposes and to ensure that the offensive took place at a time of poor weather, grounding the deadly Allied air cover German soldiers feared so much.

of food and cigarettes in captured supply dumps, while panzer commanders refilled their tanks with the thousands of gallons of high-quality American gasoline. The narrow, frozen muddy roads of the Ardennes are now choked with German armor and troops. Liberated towns in Belgium and Luxembourg are evacuated by the Americans, the locals who have sheltered them for months left to fend for themselves as the Nazis return.

It is North Africa almost three years ago and the Hürtgen Forest last month, terrified Allied troops running from battle as if they've never heard a shot fired in anger.

. . .

SUNDAY DINNER DOESN'T last long.

General James Gavin is summoned from the table halfway through his meal and ordered to send the 82nd into the fight. There will be no parachute drop. The division will be driven into battle by truck. The first order of duty is finding those soldiers now on leave in Paris and summoning them back to base. Whether they arrive in time or not, the division will depart at dawn.

Gavin doesn't have time to wait. By 11:30 the same night, he is on the road to the town of Spa, Belgium, to meet with General Courtney Hodges of First Army to coordinate strategy. He brings a driver and two top commanders. "It seemed possible I might encounter German troops before I got to Spa," he will remember. "So we made the trip in an open jeep, preparing for any eventuality. It was a wickedly miserable night. There was a steady light rain, considerable fog, and quite a few bridges were out."*

---

* The town of Spa is where self-care treatment facilities get their name. The word is an acronym of the Latin *Salus per Aquam*, meaning "health from water." In Roman times, the hot mineral springs in this Belgian city were used by soldiers to heal aching muscles and recover from battle. Other sources suggest the name comes from the Walloon word *espa*, meaning a spring or fountain. The use of the word in reference to a resort with natural springs first appeared in print in 1777.

But Gavin and his small band get through, shivering through a long night on the road, arriving at first light. By 9:00 A.M. he is reporting to General Hodges at First Army's Hotel Britannique headquarters. The fifty-seven-year-old Georgia native with the deep blue eyes and erect posture dropped out of West Point but later enlisted and rose all the way up through the ranks from private. The two men know one another, Gavin having served under Hodges in the Philippines in the 1930s, before parachutes and dreams of making general became a reality. Hodges is quiet, inarticulate. He has a famous habit of relieving commanders for failure to perform—as he almost did to General Norman Cota at the Hürtgen Forest.

The headquarters is in disarray, nobody sure of the severity of the German attack. Christmas decorations for the coming staff party but no plans for repelling the enemy advance. Hodges is calm as he speaks to Gavin, days away from locking himself in his office from a suspected nervous breakdown when it appears his army will be overrun. The two now make for the war room, where maps show the German front has expanded to one hundred miles long.

Watch on the Rhine is an Allied intelligence breach of the highest order. General Omar Bradley has taken what he calls a "calculated risk" of defending this Ardennes area with two inexperienced divisions new to the war and two other badly battered divisions awaiting replacement troops. Among these are General Norman Cota and the 28th, still reeling from the Hürtgen Forest.

None of Bradley's G-2s suggested any form of attack in this area, instead predicting that the enemy was on the ropes. Two days into the German offensive, Bradley's intelligence network is so poorly informed that he still believes the enemy attack is nothing more than a minor skirmish.

Gavin sees otherwise. It is decided that the 82nd will take and hold a pivotal crossroads at the town of Werbomont, Belgium. There, they will block any German advance.

The 101st Airborne—"the Screaming Eagles"—will defend a second crossroads at the Belgian town of Bastogne. The main east-west road runs through here, all but ensuring that Hitler's tanks must pass this way.

General Maxwell Taylor, Gavin's counterpart as commander of the 101st, is in Washington, DC, on leave. He jumped into Normandy and Market Garden but will miss this engagement. In his absence, James Gavin will lead both airborne divisions.

Gavin first travels to Werbomont, and then another hour to Bastogne. The air is thin, cold; he can see his breath. Farms. Pastures. Woods. Winding roads already pocked with shell holes.

"As I moved along, I felt I was in no-man's land," he will write. "There is a peculiar stillness and lack of activity beyond one's own front lines until you encounter the enemy," Gavin adds of his return to battle, the third time since D-Day.

"Combat veterans sense this condition quickly as they become intensely cautious and listen, seemingly with every pore of their bodies."

But despite the coming danger, Gavin stands out front at all times. "The place for a general in battle is where he can see the battle and get the odor of it in his nostrils," he believes. "There is no substitute for the general being seen."

The Battle of the Bulge, as the Allies will call this German offensive, has begun.*

The Germans are coming straight toward the 82nd and 101st.

General James Gavin is ready.

---

* The German attack was originally called the Von Rundstedt Offensive, in the belief that Germany's top tactical general was its planner. In fact, Adolf Hitler was the primary planner. Field Marshal Gerd von Rundstedt thought the operation deeply flawed. The "bulge" refers to the salient formed by the German push through Allied lines. The people of Belgium still refer to the German attack as if it were planned by von Rundstedt.

37

General George S. Patton is back in Verdun.

For the meeting that will change his life.

Four months after capturing this fortress city on the Meuse, Patton strides into a dingy second-floor French barracks. Familiar faces gathered around a bare wooden conference table: Ike, Bradley, the usual British contingent of Air Chief Marshal Sir Arthur Tedder, and Montgomery's chief of staff, Major General Francis de Guingand. No Monty. Even at this dark hour of the war, he refuses Eisenhower's every summons.

A further complement of staff officers sits and stands around the room. Unheated, save by a potbellied stove providing next to no warmth. Everyone keeps their heavy coats on. No one's smiling.

Patton has driven ninety minutes in an open jeep to be here. Willie stayed behind. Blankets across the general's lap to keep his legs warm. Patton smokes a cigar and bides his time as Eisenhower, one day from being promoted to five-star general, opens the meeting. Ike doesn't

240

look healthy, his face pale and stricken. He knows it and tries to be funny to deflect, framing the German attack as an opportunity and demanding that there be no long faces in the room. Left unsaid is that the loyal General Bradley is quietly furious. Eisenhower has once again kowtowed to politics and Montgomery, reassigning Bradley's First Army to Monty for the duration of this fight. Patton is all alone as commander of Third. Bradley has offered his resignation but Eisenhower refuses to accept it.

The response to Ike's opening line is a tepid chuckle. Patton alone tries to change the tone.

"Hell," Patton responds to Eisenhower's demand for optimism. "Let's have the guts to let the sons of bitches go all the way to Paris. Then we'll really cut them up."

"George, that's fine," answers Eisenhower. "But the enemy must never be allowed to cross the Meuse."

It was in May 1940 that the Germans launched a similar attack through the Ardennes. The pivotal moment came one week in, when the Meuse was breached by German armor, crossing on bridges and even improvised ferries. After, there was no halting their dash to the English Channel. Now, advancing in that direction with seventeen divisions, the Germans appear equally unstoppable.

"Ike had the SHAEF G-2 give the picture," Patton will remember of today's meeting, referring to Major General Kenneth Strong. "And then he said he wanted me to get to Luxembourg and make a strong counterattack with at least six divisions.

"The fact that three of these divisions exist only on paper did not enter his head."

The situation is perilous. The 101st Airborne is stuck inside Bastogne, completely cut off and surrounded. If not rescued, they will be wiped out completely. The Germans have been shooting prisoners since this attack started. No reason they won't do the same at Bastogne.

"When can you start?" Eisenhower asks Patton. With Operation

Tink due to have stepped off this morning, Third Army has tens of thousands of men aimed due east. That means trucks, tanks, jeeps, artillery pieces, and even boats to cross those swollen rivers. It is one thing for a small fighting force like the 82nd Airborne to move out from their barracks with hours' notice. It is quite another to rotate an entire army ninety degrees in winter, then have them travel one hundred miles north on narrow, frozen country roads. At one week, the schedule for Market Garden was considered extremely aggressive. The room expects to hear something similar from Georgie Patton.

"On December 22 with three divisions," Patton states calmly.

The general records the response of the assembled generals in his journal: "It created quite a commotion."

Nobody knows that, with the help of Colonel Oscar Koch, Patton has already drawn up three different battle plans. All it will take is a phone call to his headquarters for one of them to be in motion.

The British find Patton's audacious boast ludicrous. At a moment like this, even the Americans find Patton's boastful promise arrogant.

And yet . . . "A stir, a shuffling of feet, as those present straightened up in their chairs. In some faces skepticism. But through the room a current of excitement leaped," Patton aide Charles Codman will remember.

The game is afoot.

Meeting continues two more hours. Eisenhower walks Patton to his jeep.

"Funny thing, George," Eisenhower jokes, "every time I get another star, I get attacked."

Both men remember when Eisenhower made full general: North Africa and the tragedy at the Kasserine Pass.

"And every time you get attacked, Ike," Patton responds, "I have to bail you out."

THE WINTER WAR

◆

38

Martha Gellhorn grows tired of war.

First day of the new year. Thick forest lining country roads. Late sunrise and early sunsets reflecting off the blanket of country snow, fields and pastures shining pink. Pale midday sunshine making all that snow glitter like diamonds.

But this is no idyll. War is everywhere. Frozen white P-47 contrails in the winter sky. Dead cattle littering icy roads, feet sticking into the sky, as cows seem to do when they die, looking all the more massive for their bloated stomachs.

The Battle of the Bulge is almost settled as the journalist retraces its path, wondering how such a picturesque landscape cannot be viewed as some place from a Christmas card but instead as "Kraut killing country."

Yet she well knows the terrible things that occurred in and around this little town of Bastogne. The heroics will fill history books for centuries to come. Now that it has come to pass, it seems as if the outcome was predestined, known at the beginning of time, a fight between good and evil that could never have ended any other way.

. . .

GENERAL GEORGE PATTON pivoting his entire army and bailing out Dwight Eisenhower in one of the most audacious acts ever seen in warfare. Third Army races to rescue the 101st Airborne, trapped and surrounded in Bastogne. Patton's brilliant push to the battlefield turns the tide, thwarting the German attack.

. . .

GENERAL NORMAN COTA and the 28th overrun, outnumbered, and cut off—yet holding the line against nine German divisions. CBS News is calling it "one of the greatest feats in the history of the American army." The death toll on Cota's watch is again mournful. Now, once more, ranks severely depleted, he pulls his men off the line to train replacements.

. . .

GENERAL JAMES GAVIN fighting in battle after pitched battle, always at the front in a winter-white smock as the 82nd attacks and counterattacks. The German Army has been pushed back, never to advance outside their borders again. Hitler's desperate bid to sue for peace is no more.

The race for Berlin is on again: the Soviets from the east and a revived Patton-Montgomery rivalry soon to push hard from the west.

One way or another, Berlin will fall, and Adolf Hitler will pay the price for his actions.

. . .

GELLHORN FORESEES THIS coming end to the war.

And it makes her weary.

It wasn't over by Christmas like everyone predicted—that holiday was a week ago, when Patton rescued Bastogne—but she knows what's coming, for war is her job. It's all she knows. After this one, there will

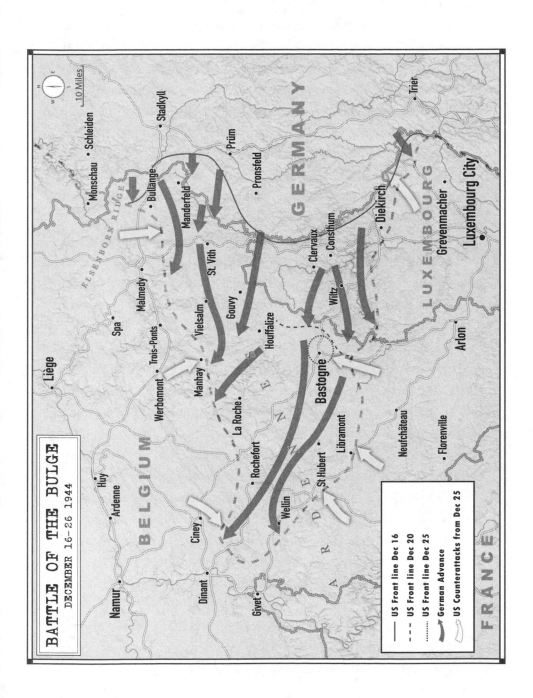

BATTLE OF THE BULGE
DECEMBER 16-26 1944

N
W — E
S

10 Miles

Liège

Huy

Ardenne

Namur

BELGIUM

Ciney

Dinant

Givet

Monschau

Schleiden

Bullange

Manderfeld

ELSENBORN RIDGE

Malmedy

Spa

Trois-Ponts

Werbomont

Manhay

La Roche

Rochefort

St. Vith

Vielsalm

Gouvy

Houffalize

A R D E N N E S

Wellin

St. Hubert

Bastogne

Libramont

Neufchâteau

Stadkyll

Prüm

Pronsfeld

GERMANY

Clervaux

Consthum

Wiltz

Diekirch

LUXEMBOURG

Grevenmacher

Arlon

Florenville

Trier

Luxembourg City

FRANCE

——	US Front line Dec 16
– – –	US Front line Dec 20
·······	US Front line Dec 25
➤	German Advance
▷	US Counterattacks from Dec 25

be another to write about. Nothing will match the scale of this drama, but she will be there nonetheless.

The journalist now travels on back roads around the Bastogne battlefield, avoiding the main thoroughfares for fear of blundering into the few remaining enemy.

German dead are everywhere, frozen and neglected. Adolf Hitler isn't sending anyone to bring them home. She takes her readers into the war, focused on the uncomfortable. "You can say the words death and destruction and they don't mean anything," she writes. "But they are awful words when you are looking at what they mean."

She tells of German staff cars, half-tracks, and tanks, all flattened and eviscerated by bombs and P-47 machine-gun bullets. The American pilots dive in single file, shooting at an altitude of just sixty feet before pulling up. No man can survive such an onslaught, plane after plane after plane firing at point-blank range.

Gellhorn mourns the enemy and their detritus: shoes, bullets, lighters, letters, keepsakes from home. "The road passed through a curtain of pine forest and came out on a flat, rolling snow field. In this field, the sprawled or bunched bodies of Germans lay thick, like some dark shapeless vegetable."

Where the battle still flickers, she sees fire. Smoke. Gutted homes. Misinformed P-47 pilots strafing even American tanks.

"The war's over," one tank crew boasts to her as she travels toward what now constitutes the front lines. "Don't you know? I heard it on the radio a week ago. The Germans haven't any gasoline. They haven't any planes. Their tanks are no good . . . hell, it's all over."

Another tells of a nearby forest filled with the bodies of dead Germans.

Still another tells Gellhorn to stay off the main road. "They're making a counterattack," a sergeant prophesizes. "They got about thirty tanks. I heard them coming this way."

"What are you going to do?" asks Gellhorn.

"Stay here," he answers.

"We got a gun," adds a nearby soldier.

. . .

GELLHORN FINDS A command post and walks inside to interview the general. "You could not easily enter the office through the front door," she writes of her new normal. "A dead horse with splattered entrails blocked the way. A shell had landed in the farmyard a few minutes before and killed one cow and wounded a second, which was making sad sounds in a passageway between the house and the barn."

She finds a way in. A forward air combat controller is on the radio talking to P-47s strafing anything that moves. She overhears a comment from one pilot talking about the beauty of a burning German tank and another pilot crowing about knocking out three Tiger tanks, and the wonderful sight of their crews splayed dead on the snow. Incoming German shells land nearby but nobody takes notice. Artillery officers and P-47 ground support staff roll their eyes at one another, showing off for Gellhorn, each bragging that their shells should get all the credit for the ongoing killing.

There is the radio; there are snacks to be made from C-rations; there is the lowing of the dying cow so obviously in pain. Gellhorn's driver is upset about the animal. "What I hate to see is a bunch of livestock all beat up this way," the young soldier confides to the reporter. "It's not their fault."

Time means little. There is just war. Christmas was not celebrated in a formal sense on the front lines, other than a meal of hot turkey for the lucky. "There was nothing to drink," Gellhorn comments about the New Year's Eve celebration for the soldiers. Her own New Year's Eve suffered from too much libation—though not on her part.

On New Year's Day, in a snowstorm, Gellhorn leaves the Battle of the Bulge for good. Artillery thunders as new snow falls over northern

France. She arrives in Luxembourg City and slides from the war for an hour, borrowing a homemade sled and joining local children on a fast hill near a stone quarry. The front lines are two miles away. P-47 Thunderbolts go about their business in the skies overhead, and the big guns do not stop firing. All around Gellhorn, even above the noises of combat, she focuses on the excited children screaming with fear as their sleds pick up speed and slide out of control.

"Children aren't so dumb," her driver comments. "What I mean is, children got the right idea. What people ought to do is go coasting."

· · ·

THAT EVENING, GELLHORN tries to summarize all she has seen this past week. Her thoughts turn philosophical. She does not tell her readers, but last night she fought a battle all her own.

Ernest Hemingway happened to also be staying at the Luxembourg City Hotel and invited himself to New Year's Eve dinner. Bill Walton from *Time* sat at the same table. The writer and painter had driven with Martha into Bastogne earlier in the day.

Over drinks and a meal, Hemingway launched a series of insults that finally got Gellhorn fighting back. The couple argued so viciously that Walton scolded Hemingway for being a bully and demanded he stop the verbal abuse. The night ended back at the hotel with a drunken Hemingway breaking into a janitor's closet and placing a bucket on his head. Dressed in long underwear and his outlandish costume, he pounded on Martha's door with a mop stick he held in front of him like a lance, as if he were a medieval knight.

"Go away, you drunk," she yelled through the locked wooden door.

Finally, Hemingway did.

This time for good.

So, on the first night of 1945, as the world waits for the war to end, Martha Gellhorn sits in that same hotel room and writes about how it feels to conclude a long battle—marriage and Battle of the Bulge feeling one and the same.

"The Bulge was ironed out," she writes from her hotel in Luxembourg City.

"This was not done fast or easily, and it was not done by those anonymous things: armies, divisions, regiments.

"It was done by men, one by one."

39

Three men decide the fate of the world.

Literally, just three men.

The whole world. Billions of people. Three men—one of them dedicated to his country, one obsessed with personal power, and one with two months to live.

Prime Minister Winston Churchill, Soviet dictator Joseph Stalin, and US president Franklin Roosevelt gather at the Livadia Palace, once the home of Russian kings and Nazi generals: long green lawns, palm trees, a low white building with perfect arches, pillars, and 116 rooms. Nazi Germany occupied this area from 1942 until last May, looting the palace like thugs on their way out. The furniture on which the many conference guests now sit comes from Moscow furniture stores, the waiters and maids from Moscow hotels, all brought down by train from the Soviet capital, 792 miles north.

The photograph of the three men posed on polished brown wooden chairs in the courtyard will become iconic, from left to right Churchill,

Roosevelt, and Stalin. They sit close, like friends, bundled in thick winter coats. In one photo, as Churchill and Roosevelt appear to be chatting amiably, a distracted Stalin is caught gazing in the opposite direction. No matter. Stalin has had every room in the palace bugged. He knows exactly what they are confiding to one another.

It's more than a year since they last gathered in Tehran, when it was decided that Russia would enter the war in the Pacific, among other agreements. The world has changed, but their posturing has not. Stalin insisted that his doctor forbade him from travel—as if anyone can tell him what he can and cannot do—forcing the American and British leaders to undertake a complex journey to reach this Black Sea resort: thousands of miles on ships and planes, and finally a ninety-mile drive over mountain roads. But this "Yalta Conference" is worthy of such effort. Seeking to avoid the punitive measures enforced by the Allies when Germany surrendered at the end of the First World War, the "Big Three" have allotted a week to discuss their hopes for a postwar Europe. "The whole world will have its eyes on this conference," Winston Churchill toasted at the opening dinner last night. "If it is successful we will have peace for one hundred years."

Roosevelt is pale and drawn, visibly ill, congenital heart condition never more obvious, cigarette in between left thumb and forefinger. Blood pressure 260 over 150.

Stalin looks robust, the picture of health, a very short man with a thick, graying mustache and wearing polished black cavalry boots. It's clear that it is the president who should not be traveling. In truth, the Soviet leader is afraid of flying.

But Stalin plays the good host. This is a celebration of coming victory, more than seven hundred British and Americans flown in as part of the delegation. Many are in uniform. Hotels are in short supply for so many visitors; even top officers sleep six to a room in the villas set aside for the Allied guests—and such is the air of optimism that nobody seems to mind, with the possible exception of those senior military personnel sharing a billet with US admiral Ernest King. The admiral is fond of reading at an unhurried pace in the quarters' only functioning lavatory, ignoring those outside waiting their turn.

"Every effort was made by our hosts to ensure our comfort, and every chance remark was met by kindly attention," Churchill will note, delighted in the villa loaned him for the duration. "On one occasion, [Chief of Air Staff Peter] Portal had admired a large glass tank with plants growing in it, and remarked that it contained no fish. Two days later, a consignment of goldfish arrived. Another time someone said casually that there was no lemon peel in the cocktails. The next day a lemon tree loaded with fruit was growing in the hall. All must have come by air from far away."

Yet hospitality goes only so far. As the first meeting begins on this gray, cold afternoon, Joseph Stalin immediately discusses how Europe will be divided after the war. Churchill, who so casually jotted down a laundry list of how lesser nations should be divided by the Allies, is most judicious about Germany. He speaks of historical borders, ethnography, and the economies of various German regions. Roosevelt suggests a small committee be formed this evening, ordered to produce a document within twenty-four hours about the "dismemberment" of Germany.

And there the matter rests.

But not for long. Soviet forces are forty miles from Berlin, even as the British and Americans remain four hundred miles away. Two million East Prussian refugees flee the Russian advance, knowing full well what capture by the Russians means, their progress slowed by snow-covered roads. Villages are set ablaze by the advancing Red Army. Those German citizens unlucky enough to get captured are brutalized—many crushed under the treads of a T-34 tank. Again, the rapes and crucifixions.

Stalin only shrugs.

"You have imagined the Red Army to be ideal, and it is not ideal, nor can it be," Stalin responds when a Yugoslavian visitor mentions the atrocities. "We have opened up our penitentiaries and stuck everybody in the army."

Over the next week, the Big Three will draw up a "Declaration on Liberated Europe." The document will touch on several points, including the unconditional surrender of Germany, trials for Nazi war criminals, reparations, development of a new international governing body known as the United Nations, and free democratic elections throughout Europe.

In addition, Germany is to be divided into four zones of occupation. Berlin itself will be split into four sections. Though French leader Charles de Gaulle is not in attendance, France will become the fourth power in the equation.

And Poland, which Soviet troops now occupy, is also "pledged to the holding of free and unfettered elections as soon as possible on the basis of universal suffrage and secret ballot."

"How soon?" Franklin Roosevelt wonders to Stalin, using a rare direct tone with the dictator. Stalin makes it clear that Poland is a vital piece of real estate for the Russians. This is the corridor through which foreign armies attack Moscow. "Will it be possible to hold elections?"

"Within a month. Unless there is some catastrophe on the front, which is improbable," Stalin answers.

As the Yalta Conference comes to an end on February 11, Churchill and Roosevelt have every faith that Joseph Stalin is telling the truth. Not just about Poland but about everything. They are committed to their ally. Roosevelt tells Stalin he made bets with his staff as to whether the Americans will capture Manila in the Philippines before the Russians take Berlin. The president is effectively ceding the German capital in return for assistance in the Pacific Theater. A coy Stalin replies that his armies are taking heavy resistance on the Oder River. The Soviet leader is quite sure the Americans will win.

"I come from the Crimea with a firm belief that we have made a start on the road to a world of peace," Roosevelt will tell Congress upon his return home. He will sail aboard the USS *Quincy*, arriving back in America on February 27, having been out of the country for over a month.

Churchill will return to London after the conference ends on February 11, enjoying brief stops in Athens and Tangiers. Beginning on February 27, he will be grilled by the House of Commons for three days about the decisions made at Yalta but will emerge with a vote of confidence. "Poor Neville Chamberlain believed he could trust Hitler," Churchill will state of his predecessor. "He was wrong. But I don't think I am wrong about Stalin."

Both leaders will soon be disabused of that notion.

Soviet foreign minister Vyacheslav Molotov approaches Stalin after the Yalta Conference. He is confused by the dictator's alliance with the Americans and British, thinking his many promises about democracy and personal liberty are at odds with the Soviet Union's agenda.

"Never mind," Stalin tells Molotov. "We'll do it our own way later."

40

It's General James Gavin's turn to wage war in the Hürtgen Forest.

Nearly thirteen hundred miles northwest of Yalta, even as the Big Three are midway through their dismembering of Germany, Gavin focuses on finally taking control of this small, wild corner of the Nazi nation.

The attack will be tomorrow. As always, the general leaves his headquarters to survey the battlefield, seeing with his own eyes the landscape over which his men will fight. He brings with him an enlisted driver and a fellow officer. The Germans have been pushed back but are still out there somewhere. The 82nd Airborne just arrived in town, tasked with finishing what the 28th Infantry could not complete three months ago: capture Schmidt. Vestiges of that November battle are everywhere, awaiting his arrival. Yet it is the terrain that immediately gets Gavin's attention.

"I learned my first lesson about the Hürtgen," he will write of his reconnaissance. Gavin firmly believes that top commanders who don't know the terrain before sending troops to fight are doomed to failure. "It couldn't be traversed by jeep. The mud was too deep and the jeep bellied down."

Gavin makes a mental assessment of the exposed ridgelines, rivers, massive dams creating man-made lakes, and the forest itself. He sees the empty foxholes, now filled with leaves and snow. The densely packed fir trees. A closer look reveals the Westwall itself, its pillboxes and rolls of barbed wire strung across the steep, wooded terrain. Trip wires, antipersonnel mines, anti-tank mines.

"They were dark and blended with the trees and landscape all around them," he writes of the now-empty enemy bunkers. Gavin has seen pillboxes before, but none as large as these, with their many rooms. "Usually, they were so covered with leaves and pine needles that they were hardly visible. I was startled when I realized I was looking right at one only a short distance away."

Gavin walks down the Kall Trail, the main transportation artery of the 28th Division—and also their November 8 escape route. This is hell on earth. The muddy path barely the width of a vehicle is cluttered with destroyed tanks, many having slid off the trail and toppled into the valley below. Gavin sees the battle clearly now, armor throwing treads in the thick mud, crews trapped inside as those tons of steel tumble into the canyon.

But there is a far more disturbing sight. Dead bodies line the side of the trail, lying stiff since November, left behind as an afterthought once the battle ended: "cadavers that had just emerged from the winter snow. Their gangrenous, broken, and torn bodies were rigid and grotesque, some of them with arms skyward, seemingly in supplication."

So much fighting has taken place in the Hürtgen Forest that it is at first hard to identify to which unit these fallen men belonged. Then General Gavin sees the telltale shoulder patch.

"They were wearing the red keystone of the 28th Infantry Division,

'The Bloody Bucket.' It had evidently fought through there the preceding fall, just before the heavy snows."

. . .

GAVIN'S TOUR OF the aftermath reveals more dead, forgotten Americans, this time at a hastily evacuated medical station where men awaiting treatment were left behind as the fighting escalated, abandoned in the haste to escape the German onslaught, now resting on the stretchers where they breathed their last. Then there are the Americans who died while laying land mines, the unexploded devices still strung across a road, just ten feet from a small cluster of German land mines. "On the other side of the mines were three or four German dead," Gavin writes. "A dramatic example of what the fighting must have been like in the Hürtgen. It was savage, bitter, and at close quarters."

Gavin and his two companions take care to remain on the muddy trail despite the difficult footing, knowing the woods have not been cleared of mines. In fact, many of these explosives, meant to maim in most horrific fashion, will still clutter the forest for the next five decades.

More carnage: "All the debris evinced a bitter struggle. There were many dead bodies, an antitank gun or two, destroyed jeeps and abandoned weapons."

The sun begins to set. Knowing the German Army might be nearby, Gavin races to leave the woods before darkness. The dramatic red hues of sunset fill the sky, leading the general to compare all he sees with Dante's *Inferno* and the lower levels of hell.

. . .

THE 82ND AIRBORNE attempts to take the village of Schmidt the next morning, where the 28th Infantry captured the church but were then devastated by unerring German artillery strikes. Gavin accompanies his men to the front, taking pity on one new replacement about to vomit at the sight of all the dead bodies. "I talked to him, calmed him down a bit, and assured him that we never abandoned our dead, that we always cared for them and buried them," the general will remember. "I knew his state of mind."

But as the attack begins, Gavin's mindset turns critical. In particular, he cannot believe the tactical blunders made by the 28th. General Norman Cota was right: The plan he was ordered to execute was deeply flawed. Having traversed the Kall Trail and seen firsthand that a jeep is useless in the muddy quagmire—which only grows worse as a ribbon of tanks and artillery pieces travels the same route—Gavin finds it ludicrous that this was the main supply route. Clearly, Cota made no attempt at personal reconnaissance—and, as the battle ended, the American men were clearly abandoned, with no thought of coming back for them. "Otherwise, the bodies would have been buried and the disabled tanks removed."

The 82nd takes Schmidt in "moderate to heavy" fighting, then digs in. Yet Gavin's dissection of what transpired will not let go of him. The sight of the unburied dead and the many lost tanks seems so easily preventable. The general is still bothered on February 17, when his victorious division is pulled off the line and returns to their training base in France.

"Reconstruction of the battle was almost too much to think about," he will write. "But as a soldier I kept thinking about it."

The daily chores of leadership do not subside for Gavin as the 82nd returns to their Sissonne barracks. There is always some task to be attended to. But Gavin remains enthralled by the mistakes made at Hürtgen, using the battle as a case study for what should be done differently next time. He comes to believe the engagement should not have been fought in the first place. And that, for the first time since D-Day, commanders went into battle without the infantry soldier's best friends: air cover and tank mobility. Simply, there was no need for the 28th to suffer six thousand casualties.

"The more senior officers frequently lacked the firsthand knowledge of the conditions under which the troops were being compelled to fight," Gavin will come to believe, not mentioning General Cota or his superiors by name.

"They had fought the battle on maps.

"And battles are not won on maps."

41

Martha Gellhorn doesn't trust Germans.

Medieval Cologne is in ruins. Two hundred and sixty-two Allied bombings since 1940. Smell of rotting flesh seeping up through the mountains of rubble. Weeds sprout in what was once the center of a great city, fertilized by corpses buried under the ruins. Downed telephone lines. Homelessness. Only the great cathedral still stands, a religious skyscraper towering over the carnage, tickling the underbellies of Allied bombers flying deeper into Germany. American troops in control, roaming the Rhine waterfront on bicycles and on foot. New green springtime grass on the far shore, where German artillery still pounds the town from a remove, killing seven civilians in the last week.

And yet, despite the horror and tragedy, there is something about this place that defies Gellhorn's sympathy.

"After the tidy villages, Cologne is a startling sight," she admits. The city's three bridges are collapsed into the Rhine. The twenty thousand remaining residents live in cellars. Millions of tons of debris are still waiting to be cleared. "We are not shocked by it, which only goes to prove that if you see enough of anything, you stop noticing it. In Germany, when you see absolute devastation you do not grieve. We have grieved for many places in many countries but this is not one of the countries."

The 82nd captured Cologne on March 5. Two days prior, while visiting British troops positioned along the Siegfried Line near the town of Jülich, Winston Churchill consecrated his first trip into Germany since the war began by ignoring the crowd of photographers traveling with his entourage. Ordering them to put their cameras away, the grinning prime minister opened his fly and urinated on Nazi soil. This display of contempt for Adolf Hitler inspired several top British generals traveling alongside him to do the same.*

That disdain for all things German is not confined to a prime minister who endured the darkest days of the London bombings.

Gellhorn's own contempt for Hitler's people is not just present but grows each day. She is traveling alone, but near enough to General James Gavin that she watches him conduct an awards ceremony on a German street and mentions him by name in her latest post. But it is the German people she watches most closely, confounded by how such ordinary individuals could have supported the Nazi war machine. "The Germans are nice and fat too," she writes with thinly veiled sarcasm. Gellhorn is horrified by the discoveries of ample food supplies in ruined Cologne. As occupied cities and countries starve, the 82nd Airborne liberates vast stores of canned fish and vegetables, cheeses, sugar, chocolate, nuts, and even syrup.

---

* Field Marshal Alan Brooke will write of Churchill's reaction: "I shall never forget the childish grin of intense satisfaction that spread all over his face as he looked down at the critical moment."

She becomes a scold: "They carry on their normal lives within seven hundred yards of their army, which is now the enemy."

None of the local citizens will admit to serving in the military, memberships in the Nazi party, or even having family serving in the fight. All claim to be innocent farmers or factory workers. "It should," she notes, "be set to music. Then the Germans would sing this refrain and that would make it even better. They all talk like this."

Gellhorn was most recently in Paris. There is a legend circulating that Gavin sent an aide to find her, insisting she leave the bar at the Lincoln and fly to the front to join him at his house at the Sissonne headquarters. She refused, so the story goes, but only for a while. Gellhorn came not just for the war, or to bed her general, but out of profound loneliness and the need to conquer that depression with work. Gavin and Gellhorn spend most nights together, playing cards and making love. "When I'm alone sorrow drowns me. This is a grief I did not know I could feel and it is very hard to bear," the journalist wrote Allen Grover of *Time* in January. Gellhorn is fond of profanity, sprinkling strong swear words into correspondence and everyday life. This candid admission to Grover, with whom she had a brief affair, is all the more profound for that lack of embellishment.

So, she travels with the 82nd—she calls them "friends," in direct opposition to her scorn for the Germans—and works on a new story for the *Saturday Evening Post*, taking a short break from *Collier's*. The local command post is a former candy factory. Her missives from the front continue to reflect the human experience of war, because she prefers to write about emotion instead of troop movements. She makes note of the 504th Regiment paddling the Rhine, observing that their boats are significantly better than the canvas collapsibles from Nijmegen. In fact, the US Navy is supplying the 82nd with legitimate invasion vessels. "These landing craft are built like enlarged shoe boxes and are propelled forward by dint of paddles, and the current is swift, and the river is wide, and on the other side was the Wehrmacht, which was not giving up by any manner of means."*

Gellhorn then leaks her insider knowledge of the 82nd's movements into her writing: "The company of paratroopers drew themselves onto a great deal of armed attention—two German divisions, it was estimated," she writes. "This small airborne action relieved pressure at another part of the front, and the company lost many men."

In fact, Gellhorn and Gavin had a blowout fight over the deaths of those paratroopers sent to form a diversion. A great number of men with whom she has grown friendly and familiar died. Gellhorn accused Gavin of negligence. The subsequent row grew so titanic that the general feared she would stumble into the night in a rage, then be shot by the enemy, because this is the sort of area where night is still a time to be vigilant. He had her placed under armed guard until tensions cooled. The fight is soon forgotten. "I have always thought that love like this was something that imaginative people wrote about in books, but something that never really happened," Gavin will write to the journalist, not sounding at all like a hardened warrior.

Martha Gellhorn has covered war in many lands—Spain, China, Poland, Finland, Sweden, and now Germany. She has seen the consequences. But there is an arrogance in the German manner that deeply nettles her. It is the people and the destruction and the fact that no one says a word she believes.

She witnesses displaced persons by the tens of thousands now released from years of slave labor by the Allied arrival. They speak of starvation rations, twelve-hour workdays, lime-filled pits in which the bodies of the dead are hurled.

---

* The United States Navy provided men and boats for the Allied river crossings of 1945. The LCVPs in use were thirty-six feet long and eleven feet wide, and were transported to the front lines on flatbed trucks. The 82nd also made use of smaller M2 assault boats on their nightly raids across the Rhine into German positions.

Recently freed British prisoners of war tell of their time in captivity: long marches, dead men left unburied, starvation. "They're not human at all," a soldier from New Zealand tells her.

"I wish they'd let us guard the German prisoners," adds one from Wales.

Gellhorn greedily writes their words in her notebook, then transfers those quotes into her story.

Not even a simple flower vendor escapes Gellhorn's derision. The man selling tulips and daffodils approaches while she sits with two soldiers in a jeep, telling that his entire family was killed by American bombers. Everyone. Forty-two relatives. All were buried when a bomb struck a cellar. He shows a photo of his sister, found headless and limbless afterward.

Rather than show sympathy, Gellhorn senses something amiss. "If forty-two members of our families had been killed by German bombs we would not talk pleasantly to Germans," she states in print.

. . .

AN AMERICAN B-26 bomber crashes on the far shore of the Rhine. The area is still in German hands. Thick pillar of black smoke rising from the wreckage. One o'clock in the afternoon. Gellhorn compares the sight to a Viking pyre. Five hours pass.

"At six o'clock began one of the strangest episodes anyone had yet seen in the war," she will remember of what follows, adding that "anyone" included members of the 82nd who had jumped into combat four times and fought at the Bulge, men who "could be expected to have seen everything."

A white flag of surrender waves near the wreckage. Then a pair of German soldiers appears, accompanied by a priest and medic carrying a stretcher. An American landing craft crosses the river, covered by gunners from the 82nd, just in case. Three more litters of US fliers are borne to the water.

Suddenly, a crowd of civilians emerges from hiding on the opposite shore to witness the handoff. As the stretchers are loaded, more German soldiers come out to the water. They promise to allow the landing craft time to return to the American side and load the wounded into ambulances. US troops, who now stand to witness the proceedings, form a crowd, gazing over at their enemy. "Everyone was out staring at everyone else," writes Gellhorn. "We could not believe it and were still prepared to dive for cover quickly."

But as the landing craft moves across the Rhine, to the middle where the current moves quickest, then near to the American shore, both sides retreat into hiding.

The intermission takes a little more than an hour.

Then war resumes.

And Martha Gellhorn's dislike for Germans continues to grow.

"You can't really learn to like these people," she will quote a British soldier.

"Unless they're dead."

42

General James Gavin prepares to lead the most dangerous jump in history.

A drop into Berlin.

Operation Eclipse, as the parachute assault is known, will beat the Russians to the German capital. The war room here at 82nd headquarters contains a secret closed compartment. Within that space, a map reveals Eclipse planning details. Eyes only. Draped in fabric whenever the door is opened or closed so that the top secret escapade remains so. Gavin will jump wearing his traditional field uniform but carry with him a spit-and-polish dress uniform to conduct diplomatic negotiations with the Germans.

"I found an abandoned military airfield not far from Sissonne, and rehearsals for the Berlin operation were commenced at once," an excited Gavin will write.

Just yesterday, the American 9th Armored Division crossed the Rhine at the town of Remagen. The bridge was destroyed in a German counterattack, but the solid Allied presence on the German side of the Rhine was the first concrete movement toward Berlin since the Battle of the Bulge. Hitler's unsuccessful offensive now a thing of the past, Dwight Eisenhower is holding several divisions in reserve to prevent another such surprise, while also acting aggressively to beat the Russians to Berlin.

Operation Eclipse is just such a mission. And the Russians are not invited to take part. It's fair to wonder whether the Nazis or the Soviets will be more shocked by the sight of thirty thousand American parachute canopies billowing down on the German capital.

The plan revolves around the 82nd landing south of Berlin's Tempelhof airfield. After capturing the facility, units will block any German attempts to counterattack while others will travel into the city, taking control long before Soviet forces can arrive. German resistance groups will guide the paratroopers, avoiding known Nazi defenses. In addition, the 17th and 101st Airborne Divisions, as well as a British airborne brigade, will play a role, capturing Rangsdorf, Gatow, Staaken, and Oranienburg airfields. Due to the high stakes of accepting the surrender of Nazi Germany, a highly detailed list of rules is being drawn up by SHAEF, outlining precisely how that is to take place, with orders that no promises be made to high-ranking German officials. For a soldier who began the war as a captain, this is a tremendous honor for Gavin.

And with the fighting coming to an end, the general knows this will likely be his last-ever combat jump—not just now but in his entire career. He will watch from the ground as 17th Airborne gets the call to drop ten thousand paratroopers across the Rhine on March 24. Calling it "an awesome spectacle," Gavin can only hope to duplicate the precision of Operation Varsity as he drops into Berlin.

"It was exciting," the general will remember of the planning. "This was to be the final battle, and to be in at the finish, after a long road from North Africa, was very much to our liking."

. . .

In Moscow, Joseph Stalin's spies tell him all about Eclipse.

Despite the secret chamber within the 82nd Airborne's war room. Despite the cloth draped over the top secret maps of Tempelhof. Despite the "need to know" restrictions about who is allowed to enter and exit that secret room, Stalin knows everything.

On March 28, Stalin meets with his top generals, Georgy Zhukov and Ivan Konev.

Zhukov is inscrutable, pugnacious, a short-tempered martinet. He led the northern flank of the Red Army as it pushed from Belorussia into Poland. His army crossed the Oder River on January 27. After a break to correct his lengthy supply lines, he is once again racing to Berlin.

Konev is bald, confident, forty-seven. He pushed the Soviet force into Germany from the south, through Ukraine and Romania. His army also crossed the Oder on January 27.

All of Central and Eastern Europe is now under Soviet control—and Joseph Stalin is not letting any of it go. His promises to share power with Britain and America are a sham. There is minor popularity for communism in France, Scandinavia, and even England. In this way, the Soviet Union and its avowed religion are creeping forward, almost totally in control of Europe.

Yet all that is in the future. Right now, the Soviet dictator craves a very specific prize.

"Two Allied divisions are being readied for a drop on Berlin," Stalin tells them, underestimating the airborne force yet aware that the element of surprise alarms his generals. Nobody would have dreamed the Allies would concoct such a bold plan. Stalin will soon sign a directive known as Stavka 11074, dividing Berlin between Zhukov's First Belorussian Army and Konev's First Ukrainian.

The dictator adds a single command: *Get there first.*

43

General George S. Patton follows in the footsteps of Julius Caesar.

Patton is in full reincarnation mode. The general claims to smell "the coppery sweat of the legions and see the low dust cloud" as he pushes his army to the Rhine. Roman roads, ruined ancient amphitheater, triumphal entrance into the city through Caesar's ancient route from Wasserbillig to Trier. The next step is crossing the Rhine, like the emperor for whom he believes he once fought as a legionnaire.

Once again, Patton's Third is along the German border, in the nation's oldest city, frustrated that Field Marshal Montgomery has been given preferential treatment for supplies and men for yet another "full-blooded thrust." The Romans captured Trier in the first century BC, naming it Augusta Treverorum. Patton took it on March 1, then enjoyed a laugh when he received official orders to detour around the city or risk losing his army.

"Have taken Trier with two divisions," he replied to the command from Eisenhower. "Do you want me to give it back?" In the past month, with heavy winter snows, subzero temperatures, and Montgomery getting the guns and gas, Patton took a short leave in Paris. He found the time away from the front a distraction, his thoughts slipping back to war even while attending the nude Folies Bergère dance revue. He used a bout of food poisoning as an excuse to return to the front lines long before his leave was over. Yet the rest before the final spring push reinvigorated the general, now nearing sixty—as did the news about Ninth Armored's Rhine crossing. Patton's own Fourth Armored now rests along the Rhine, waiting on the signal to go.

Now that Patton is back from Paris and given full permission to proceed on to Berlin, his first priority is crossing the Rhine before Montgomery. "I am going to attack as soon as possible," he recently announced. "Because at this stage in the war, time is more important than coordination."

Montgomery's Operation Plunder will see him cross the line at Wesel. Yet again, his passion for the set piece battle delays his attack. Crews of engineers from his 21st Army Group will lay down pontoons to build a bridgehead over the Rhine. In a repeat of Market Garden, Montgomery is working American general Lewis Brereton to add a paratroop element. Sixteen thousand British and Americans will drop. Plunder will be the largest offensive since D-Day.

But Plunder will not happen until March 23.

Meanwhile, Patton goes. He delights in fighting by "sixth sense," not needing weeks and months of preparation. No big buildup. No paratroops. Patton is an ardent innovator and proponent of ground troops working in close symphony with forward air protection. But his crossing of the Rhine will be much more quiet, if all goes as planned. "Without benefit of aerial bombardment, ground smoke, artillery preparation, or airborne assistance," one of Patton's officers will note.

Crossing the Rhine first represents "a glorious opportunity to score

off Montgomery." Patton has quietly collected enough bridging mate-
rial and landing craft to get his army across quickly. On March 22,
less than a week after sallying forth from Trier, advance elements of
Third Army cross the Rhine at Nierstein. Another soon crosses farther south.*

"Brad," Patton tells Omar Bradley by phone on the morning of
March 23, "don't tell anyone, but I'm across." Journalists with Third
Army were ordered to temporarily keep the moment quiet to prevent
the Germans and the Russians from knowing his exact position.

"Well, I'll be damned," Bradley responds. "You mean across the
Rhine?"

"Sure am. I sneaked a division over last night. But there are so few
Krauts around here they don't know it yet. We'll keep it a secret until
we see how it goes."

Third Army shoots down thirty-three Luftwaffe fighters attempting to destroy the new pontoon bridges. The Krauts know about him.
Only then does Patton request the glory for which he so longs.

"Brad," he states in a second call. "For God's sake, tell the world
we're across."

The next morning, Patton is just hours away from joining the
ranks of two great emperors—Napoleon and Caesar—as he is driven
across the Rhine. Montgomery has yet to launch the withering artillery fire that will presage Plunder.

"Time for a short halt," Patton orders his driver, Sergeant John
Mims. The general steps from his special jeep and ambles to the edge
of the pontoon bridge. Photographers take pictures of the promised
blending of the waters.

Warm spring day. Sun shining. Bare trees on both banks. Rhine
running brown and cold. The general balances on a plank, one boot

---

* A memorial marking the exact location of this crossing was unveiled in March
2017.

sticking out over the water. A fall here would be comical. Patton unzips his fly. Soldiers and press all around, some averting their gaze and others watching to see if this is really happening.

No time for stage fright.

Patton carefully adjusts himself.

"I've looked forward to this for a long time."

44

---

ollier's readers open today's edition to read about Martha
Gellhorn studying the ready room map.

But only from a distance. Too many P-47 pilots gathered
around the large image of Germany and its many targets in this shack.
She certainly doesn't want to stand in the way.

The flight took place weeks ago, but the story makes it into *Collier's*
only on St. Patrick's Day. For Gellhorn, it all began with fighter planes
and transports. Nonstop aircraft noise making everyone talk too loud.
Commotion. P-47 pilots going out on a mission study the map. P-47
pilots coming back confirm their kills. Outside, bitter cold, snow
swirling from prop wash, frozen mud puddles the dark burnt umber
of Georgia clay. The Luftwaffe is hardly the aerial force from the war's
early days. The fighter and bomber armadas that used to darken European skies are a thing of the past, done in by lack of airplanes, pilots,
and gasoline. Yet they still fight. German air force use of the Me 262

jet aircraft and an experienced pilot cadre still makes any aerial operation over Germany a calculated risk.

Gellhorn is not allowed to fly. But a night fighter unit has offered her a flight over Germany tonight. With the race to Berlin picking up speed, the war might be over before she has another chance. Her days of asking permission are long past. So is the need to beg forgiveness. Gellhorn just makes up her mind and finds a way, still not possessing press credentials or military identification. But it helps to be a little famous—and not the famous that came from being Ernest Hemingway's wife. Her dispatches for *Collier's* reach around the globe as her American readers send press clippings to family members on the front lines. So, when Gellhorn shows up at a very busy forward air station in the dead of winter, there's a good chance someone will let her do something dangerous if she works it hard enough.

"Across the field," Gellhorn writes in today's *Collier's*, once again pointing out the uncomfortable side effect of war known as casualties, "a fleet of C-47s was lined up and ambulances and orderlies lifted the blanketed wounded into the planes. When the cargo was completed, tier after tier of pain, the heavy freight planes moved down the runway en route to England."

Gellhorn waits. And waits. Only woman in the room. Takes notes. Flirts when she has to. The airfield in Verviers gets dark early. A disturbing quiet. Personnel disappear into their tents and makeshift squadron buildings. The daily routine of flying is done, replaced by the need to eat and sleep. Wind billows the hospital tent flaps. "A wasteland in Siberia, a plateau on the moon, the very end of the world," she sighs into her notebook.

It's not even 4:00 P.M.

"Pilots, according to myth, return from their hazardous work and have a hot bath and step into perfectly tailored uniforms and while away their spare time in a frolic of stout-hearted laughter and singing," she informs her *Collier's* readership. "Actually, they live like hell at these forward fields.

"It is only one step better than the foxhole."

. . .

THEN COMES THE night shift.

"If you're going, you'd better come with me," the major calls to the reporter. This is the moment Gellhorn has been waiting for. She is about to become one of the first female journalists to fly into combat. It is well known that the Soviet air force has a large contingent of women, many of them pilots. But tonight, Gellhorn will also become the first American woman to fly over wartime Germany. There is no telling what might happen. Last night, the same fighter squadron lost a plane in combat. A burial crew drove to the site in the morning. All they found were the four feet and two remaining hands of the pilot and radar operator.*

The night starts with dinner. Pilots and radar operators in a cold, dark house. Potbellied stove. Flight suits, fur-lined boots, brown leather jackets with unit patch on the left breast. "They passed heavy dishes of lukewarm unpalatable food around the long tables and laughed and shouted to each other, eating in haste," Gellhorn writes

---

* However, Gellhorn was hardly the only American woman to fly. Women Airforce Service Pilots (WASP) was an organization of 1,100 female pilots (out of 25,000 applicants) who ferried aircraft from factories to European bases and performed other necessary duties such as towing targets for aerial gunnery practice and serving as flight instructors. In October 1944, Ann Baumgartner, in a Bell YP-59A Airacomet, became the first American woman to fly a jet. Thirty-eight WASPs were killed in the line of duty. The WASP program was officially ended in December 1944 as the end of the war drew near. The first known female American journalist to fly into combat was photographer Margaret Bourke-White in January 1943. Female US pilots were not allowed to fly combat aircraft until 1993.

as she settles in with the men with whom she will spend a terrifying night.

There is no training. The reporter is led to Squadron Headquarters, where she is kitted out in the same warm flying pants, jacket, and boots as the men. Someone hands her an oxygen mask, which doesn't quite fit because it's made for a male head. She stands like a mannequin as a parachute is strapped onto her lithe frame. Gellhorn is sworn to secrecy, allowed to accompany the mission but censored about some of the things she will see and hear.

Among those are names. Which is why America knows her escort only as the major. Her description will have to suffice. He is blond, she notes, "a man of twenty-six but with the ageless hard tired look one is used to seeing on the faces of all the young."

Once again, the major is now at her side, handing Gellhorn an escape kit, pointing to a map, showing her how to find safety if she is shot down. "Walk southwest," he tells her.

Gellhorn will be flying in a P-61 "Black Widow," specifically designed for night fighting. Created in 1940 through a collaboration between America's Northrop Aviation and the Royal Air Force, the plane's sleek, low-slung fuselage with its long bulbous nose housing a complex radar system is painted all black. The aircraft has a high ceiling, gas tanks capable of carrying almost 640 gallons—allowing each crew to loiter over a target area—and a top speed fast enough to close quickly on the enemy. Each crew consists of a pilot, gunner, and radar operator—the last position still a novelty in aviation. Until recently, radar has been operated from the ground, then radioed to aircraft in flight. This new addition allows Black Widows to find objectives in real time, in complete darkness. Low red lighting on cockpit instruments further aids the pilot's vision. When it comes time to kill, the Black Widow can match any plane in the sky. Four 20mm Hispano M2 autocannon in the lower fuselage launch 700 rounds per minute. Another four Browning .50-caliber machine guns fire from the dorsal gun turret, controlled remotely by either the gunner or radar operator. Should he choose to do so, the pilot can lock those machine guns into a forward position and fire them himself.*

"A night fighter pilot is directed by radar to his quarry, which he cannot see, and he must not fire until he has a visual target," Gellhorn will describe. "He can be as close as two hundred yards from an enemy plane before he is certain of it."

Cold jeep ride to the plane. Dinner levity gone. No one speaks as the crew approaches the long line of black silhouettes that will soon climb into the night. "This is the worst part of any mission," says a radar operator.

Gellhorn will be nothing more than a passenger, but there is additional last-minute instruction: where to plug in her oxygen mask, where to plug in her headset, how to open the door if the plane is going down, how to jump, how to pull her rip cord. The journalist has been unusually nervous all day. Now the reality of taking flight settles over her. Cold permeates her body, so she forces herself to think of something else. This leads to irrational fears of accidentally making a mistake that will spill her into the night sky at a high altitude. Her improvised seat is a sofa cushion and a crate—the P-61 was never meant to carry four.

She hears the major in the cockpit making last-minute decisions as he talks to ground control and pilots in other planes, "as calm and sensible as if you were talking about whether there was enough gas in the car to get to the country club."

And then they are airborne. Gellhorn struggles to take in the

---

* Northrop will later go on to become a major power in the aviation industry, but at the time it bid for the Black Widow project, the company was only one year old. With more established companies like Grumman Aviation already committed to other projects, Northrop was able to win the contract and establish itself. Northrop and Grumman will merge in 1994. Northrop Grumman is now a $30-billion-per-year company.

competing sensations of speed, loft, and the sudden appearance of a bold moon drawing nearer and nearer as the major lifts the Black Widow higher into the sky at 265 miles per hour.

"We were over Germany, and a blacker, less inviting piece of land I never saw. It was covered with snow. There were mountains, there was no light and no sign of human life, but the land itself looked actively hostile," she writes.

Gellhorn hears a voice over the radio—someone on the ground passing instructions to the major. "Roger" is his only reply.*

The plane lurches sharply upward, as if pulled by a galactic rope, doubling altitude from eleven thousand feet to twenty-two thousand in seconds. Gravitational forces press Gellhorn down into the crate. Straps from her too-large oxygen mask wrap tightly around her throat. Her nose won't stop running. The temperature inside the plane drops to thirty below zero.

"I thought," she will write, "that my stomach was going to be flattened against my backbone."

Up front, she knows the major wears far less clothing as he flies. The small cockpit won't allow him a full range of motion to maneuver if he wears the same bulky gear as Gellhorn and the rest of the crew. She marvels that he endures this bone-crushing cold for two to three hours at a time, night after night.

The Black Widow continues climbing. Abruptly, the major banks hard and shoves the nose down, racing back to earth. As airspeed approaches the aircraft's maximum of 366 miles per hour, the journalist struggles to remain atop her crate. Whatever novelty she once felt about flying a combat mission is past. A miserable Gellhorn questions her decision to fly, even irritated by the calm voice of the major speak-

---

* "Roger" grew out of the word "received," as a radio acknowledgment of instructions. "Received" was shortened to "r" because non-English speaking pilots have trouble with that word. "Roger" was the solution, its jaunty formality belying the elaborate acronym "Received Order Given, Expect Results."

ing to her over the intercom. The communication is one-way. All she can do is listen. Gellhorn has no frame of awareness, no sense of what is happening or what she is seeing. The major, when he is not seeking out targets, thoughtfully educates his passenger.

"Everything was calm now, except for the fact that we were still over Germany," she writes. "Then the pilot called to me on the intercom, and, looking where he told me, I saw the trail of a V-2. It came from somewhere deeper inside Germany and was at this distance a red ball of fire."

Gellhorn, still nauseated from the abrupt climb and descent, is nonetheless fascinated. She fixates on a bright star in the nighttime sky, thinking it might be enemy fire. So far, the night has been a bust in terms of shooting down German planes—"hose the Huns" as the Black Widow pilots like to describe their kills, finding nothing poetic in "clobber the Herman," as P-47 pilots call the same act.

Almost two hours into the flight, Gellhorn wants it to be over. The major points out antiaircraft fire in the distance and she feels sorry for the Allied pilots enduring the barrage. Only then does she realize the flak is aimed at her.

"We did another quick aerial pirouette," she writes, "and roared for home. We landed as we had taken off, which is to say like a bolt of lightning."

Later, the major laments that tonight was boring. He takes Gellhorn for drinks with the P-47 pilots, who are alternately celebrating the birth of one young flier's baby daughter and mourning the loss of a beloved squadron leader. Cigars. Backslapping. No names.

Gellhorn and the major say their goodbyes at the headquarters shack. "Well, so long," he tells the reporter.

"Come and see us again. Give you a ride anytime."

TAKING BERLIN

——◆——

45

General George S. Patton's race to Berlin is over.

So is General James Gavin's Operation Eclipse.

Patton stays up late, absorbing the news. Ike and Omar Bradley paid a visit to Patton's headquarters to deliver the message in person just moments ago. Willie rests at Patton's feet.

We "had a very pleasant evening, in the course of which General Eisenhower gave me a stop line and explained his reasons," Patton will remember. It's been an emotional day. Patton, Ike, and Bradley toured the horrors of the Buchenwald concentration camp. They also stepped into a salt mine discovered by Patton's troops, filled with art and cash pilfered by the Nazis.

Upon taking command of SHAEF early in 1944, Eisenhower's orders from the Allied Combined Chiefs of Staff were to "enter the continent of Europe, and, in conjunction with the other United Nations, undertake operations aimed at the heart of Germany and the destruction of her armed forces."

Ike believes he has done all that. Now, the zones of German occupation having been determined at Yalta two months ago, Ike is handing Berlin to the Russians.

"From a tactical point of view, it was highly inadvisable for the American Army to take Berlin, and he hoped political influence would not cause him to take the city. It had no tactical or strategical value and would place upon American forces the burden of caring for thousands and thousands of Germans, displaced persons, Allied prisoners of war," as fellow general Hobart Gay will remember of Eisenhower's comments.

Soviet marshal Georgi K. Zhukov is only forty-three miles from Berlin. He has nearly a million men arrayed along the eastern banks of the Oder River. Fearing heavy German resistance, he has delayed his assault on the capital for two months but is now just weeks from launching the final attack. The Allies, in order to beat Zhukov and the Russians to Berlin, must first cross the Elbe River, then cross fifty miles of lowland lakes, streams, and canals. Expected casualties number one hundred thousand British and American troops.

Yet even if that high price is paid off with the great success of Americans reaching Berlin first, the boundaries agreed upon in Yalta mean that the conquered land must be immediately given over to Russian control when the war ends. "A pretty stiff price to pay for a prestige objective," Bradley has informed Eisenhower.

More than two weeks ago, on March 28, Eisenhower requested that the Allied military missions in Moscow inform Joseph Stalin of his intention to halt at the Elbe River. Eisenhower does not say as much, but his plan from there is to send one army north to prevent the Russians from seizing Baltic and North Sea ports. A second force, led by George Patton, will remain in the south, pushing into Czechoslovakia and Austria.

In London, Winston Churchill is furious. He wants to take Berlin at all costs, politics and Yalta agreements be damned. He now knows Stalin has no intention of keeping his promises. Churchill's commanders are outraged that a soldier like Eisenhower has ventured into the realm of diplomacy.

Patton doesn't like it. He believes the Russians are going to take and hold as much land as possible. It is up to the Allies to get there first. His advance across Germany since crossing the Rhine has been yet another triumph. The German High Command spends an inordinate amount of time locating Patton, considering him the Allies' top general. Every day, the Nazis worry about his next phantom attack. "Where is he? When will he attack? Where? How? When? With what?" one captured German officer will admit under interrogation.

Robert Reid of the BBC marveled at the pace of Patton's progress. "This is surely the fastest advance in the history of war," Reid told his listeners. "An advance where divisional command posts make big jumps forward two or three times a day, which is some indication of the way things are going out here."

But now Patton is halted. He has been ordered to stop on the west bank of the Mulde River, west of Dresden, a city destroyed in two nights of incendiary bombing in February.

"Ike, I don't see how you figure that one," Patton replied. "We had better take Berlin—and quick—then go on to the Oder."

The general stays up long after Eisenhower and Bradley leave his headquarters. Before turning in, he notices that his watch has stopped. Patton turns on the radio to get the time. Instead, he hears the shocking news that President Franklin Roosevelt is dead.

A stunned Patton goes out into the night. Willie follows.

Crossing the Rhine was a moment of supreme glory. But winning the ultimate battle in Berlin would have been the perfect finale to a life in uniform.

"Sometimes I feel I may be nearing the end of this life," he writes Beatrice. "I have . . . licked the Germans, so what else is there to do?

"Remember that I love you."

. . .

ONE WEEK LATER, on April 19, Patton's Third Army is in Czechoslovakia. He is pushing east as fast as he can to prevent a Soviet takeover. Third Army's tanks advance at the rate of fifteen miles per day. The Soviets are headed directly at the general's army, marching in his direction from Vienna. Patton is unsure whether or not he will fight America's "Allies," but he will definitely fire if fired upon.

The general is summoned to Omar Bradley's headquarters in Wiesbaden. There, Dwight Eisenhower tells him to halt.

Once again, a frustrated George S. Patton does as he is told.

46

General James Gavin will not fight in the final battle.

But this morning he sets out on one last mission.

Operation Eclipse is off. There will be no aerial drop on Berlin. Instead, the general crosses the Elbe in search of Germans, Russians, and anything else he might find. The general's jeep glides through quiet countryside. British field marshal Bernard Law Montgomery refused to send his troops across the Elbe, concerned about major combat with a large, entrenched German force. Gavin has no such fears.

First light. Gavin drives out with a reconnaissance patrol on a morning so beautiful he will remember it for decades: green fields, white chestnut trees, orange poppies, bright yellow crocus.

No sign of war.

As Gavin's jeep enters a small town, a lone German soldier on a motorcycle tries to flee but instead crashes into a ditch. Gavin and his patrol take the man prisoner and begin immediate interrogation. Yet

289

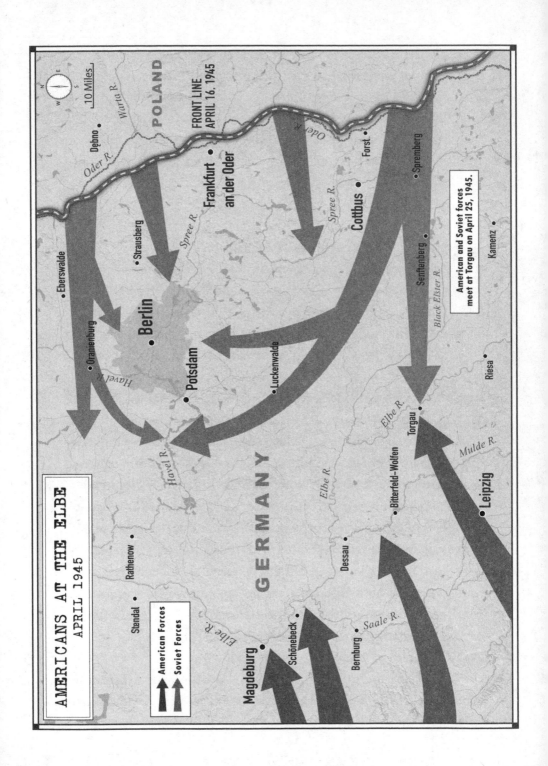

AMERICANS AT THE ELBE
APRIL 1945

American Forces
Soviet Forces

10 Miles

N
W E
S

POLAND

FRONT LINE
APRIL 16, 1945

American and Soviet forces
meet at Torgau on April 25, 1945.

GERMANY

Warta R.

Dębno

Oder R.

Oder R.

Frankfurt
an der Oder

Spree R.

Spree R.

Forst

Cottbus

Spremberg

Kamenz

Strausberg

Eberswalde

Berlin

Oranienburg

Potsdam

Havel R.

Luckenwalde

Senftenberg

Black Elster R.

Riesa

Havel R.

Elbe R.

Torgau

Mulde R.

Rathenow

Elbe R.

Bitterfeld-Wolfen

Leipzig

Stendal

Dessau

Elbe R.

Saale R.

Magdeburg

Schönebeck

Bernburg

there is something quite different about this prisoner: "He was the last German in the war we were to see running away," Gavin will write with unintended sentiment.

Instead, Wehrmacht soldiers soon emerge cautiously from the woods along the road. But they no longer wish to fight. The Russians are somewhere not far behind. These Germans are walking west to surrender to Americans. They are mostly young men, some still teenagers. Hungry, unkempt, dirty from sleeping rough, they are very much a beaten army.

But Gavin is rattled. The war is ending, that is for sure, but before him stand the men who laid the mines that killed and maimed thousands of Allied soldiers, aimed the deadly 88s, fired machine-gun bursts from pillboxes, sniped. There is a *very* good chance someone here fought and killed men of the 82nd. "It was an eerie sight for those of us who had fought for more than three years all the way from Africa, for the mere sight of the bucket helmet meant certain death unless someone reacted instantly and instinctively, taking cover and firing," the general will write.

Soon, the 82nd is taking prisoners by the thousands. Montgomery was right in believing a large German force existed across the Elbe, but very wrong in his belief about their intentions. Gavin will capture 150,000 prisoners—a complete German Army Group—today and tomorrow. The Germans are told to throw down their guns and make their way to the American lines. It is a reversal of France in 1940, when the German advance was so quick that the surrendering French soldiers voluntarily walked to prison camps. Now, the Germans load into their own vehicles and drive west, some two thousand trucks in all. The narrow country lanes cannot support the traffic. Movement slows. Refugees eager to flee the Soviets join the column, adding to the chaos. "The confusion," Gavin writes, "went on day and night."

Only later will the general learn that his division just captured the entire German 21st Army.

The war is over for the Germans. It is almost over for James Gavin and the 82nd. But there is still no end to death. And as callous as Gavin has become to the sights and smells of corpses, more horrors await.

· · ·

GENERAL GAVIN SETS up his headquarters in the enormous Ludwigs-lust Palace. There, among walls lined with oil paintings and mirrors, ornate chandeliers hanging from the ceiling, he accepts the surrender of German general Von Tippelskirch. The 82nd soon learns of a nearby concentration camp named Wöbbelin, where they liberate four thousand emaciated prisoners slowly being starved to death. "The dead we buried in a park in front of the palace, where we required the German citizens to dig the graves and place the bodies in them. The entire population of the town was required to attend the burial service," the general writes matter-of-factly.

Gavin is appalled by the camp but not stunned. Death has become commonplace. The concentration camps were a more barbaric version of war, if only because the weak, young, and innocent were among the murdered.

· · ·

GAVIN IS TWENTY miles east of the Elbe River—twenty miles more than he is technically allowed by Eisenhower's agreement with Joseph Stalin.

With that in mind, General Gavin and the 82nd go forth to find the Russians.

47

Americans aren't welcome on the Soviet side of the Elbe River. Not even a very persistent Martha Gellhorn.

Two hundred miles south of General James Gavin and the 82nd Airborne's position on the Elbe, the reporter is also meeting the Soviets. An old Saxon castle looks out over the river, where a pontoon bridge stretches several hundred yards from the US side to the Russian-controlled shore. Sunny spring day. A single Soviet guard who calls everyone "Amerikanski" guards the crossing. Unwashed. Small. Eager.

The Elbe is the agreed-upon line where American troops must halt their advance through Germany. On April 25, for the first time in the war, soldiers from the United States and the Soviet Union linked up south of this old village. An American reconnaissance patrol spotted Soviet troops on the far bank among hundreds of German refugees fleeing the fighting. The Americans found a boat and rowed across, completing the ceremonial linkup between Allies who had never before fought together or laid eyes on one another. There were no journalists or cameras to record the moment, so it was agreed that the meeting would be repeated later that afternoon here in Torgau for the media. Which it was.

But once the backslapping was done, and with it the hugs and awkward attempts to speak each other's language, the Russians pronounced that the Americans were no longer welcome on the eastern side of the Elbe. Which is precisely the sort of challenge Martha Gellhorn delights in defying.

As she badgers the Soviet guarding the pontoon crossing, she notes the overall lack of hygiene on the part of the Allies, writing that "the Russians all looked like they hadn't had time for a bath since Stalingrad."

The journalist and her driver use their partial knowledge of several languages to request permission to get to the other side: Spanish, English, German, even a little Russian.

"*Nyet,*" comes the response. No.

Gellhorn sees female Russian soldiers, a novelty. A nurse wearing a gun on her hip. The Russians go back and forth all day, but Americans are forbidden from crossing.

Getting over to the fresh green grass on the Soviet shore becomes the writer's mission. She finds a headquarters and pleads with a Russian colonel whose "handshake has the death squeeze of a grizzly bear." Gellhorn even accepts his offer of hard-boiled eggs, sausage, and honey for dinner. She flirts and smokes.

Still, "*Nyet.*"

A second colonel arrives. The drinking starts. Toasts to "Treeman." Gellhorn thinks it's a Russian toast until she realizes America's allies are invoking the name of the new president.

Gellhorn acquires an interpreter, a Polish Jew whose family was murdered by the Germans. His four-month-old was killed with a pistol butt to the skull, he tells her. But the sad talk makes the colonel uncomfortable and he pulls Gellhorn away. Together, they walk the streets of Torgau after dark, where she gets her first real glimpse of the tapestry known as the Red Army, but gets no closer to crossing the pontoon bridge.

"Blonds and Mongols and fierce-looking characters with nineteenth-century mustaches and children about sixteen, and it felt like a vast encampment of nomad people, where everyone is eating around campfires, singing, playing cards, and getting ready to roll into blankets and sleep," she writes.

Gellhorn asks the colonel when she can cross the Elbe.

"Two weeks," she is told, to which the reporter grimly assures herself she will be very far from Torgau in two weeks.

Gellhorn explodes. She reminds the colonel, through her Polish interpreter, that Soviet correspondents are allowed to travel freely with American units. She accuses the colonel and all the Russian people of being suspicious and overtly political, focused on the divide between capitalists and communists. "They agreed to this but said that nothing in their army was done without permission; the permission had not been granted yet," she writes.

Stonewalled, she returns to the pontoon bridge in the morning. Gellhorn makes small talk with the American soldiers on hand, smoking and watching the river flow in the pale morning light. Someone has painted the boats supporting the bridge the color green. Small trees have been placed in bows and sterns, forming a lovely esplanade.

A progression begins. While the American army is asking permission to cross the Elbe, a massive Soviet force marches west, taking over the bridge as if all Germany belonged to them. "It came and flowed over the stone quay and up on the roads like water rising, like ants, like locusts. It was not so much an army as the whole of the world on the move," Gellhorn writes of the horde.

There is no formation, no order of battle. Just soldiers in all sorts of uniforms carrying all sorts of weapons. Clearly, these troops are not headed for Berlin, one hundred miles north. It seems their goal is nothing less than pushing as far westward as possible. The Americans are respecting the Elbe as a line of demarcation, but the Soviets see it as just one more river in the hundreds of rivers they've crossed in this long, dirty war. "They looked tired and rather indifferent," she jots in her notebook, "and definitely experienced."

Trucks, handcarts, old horses pulling wagons. Geysers on the smooth river surface as playful Soviets hurl grenades into the current.

And wives. And girlfriends. The Soviets have no issue with women going to war with their lovers. The journalist shrugs, thinking the notion a fine idea. But Gellhorn also reminds her readers that no ordinary woman can make it in wartime. "These were no glamour girls," she writes with a bit of pride, not letting on that she's maintained her polish and sharp appearance despite a year of hardship. The Lincoln Hotel might be home base, but she's at the front far more often than Paris. Yet Gellhorn knows a thing or two about camp followers. These Soviet women are of a completely different stripe.

"They were peasants and they looked as if no hardship could be too much for them, no roads too long, no winter too cruel, no danger too great."

The long line of Soviets continues to cross—bicycles, more trucks, an ambulance with little red crosses painted on the side. Gellhorn remains sitting on a low wall on the bank. She notes a few soldiers wearing medals from the Battle of Stalingrad, three thousand miles away.

Two nearby American soldiers marvel at the Russians, admiring their obvious toughness.

"I guess they'll push us back to the Rhine pretty soon," one says.

"I hope they push us back quick," replies his buddy, the taller of the two. "I hope they take all of Germany. They'll know how to handle it, brother. They really know. Suits me. What I want is to go home."

48

Martha Gellhorn bears witness.

Her father is Jewish. So is her maternal grandfather. Now, just inside the electric fences of this place known as Dachau, on the edge of a leafy Munich suburb on this glorious spring morning just hours after the war ended, among rows of barracks and torture chambers and crematoriums where the dead were burned and simple walls where men and women were lined up and shot by teen-aged German soldiers, the reporter who has seen everything now sees the unthinkable. It is a moment that will change her forever.

The air smells of rotten flesh, dried blood, feces.

"The skeletons sat in the sun and searched themselves for lice. They have no age and no faces. They all look alike and like nothing you will ever see if you are lucky," Gellhorn writes of the survivors of Adolf Hitler's horrific attempt to kill every Jew in Europe. "They watched us but did not move; no expression shows on a face that is only yellowish, stubby skin, stretched across bone."

There have been rumors of places like this for years. Citizens escaping European countries have long told of death camps where Hitler kills those he despises: attorneys, priests, Roma, homosexuals, and any other individual deemed subversive. But mostly he kills Jews.

Beginning in July 1944 and the Soviet rampage through Eastern Europe, rumors of these camps proved true. Majdanek, Belzec, Treblinka, and Auschwitz were revealed as Poland fell into Russian hands. The British captured Bergen-Belsen three weeks ago. General George S. Patton was so enraged after visiting Buchenwald that he forced the local population to come see for themselves the piles of naked dead bodies. "We are told that the American soldier does not know what he is fighting for," Patton pronounced. "Now, at least, he will know what he is fighting against."

· · ·

GENERAL JAMES GAVIN and the 82nd Airborne liberated the Wöbbelin concentration camp on May 2, coming across one thousand dead. "Even our hatred for the German, deep-seated and intense as it was, was to be added to when we found the concentration camp a few miles from here," the sickened general wrote afterward. "The first burgomeister committed suicide with his family the night that I arrived. We couldn't understand why until we found the camp.

"Those things must never be forgotten."

· · ·

So, MARTHA GELLHORN knows in advance what she will see today. Marguerite Higgins of the *Herald Tribune* has already written extensively about Dachau. Soldiers of the US Seventh Army are talking in shocked tones about the fifty boxcars filled with the dead they found while liberating the camp last week. In a final rush to exterminate Jews, thousands were immediately hauled by train to Dachau to continue Hitler's "Final Solution," only to die from thirst and suffocation, locked in cattle cars on railroad sidings as they awaited murder. When they didn't die fast enough, pleading with their captors to unlock the boxcars, German soldiers fired through the wooden doors.

When Gellhorn writes of Dachau, it is like confiding in a dear friend. "I do not know how to explain it, but aside from the terrible anger you feel," she notes of all she sees today, "you are ashamed for mankind."

The journalist interviews liberated prisoners. One tells of experiments performed on inmates, all of whom knew of their use as guinea pigs to gauge the effects of water, cold, and oxygen deprivation on the human body. She is perplexed. "Didn't they scream? Didn't they cry out?"

The Polish doctor explaining the experiments has been in captivity five years, first at Buchenwald and now Dachau. "There was no use in this place for a man to scream or cry out. It was no use for any man, ever," he explains with a smile. He is six feet tall and weighs one hundred pounds. That smile missing four teeth looks like a broken comb.

Gellhorn does not so much listen to the men guiding her around the camp as endure the endless monologue of tortures and punishments: castration and sterilization; lashing, standing for days on end without food or a place of relief, wrists bound behind backs and then lifted upward on a hook until shoulders separate.

And Dachau is not new. First built in 1933, it is the original concentration camp. Thousands have died here through starvation, working as slave labor, or being gassed. "Last February and March," Gellhorn writes, "two thousand were killed in the gas chamber because, though they were too weak to work, they did not have the grace to die, so it was arranged for them."

So it is that Gellhorn walks to the far end of Dachau, site of the vast brick crematorium. Ironically, it rises next to the glass house where prisoners grew flowers and vegetables for their Nazi captors. "We have all seen a great deal now," Gellhorn tells her readers. This will be her last missive from World War II. "We have seen hospitals, bloody and messy as butcher shops; we have seen the dead like bundles, lying on all the roads of half the earth. But nowhere was there anything like this.

"Nothing about war was ever as insanely wicked as these starved and outraged naked, nameless, dead."

. . .

MARTHA GELLHORN IS speaking to the tall Polish doctor with missing teeth when another former prisoner shuffles over and whispers something in his ear. She is surprised to see the doctor clap his hands together. She intrudes, asking to be told the message.

Word has arrived that Field Marshal Bernard Law Montgomery accepted the enemy's terms of surrender at six P.M. last night.

"War is over," the doctor tells Gellhorn.

"Germany is defeated."

49

The doctor is wrong.

The final battle rages.

"Hitler made his final and supreme decision to stay in Berlin to the end," Winston Churchill will write. "The capital was soon completely encircled by the Russians and the Fuehrer had lost all power to control events. It remained for him to organize his own death amid the ruins of the city."

As the Russians close in, Hitler poisons his dog, watches his wife, Eva, take poison, then shoots himself in the head. Loyal staff carries him from the bunker where he died, then burns his body until only dental remains are left.

Berlin is left to the Russians. The atrocities carried out in villages far from the capital are even worse. No woman is safe from rape and the most horrible forms of mutilation. Men fighting to defend their homes are shot, their bodies defiled with bayonets and more bullet holes. The city burns everywhere, fires big and small, grand boulevards reduced to rubble by Russian bombardment. The Soviet flag flies from the bullet-pocked Reichstag, once the seat of German power.

Berlin has been taken.

And it will not be free again for more than four decades.

. . .

FOUR HUNDRED MILES south in the village of Riedlingen, a teenaged German soldier too young to shave deserts his post. His mother is already in Allied custody, being questioned about her famous late husband—telling interrogators the truth about his cause of death rather than allowing Hitler's lie to define Erwin Rommel's final moments.

It was May 10, 1940, when Rommel played a vital role in the first hours of the war on the Western Front by attacking through the Ardennes, then racing across France, accepting the surrender of thousands of French soldiers. Five years later, almost to the day, sixteen-year-old Manfred Rommel—once a patriot but now a deserter from the lost Nazi cause—throws down his rifle and raises his hands in the air.

The French First Army takes him into custody.

EPILOGUE

Winston Churchill is not a good poker player.

Today's speech is entitled "Sinews of Peace." Churchill rises and approaches a lectern wrapped in floral garland. Elevated stage. Off-white curtain, two American flags, and bouquet of lilies as backdrop. He wears crimson cap and gown over his black waistcoat for today's lecture in the Westminster College gymnasium. A single Paramount movie camera purrs, recording this moment. President Truman, to whom the former prime minister lost several hundred dollars playing cards on the eighteen-hour train ride from Washington, sits to Churchill's right, in black graduation gown and mortarboard.

. . .

IT IS LESS than a year since the war's end, but so much has happened.

"Death, in time," General George S. Patton told Third Army in his memorable speeches, "comes to all men." And so it has come for Patton. Tragically, the general is dead, the result of a car accident. There is suspicion of Soviet involvement. Willie was flown home to live with Beatrice.

General James Gavin is posted to Berlin. Martha Gellhorn fre-

303

quently visits, their affair in its second year. The general plans to propose marriage. But love in wartime is one thing; daily life on a peacetime post is another. She will say no.

General Norman Cota is retiring from the army.

Manfred Rommel has been interrogated by the Allies and released. Manfred and George S. Patton's son, also George Patton, will become great friends—but only decades from now, when Manfred becomes mayor of Stuttgart—a post he will hold for over twenty years—and the younger Patton returns to Germany as a general in the United States Army.

Winston Churchill has been voted out of office. Just weeks after victory in Europe, the people of Great Britain decided it was time for change.

The former prime minister wants back in the game. The journey starts this afternoon.

. . .

EARLIER, THE PRESIDENT and the prime minister were driven through the streets of Fulton, standing side by side in a top-down convertible Cadillac draped in red, white, and blue bunting. Warm day. Still no leaves on the stately maples and elms lining Main Street. Missouri is Truman's home state. He is unpopular with many Americans who still pine for the paternal leadership of Franklin D. Roosevelt but clearly loved in the American heartland.

Churchill is adored no less. He doffed his hat and waved to the crowd, grinning as he flashed his two-fingered "V for victory" salute. His fingertips were not turned inward, in the defiant pose of Britain's Agincourt archers, but outward in a show of solidarity, as he did so many days and nights during World War II.* The former prime

---

* The Battle of Agincourt, fought on October 25 (St. Crispin's Day), 1415, was a triumph for Great Britain. This is the same battle celebrated in Shakespeare's *Henry V,* best known for the king's speech to his troops. The British archers were highly feared by their French foes for incredible accuracy—capable of firing an arrow through the

minister likes Truman a great deal, describing the president as having a "gay, precise, sparkling manner and obvious power of decision."

"Welcome Churchill" pronounces a banner suspended over the street, fluttering like a flag in the stiff breeze.

More applause as Churchill and Truman amble through a corridor of photographers, reporters, and local citizens outside the gym. Then still more standing-room cheers as the two men walk into the gymnasium for the awarding of an honorary degree and then this speech by Churchill.

The former prime minister has long been troubled by the behavior of Joseph Stalin and the Soviet Union. His own role in the division of European nations between the former Allies has been a fool's game. It sickens a seasoned politician like Churchill to know he has been played. Millions of non-Soviets now suffer under Stalin's rule, all because Churchill and Franklin Roosevelt labored under the false belief that the dictator was their friend. Right now, even the grinning Truman feels that way—although he has decided to send the USS *Missouri* to Asia in a show of strength against Soviet saber-rattling.

For all Churchill's misgivings, it is a speech Stalin made just last month that fuels his oratory motivation. Stalin spoke to his party congress, stating that the Soviet Union was placing the production of arms before consumer goods. He blamed this need on the capitalist influence over the rest of the world. But the undercurrent was war— whenever and wherever he might insert Soviet influence to complete a course of global domination. Stalin and Churchill have long jabbed at

---

eye slits of facial armor from a hundred yards across the battlefield. When the French captured a British archer, their common practice was to cut off the first two fingers of the bow hand so their enemy could never fire his weapon again. For this reason, British archers taunted the French from the other side of the battlefield by holding up a two-fingered salute. Incidentally, this gesture is different from the waving of the middle finger, which dates to Athens, in the fourth century BC—extended finger representing a phallus.

one another through their public comments. But the wording was always coded, meant to be understood by reading between the lines.

This time, Stalin's comments were as direct as he could have possibly been.

Tonight, Churchill will do the same.

Churchill was in Florida at the time of Stalin's address, enjoying a warm February away from poverty-stricken postwar London. But the dictator's words sent a chill through the former prime minister. Since his removal from office, Churchill has sought a way to reinsert himself into global politics. After he spent five years not just immersed in that arena but as one of its key players, being shut out brings him little happiness. But the warmth of the Missouri crowd and this small-town fanfare are cause for enthusiasm.

So as Churchill stands before the gymnasium audience, smile on his face, he delivers the speech he wrote on the train before being beaten so badly at poker. Truman had originally preferred not to pre-read the text but gave in. "Brilliant," the president told Churchill, handing it back, adding that it would "create quite a stir."

Winston Churchill would love nothing more.

.   .   .

"I AM GLAD to come to Westminster College this afternoon, and am complimented that you should give me a degree. The name 'Westminster' is somehow familiar to me," the prime minister begins, to polite chuckles. The Missouri crowd enjoys the comparison between their college and the London centerpiece.

Churchill continues with words of thanks and of the freedoms to be found in America. Then he begins the slow descent into the meat of his message. "Let me, however, make it clear that I have no official mission or status of any kind, and that I speak only for myself. There is nothing here but what you see.

"I can therefore allow my mind, with the experience of a lifetime, to play over the problems which beset us on the morrow of our absolute victory in arms, and to try to make sure with what strength I have that what has been gained with so much sacrifice and suffering shall be preserved for the future glory and safety of mankind."

A restlessness in the crowd. Churchill was originally asked to set up temporary residence here and deliver a series of messages. The president of Westminster College's request made its way to Truman's Oval Office desk, where Truman wrote a personal endorsement before sending Churchill the invitation.

But several lectures are too much for the former prime minister. One is enough to say what is on his mind. And today, for the first time, those thoughts publicly confess that Great Britain is no longer the world's greatest power. Her empire is gone, and she can barely feed her people. Even Churchill himself is under enormous personal financial strain.

"The United States stands at this time at the pinnacle of world power. It is a solemn moment for the American Democracy. For with primacy in power is also joined an awe-inspiring accountability to the future. If you look around you, you must feel not only the sense of duty done but also you must feel anxiety lest you fall below the level of achievement. Opportunity is here now, clear and shining for both our countries . . . We must, and I believe we shall, prove ourselves equal to this severe requirement," Churchill states.

The room is still. Thirteen men are arrayed on the dais—politicians, university staff, local dignitaries—but none of them matter on the *world* stage. It is the presence of Harry Truman within reach of Churchill that reinforces his remarks. Stalin will surely be informed that the president of the United States, until now so forgiving to the Soviets, agrees with these sentiments—otherwise, he would have found a way to remain off this platform.

"The awful ruin of Europe, with all its vanished glories," Churchill continues, "glares us in the eyes. When the designs of wicked men or the aggressive urge of mighty States dissolve over large areas the frame of civilized society, humble folk are confronted with difficulties with which they cannot cope. For them all is distorted, all is broken, even ground to pulp."

He speaks of famine, the United Nations, the atomic bomb, Magna Carta, habeas corpus. The audience came this afternoon to hear the inspiring words of a seventy-one-year-old friend of America. What they did not expect was the most concise and overarching analysis of world affairs many have ever heard. Ten minutes into his speech, Churchill brings the words into tighter focus.

"Now, while still pursuing the method of realizing our overall strategic concept, I come to the crux of what I have traveled here to say," Churchill tells the audience.

"Neither the sure prevention of war, nor the continuous rise of world organization will be gained without what I have called the fraternal association of the English-speaking peoples. This means a special relationship between the British Commonwealth and Empire and the United States."

"Special relationship" will be one enduring phrase emerging from this speech. The bond of trust forged during World War II will continue.

The other phrase will be even more defining.

"From Stettin in the Baltic to Trieste in the Adriatic, an iron curtain has descended across the Continent. Behind that line lie all the capitals of the ancient states of Central and Eastern Europe. Warsaw, Berlin, Prague, Vienna, Budapest, Belgrade, Bucharest and Sofia, all these famous cities and the populations around them lie in what I must call the Soviet sphere, and all are subject in one form or another, not only to Soviet influence but to a very high and, in many cases, increasing measure of control from Moscow."

No one talks about the Soviets like that, certainly not to the American public. Churchill addresses the former ally as a toxic entity, certainly not a friend. It's a little confusing to the audience.

And yet: Iron curtain.

A description so apt and easy to see.

Churchill mentions Yalta, when everything was given away. Takes full blame.

"I am convinced that there is nothing they admire so much as strength," Churchill adds. "There is nothing for which they have less respect than for weakness, especially military weakness."

The former prime minister ramps up for the grand finale with a dire warning: "Catastrophe may overwhelm us all . . .

"Last time I saw it all coming and cried aloud to my own fellow-countrymen and to the world, but no one paid any attention."

AFTERWORD

At the time of this writing, Winston Churchill's words are proving as true now as they did in 1946. The "Iron Curtain" was very real at the time of his Missouri speech but ceased to exist after the fall of the Soviet Union on Christmas Day, 1991. Churchill's metaphor became very real in August 1961, when the Soviets built a barrier around their portion of Berlin so that citizens could not escape to freedom. That "Berlin Wall" was knocked down on November 9, 1989, heralding the coming end of the Soviet Union.

The Anglo-British "special relationship" became a bedrock world alliance after Churchill's 1946 speech, never stronger than the connection between President Ronald Reagan and Prime Minister Margaret Thatcher, which ultimately brought down the Soviet Empire.

Yet in 2022, Russian president Vladimir Putin, a ruler with a Stalin-like determination to expand his nation's sphere of influence, sought to rebuild the Iron Curtain. Russian troops invaded the former Soviet territory known as Ukraine, mercilessly slaughtering and torturing civilians.

Putin had notably meddled in the 2016 United States presidential election, ensuring that a candidate favorable to his regime was elected. His invasion of Ukraine was lauded by former president Donald Trump, an individual who previously sought the end of Churchill's "special relationship" by downplaying the need for an Anglo-American alliance.

Yet the special relationship endures.

As does the Russian threat to world peace.

. . .

WINSTON CHURCHILL SUCCESSFULLY returned to the prime minister's role on October 26, 1951. He focused his foreign policy on maintaining a defensive buffer with the Soviet Union and reluctantly overseeing the independence of several former British colonies. This time in office also coincided with Dwight Eisenhower's presidency. While they were once friends, Churchill grew impatient with Ike, in particular the president's faith in nuclear weapons as a means of deterrence. Churchill remained prime minister until resigning in 1955. He continued to serve in the House of Commons but finally stood down for health reasons in 1964. First elected to Parliament in October 1900, he served as a member continuously from then until his retirement, with the exception of a two-year departure from 1922 to 1924. Winston Churchill died in London on January 24, 1965, at the age of ninety. He lay in state at Westminster Hall for three days before funeral services at St. Paul's Cathedral. His coffin was then borne down the Thames by boat before traveling by train from Waterloo Station to his final resting place at St. Martin's Church in Bladon, near his birthplace at Blenheim Palace.

. . .

GEORGE S. PATTON's catastrophic automobile accident meant he endured paralysis from the neck down in his final days. Upon his death on December 21, 1945—less than one year after his brilliant leadership during the Battle of the Bulge—he was buried at the Luxembourg American Cemetery in Luxembourg City, where he remains to this day. Upon her death in 1953 at the age of sixty-seven, Beatrice's ashes were smuggled into that European nation and scattered across his grave.

.   .   .

IT SHOULD BE noted that Private Harold Garman, Private Barney Hajiro, Private George Sakato, Technician Fifth Grade James Okubo, Private First Class Joe Nishimoto, Staff Sergeant Robert Kuroda, and Sergeant Bud Hawk received the Congressional Medal of Honor.

.   .   .

GENERAL JAMES GAVIN remained in Berlin on occupation duty following the war in Europe, all the while preparing for one last jump—this one intended to be Operation Downfall, over Japan. But the dropping of two atomic bombs and the end of fighting in the Pacific Theater meant that jump never happened. After leaving the army in 1958 as a three-star general, Gavin went on to serve as President John F. Kennedy's ambassador to France in 1961. He died in 1990 at the age of eighty-two. General Gavin was survived by his wife, Jean, whom he married in 1948.

.   .   .

MARTHA GELLHORN NEVER stopped covering war: Vietnam, Central America, and finally the American invasion of Panama in 1989 were among the conflicts she wrote about after World War II. Her final assignment was to report on poverty in Brazil at the age of eighty-seven. Gellhorn retired to London, where she first bought a home during World War II. Suffering from blindness and ovarian cancer, she took her own life on February 15, 1998, with a cyanide capsule. Her flat at Cadogan Square in Chelsea bears the blue English Heritage plaque accorded to all great historical residents of London. At her request, Martha Gellhorn was cremated and her ashes scattered over the River Thames.

THE PROCESS

Thankfully, Covid was winding down as I began researching *Taking Berlin*. Travel opened back up, allowing the chance to visit battlefields, museums, and other historical sites once again. Walking the scene of an historic moment is one of the great thrills of writing history. It is almost self-indulgent to stand on what is now a simple riverbank, for instance, next to a CrossFit gym that certainly did not exist seven decades ago, to imagine that moment the 82nd Airborne carried heavy collapsible British boats over a tall earthen berm, then down to the Waal for their heroic paddle.

That is the way of historic travel, stitching together facts beforehand, then visiting a location to smell the air and feel the soil. Sometimes these places seem mundane. Others are hard to imagine.

When you are standing before the great cathedral in Cologne, it is difficult to conceive that every city block surrounding it was once mountains of rubble, where the act of crossing a street was accompanied by smells of friends and lovers buried beneath those bricks and twisted metal.

Others, like Omaha Beach, are even more massive than previously imagined, magnifying the mental image of the death and destruction. Dunkirk, for what it's worth (and not included in this book), is a vast, eerie strip of barren sand. Dachau will fill you with rage and break your heart.

It should also be pointed out that research is sometimes as simple as riding from one side of a country to another by train, looking out the window at simple farms and rolling hills, making a mental catalog of the terrain but not really looking for an historic monument—then suddenly becoming aware of how demanding it must have been to push tanks and men across those same vast distances with their valleys, bridges, and rich black soil that turned into a bog with every day of snow and rain—all the while being shot at and losing good friends.

Yet trains, planes, automobiles, and remembrances do not constitute *all* research. Places like the Imperial War Museums in London and Duxford, Topography of Terror in Berlin, and the Museum of Military History in Budapest offer a close look (sometimes hands-on, more often "do not touch") that allows precise description and a tactile sensation of uniforms, weapons, and even tanks. Rap on a Sherman's forward protective plates and you'll marvel instantly that anyone could call those thick layers of steel "lightly armored."

I lament the change in modern libraries, rows of bookshelves being replaced by the digital world. I love the musty smell of books waiting to be read. Internet I can do from home.

Newspapers are different. There was a time when immersive research meant traveling to the local university library or even as far away as London, where, after taking a train to Colindale, the British Newspaper Library offered microfilm of dailies going back to 1840. That journey was always a fond adventure, but the research world is

an easier place for the instant gratification of sites like newspapers
.com and the various online archives of big-city papers.

Finally, the books. I relied heavily on the personal writings of
George Patton, Winston Churchill, James Gavin, and Martha Gellhorn in telling their stories. Their words formed a road map and also
a jumping-off point, guiding the research toward statistics and dates
and events occurring simultaneously. I preferred to read their thoughts
from the printed page rather than digitally, if only because that's the
way they were written and the connection feels stronger.

Of course, there were many more books. The mountain next to my
writing desk grew higher every day that I wrote, eventually becoming
a barrier to stepping into and out of my office. I have little room on
my shelves, so I donate most research books to the local Friends of the
Library when I'm done.

If you're ever in Orange County and looking for lovingly used history books, you know where to go.

Thanks for reading. Let's do this again soon.

ACKNOWLEDGMENTS

It took me a while to break up with *Taking Paris*—as all authors must do when moving from one beloved project to the next—and find the voice for *Taking Berlin*. Throughout that process, which involved a lengthy period of creative self-doubt as I sought to find the story (Chapter One, for instance, became Chapter Thirteen as historical figures made it known they wanted to find their way onto the page), I relied on the professionalism, patience, and belief in this work provided by my editor, Brent Howard, and the entire editorial and marketing team at Dutton Caliber. My most heartfelt thanks.

To my agent, Eric Simonoff, thank you for reading the early pages, providing always insightful comments, and listening with a friendly ear when I call to talk about words on the page. It's been more than twenty years since I cold-called you from a boat dock pay phone in South Dakota, asking for representation. The fact you took that call, and the magic and friendship that have happened since, is one of the great joys of my life.

ACKNOWLEDGMENTS

To Mike Di Paola, granular fact-checker extraordinaire, thanks for the attention to detail—and those intriguing footnote suggestions.

To Brian Sobel, for the unforgettable Golden Gate Bridge tour and your unsurpassed knowledge of World War II.

To Yifan Yang, the hardest-working man I know. It's okay to take a holiday now and then.

To my sons: Devin, Connor, and Liam. I want to gush here, going on and on about the wonders of who you are as individuals and the men you've become. But I'll do that in person. I am truly blessed to watch you grow and challenge yourselves. My love for you is mighty.

And finally, for Calene: You are my sunshine.

INDEX

ABOUT THE AUTHOR

Martin Dugard is the *New York Times* bestselling author of several works of history, among them *Taking Paris*, *Into Africa*, and the dozen books of the Killing series, which has now sold more than ten million copies. Mr. Dugard is also a Fellow of the Royal Geographical Society. In addition, he spends afternoons coaching high school cross country and track and field near his Southern California home, an avocation in which he has indulged for the past twenty years—as documented in the essay collection *To Be a Runner*.